ANGLO-SAXON ART
To A.D. 900

By *T. D. KENDRICK*

THE AXE AGE

★

THE DRUIDS

★

THE ARCHAEOLOGY OF THE CHANNEL ISLANDS

★

A HISTORY OF THE VIKINGS

By *T. D. KENDRICK and C. F. C. HAWKES*

ARCHAEOLOGY IN ENGLAND AND WALES 1914–1931

ANGLO-SAXON ART

To A.D. 900

by

T. D. KENDRICK, M.A., F.S.A.

KEEPER OF BRITISH AND MEDIEVAL ANTIQUITIES
IN THE BRITISH MUSEUM

WITH 104 PLATES
AND 25 TEXT ILLUSTRATIONS

METHUEN & CO. LTD. LONDON
36 Essex Street Strand W.C.2

First published in 1938

PRINTED IN GREAT BRITAIN

PREFACE

THIS book is based on lectures given at the Courtauld Institute of Art, and under the auspices of the Rask-Örsted Foundation in Copenhagen. It deals chiefly with the art of the period covered by Dr. R. H. Hodgkin in the first two volumes of his *History of the Anglo-Saxons* (Oxford, 1935), though I have not included an account of the art of the Vikings and have added two introductory chapters dealing with Celtic and Romano-British art. I hope to describe the Late Saxon art of the Viking Period and the time of the Conquest in a subsequent volume, and my aim is that the two books together should form a fairly complete account of the foundations of the English medieval style.

The task of writing this first volume has been appreciably lightened by the generous assistance of many of my friends. I should like especially to thank Mr. A. W. Clapham, Mr. F. Cottrill, Mr. O. G. S. Crawford, Mlle Françoise Henry, Mr. E. T. Leeds, Mlle G. L. Micheli, Mr. V. E. Nash-Williams, Mr. John Piper, Professor D. Talbot Rice, Mr. T. E. Routh, and Mr. J. E. Tetley. I must also record my grateful recognition of the valuable help I have received from my colleagues in the British Museum, Christopher Hawkes, Roger Hinks, Ernst Kitzinger, Elizabeth Senior, and Francis Wormald ; for they have not only given me advice and criticism, but also information that was new to me and the results of their own researches. I am indebted furthermore to numerous authors, institutions, and societies for permission to use illustrations already published, and I have given their names, and the names of those who have provided me with photographs, in the Lists of Plates and Figures. Finally, I desire to thank most warmly all those who have so very kindly allowed me to take photographs in the churches, museums, libraries, and private collections that I have visited during the writing of this book.

T. D. KENDRICK

BRITISH MUSEUM, <i>1938</i>

CONTENTS

TEXT ILLUSTRATIONS

ix

xi

PLATES AT END OF BOOK

xiii

xiv

PLATES AT END OF BOOK

xxi

ANGLO-SAXON ART
To A.D. 900

I

EARLY BRITISH ART

THE early history of art in England, by which I mean the art of the period covered by this book and of the succeeding Viking Age, is best understood if we regard it as being in the main the recital of a protracted series of conflicts between the mutually irreconcilable principles of the barbaric and the classical aesthetic systems. It is true that we have to record temporary eclipses or phases of ascendancy first of one and then of the other of them ; but at no point do we lose sight of the salient fact of a sustained struggle between fundamentally opposed types of artistic expression. Put simply, the issue between them is, of course, that barbaric art (in the sense in which I use the expression throughout this work) seeks to satisfy by means of dynamic abstract patterns and by the statement of organic forms in terms of inorganic or surrealist symbols ; whereas classical art gives pleasure by means of a sympathetic and obvious naturalism. You were asked to decide, as it were, whether you wanted to look at the strange, glittering brilliance of the lively mosaic pattern seen through the kaleidoscope, or the familiar and friendly picture in a mirror held up to reflect the visible world. There was no common ground at all ; no possible harmony in method or purpose. The only form of fusion that could take place was an attempt to achieve the purpose of one of the two systems by using the materials and methods of the other. Thus you might try to render or suggest the natural forms of the mirror-subject by an arrangement of the kaleidoscope pieces ; or you might make an abstract kaleidoscopic pattern out of the separate organic elements of the mirror-subject. And whether such attempts turned out to be felicitous or unfortunate, the chief effect of them was to add to the sense of aesthetic discord and restlessness that I believe to be a characteristic of Anglo-Saxon art.

To make the story plainer, and to complete the account of this duel between the rival aesthetic sensibilities, I am going far behind the age of the Anglo-Saxons. I begin, in fact, with a brief reference to ' Early British ' art—that is to say, the prehistoric phase of Celtic art in Britain that is characteristic of what archaeologists call the ' La Tène ' Period. I do this because the Early British style is the first organized expression in our country of the kind of barbaric aesthetic sensibility that we are going to study in the Anglo-Saxon Period. It may seem surprising that we do not have to carry the story farther back; for in England the earliest manifestations of the art to which I refer do not take us a very long way behind the dawn of the Christian Era, probably not much, if at all, behind 200 B.C. But the fact remains that before this time our primitive art was almost entirely occupied with the development of static forms and lifeless surface-ornament, whereas Early British art abruptly sets aside this venerable tradition of inert solidity and dead geometrical decoration. It introduces us to an entirely new concept of art, and by so doing becomes the true antecedent of the major flowerings of Celtic and Saxon art that are to follow; because, in the first place, it is animated, and shows the dynamic movement of life reflected in form and pattern; and, secondly, because this movement is reassessed, as it were, in super-real terms, so that the life represented is that of an eerie world of the imagination.

It may be that we are over-exaggerating the abruptness of the change, and a fuller knowledge may yet show us that this insurgent vitality and imaginative quality of Early British art did after all have some roots in our own past; but, in general and as a working rule, the distinction we have drawn holds good, and the difference between the inanimate solidity of a Bronze Age beaker of 1800 B.C. and the lively harmony of a Belgic funeral-urn of 50 B.C. is fundamental. Therefore, though we need not doubt that Early British art is, as I say, our natural starting-point, we should, nevertheless, do well to bear the fact of the long prehistoric past in mind. We know that the change to the new style cannot conceivably represent an instant aesthetic revolution in all sections of the population of Britain ; for it was an art of the princes rather than of the people, and may have been far less general than is sometimes supposed. So throughout the period during which it was manifest, and perhaps in the Roman Period after it, we must make allowances for the existence of an underworld of simple peasant art that could still express with genuine sympathy and understanding the feeling for static form and dead ornament that was the accumulated heritage of at least two thousand years.

The name ' La Tène ' is taken from a site on Lake Neuchâtel in Switzerland where the continental ' Greek ' variety of Celtic art was believed to be typically represented. The beginnings of this so-called ' La Tène Style ' go back to the fourth century B.C., and it is found at first among the Celtic peoples of eastern France and the middle Rhineland ; and subsequently, following the expansion of the Celts, in Italy, along the Danube as far as Eastern Europe and Asia Minor, and, going northwards, in Great Britain and Ireland ; but I do not propose to say much about the continental work. Its most obvious characteristic seems to me to be a fondness for animated designs of a fantastic unreality that suggests a deliberate rejection of the ordinariness of natural forms, as one sees particularly well in such obvious example as the treatment of the mask. In the use of close-set decorative arrangements and in the handling of masses, La Tène art abroad owes more than is commonly realized to the still earlier ' Hallstatt ' art of the Continent ; but its details also include an Oriental Scythian-type animal

3

and certain bastard Greek ornaments, two of which, the palmette and the tendril-scroll, play an important part in Celtic design. In a robust, lively, and usually ' Baroque ' manner, this curious fusion of Hallstatt, Greek, and Scythian elements developed harmoniously and successfully ; and though the palmette and the scroll are at first the weakest part of the La Tène style, the initial clumsiness wears off, and these patterns were skilfully re-edited into dynamically distorted ' Celtic ' patterns. Moreover, having lost their classical stolidity, they infused the whole decorative scheme with a distinctly vivacious curvilinear quality ; so that movement of flowing lines and soft swelling curves became characteristic of the developed style.

In the third or second century B.C. this art reached Britain, the result of invasions by Celtic peoples. The new-comers were not the first of their race to invade our shores, but they are distinguished from the Celts who had preceded them by this hallmark of the La Tène style, now to become our Early British art. It is generally recognized by its dominant note, the foliate scroll ; but though this had become a rather stringy relic of the original La Tène experiment with a Greek pattern, and though the palmette still survives in recognizable form, Early British art has nothing to do with the distilled classicism that had been an element in the continental beginnings of the La Tène style. On the contrary, it is an unpolluted barbaric style of brilliant vigour, the complete antithesis of classicism in its urgent eccentric vitality, its hard intense abstraction, and its Celtic unfriendliness. So far as the outward appearances of our Early British works of art are concerned, I think we should do well to realize that an extraordinary sensitive-ness to dynamic use of form is incontestably their principal characteristic and the chief witness to their revolutionary character. The example of the Torrs *champfrein* (Pl. 1) is an illustration of this. We see that the surcharged ornament of the scroll, usually regarded as the distinctive feature of Early British art, is really secondary to the principal statement. Its virtue lies in its use as a cunning accentuation of the liveliness of the form itself by means of an appropriately placed boss or roundel and the loosening and tightening convolutions of the overlaid pattern.

This sensitive control of the spread of the ornament is, however, not much less important than the form it decorates. We observe the clever treatment of selected nuclei in the design, where emphasis is increased with all the full-blooded barbaric zest for concentrated pattern. The magnificent shield (Pl. 1) in the British Museum, probably made just before 100 B.C. and found in the River Witham near Lincoln, shows us this principle of the nuclear assembly of ornament as a restrained enhancement of a taut and noble shape, the eye, ranging the central spine up or down from the middle boss, coming to rest at an exactly appropriate roundel, heavily moulded and frilled, in which is a sunk field bearing an engraved scroll that adds, as it were, ' spin ' to this necessary ornamental oasis.

The most remarkable thing about the Witham shield is best seen in a drawing (Fig. 1), and that is the outline of the animal-figure, probably a thin applied plate of metal that was pinned across its front. This astonishing boar, so proudly flaunted over the whole great work, is one of the finest animal-drawings among all British antiquities. It is stylized to the point of absurdity, a grim heraldic grotesque ; but as an abstract and consciously distorted silhouette impression of a boar, it is doubtful if it has ever been surpassed. We see here the Celtic genius expressing its instinctive tendency to transmute the real into the super-real, to reduce a natural form into a calligraphic pattern-statement of itself that is nothing less than the profoundly moving interpretation of a visionary. It is, in fact, one of the chief strengths of northern barbaric art, this power to transmute the natural world into a system of appropriate and convincing symbols that are in themselves comments upon nature. They reveal a new apprehension of the facts of the living body. Thus, of the little bronze boar

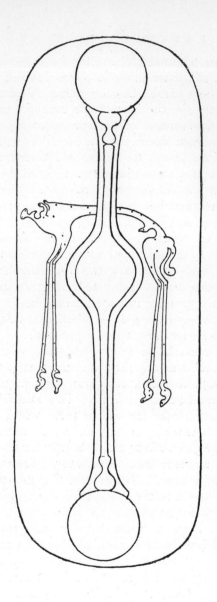

Fig. 1.—Bronze shield from the R. Witham, Lincs (⅛)

(Pl. 2) from Hounslow, which was probably nothing more important than a helmet-crest, we may fairly say that it is not an heraldic comicality, but a brilliant shorthand statement of the force and form of the animal in terms of an economically selected arrangement of abstract masses. The bold cresting on the back is as truthful in observation and rendering as any naturalistic modelling or cutting of the spine-bristles, and a profound knowledge of the animal is implied by that alert preposterous head and fantastically waisted body, so menacingly strong and yet so delicately imagined.[1]

Of the same order is the animal-art of the Aylesford bucket (Pl. 2), though here in the embossed creatures on the rim with their leaf-like snouts and their foliate tails the intensity of the abstract pattern-statement is increased. They are not interpretations of horses, but cunning symbols better described as a generalized reference to the horse-type of quadruped. Similarly the human mask on the escutcheon of the handle, to be numbered among the grandest of the minor pieces of Celtic metalwork in this country, is a sublimation of the human countenance, as though it were the supernatural aspect of man's form, its mystery and its religious background, that the artist sought to portray. The huge eyes, the long geometrical nose, and the unnatural fall of the hollow cheeks, are the Celtic symbolization of the link between the face of man and the face of God, and, surmounted as they are here by the monstrous crest of the helmet, they constitute an example of that terrifying formal distortion whereby primitive man knew how to create a vision of the super-real.

Fine figure-work of the kind we have been considering seems to be on the whole characteristic of the earlier rather than the later phase of British La Tène art. But the Celtic style retains its individualism and its barbaric quality until

[1] The bronze head of an ox from Ham Hill, Somerset, is another example of this British La Tène animal-style, *Proc. Soc. Ant.*, XXI (1905–7), p. 133.

7

the Roman occupation was complete, and examples of the latter part of the La Tène Period, roughly the century between 50 B.C. and A.D. 50, offer illustrations of a persistent aesthetic taste that we may now call native, though it would still be untrue to describe it as a universal people's art. In so far as the principle of movement in design is concerned, we may say that Early British art was steadily developing, and the sinuous exciting liveliness of the flamboyant scroll-pattern that adorns the back of the bronze mirror (Pl. 3) from Desborough in Northamptonshire is a masterpiece of dynamic drawing. This magnificent object is most deservedly admired by visitors to the British Museum, and indeed, with the possible exception of the equally handsome mirror from Birdlip, now in the Gloucester Museum, it bears the most ambitious piece of scroll-work that a prehistoric artist in this country ever drew ; yet it is to some extent embarrassed by the obvious confusion that exists between background and pattern. The bronze field intrudes staringly around and through the scroll ; it is cut up into an unpleasantly assertive pattern of its own ; the eye does not fasten in a flash on the drawing, and there is just that instant of confusion which suggests some miscarriage of purpose. Another point about this scroll is that the design does not attain to the fullest degree of rhythmic movement on account of its ostentatious fold-over symmetry, this introducing, as it were, an alien harmony of a kind that the Celtic artist often found difficult to use successfully.

Not that he had ever rejected this symmetrical type of pattern. But his genius was more at home with compositions having a distributed balance, as we see from the example of the iron spearhead with ornamental bronze plates on the blade (Pl. 1) that was found in the Thames and has been lent to the British Museum by Captain John Ball. It shows how at a late date, assuredly in the first century A.D., the Celtic craftsman had attained to the highest pinnacle of sensitive brilliance in form and design.

His scroll, the antique theme as used on the Desborough mirror and the Witham shield, is stylized and hardened almost beyond recognition ; but his use of it is the work of a great master. Though the weapon itself is faultlessly symmetrical, the four sinuous plates on the wings are all of different shapes, and of the surcharged scroll-patterns no two are the same. And yet the result of this asymmetrical ornament is complete harmony and perfect balance.

It might be objected that the incised scroll was an unnecessary and irritating embellishment, for as a decoration of the iron blade the comely plates were in themselves sufficient. But this the Celtic artist did not allow, and it is a further characteristic of his work that he would often superpose one decorative element upon another. In his eyes, it seems, a shaped field could not function as an ornament in itself. It must contain something. And this trait, going back to the beginnings of Celtic art, is one of the sources of the over-elaboration so typical of later Celtic manuscripts. But it is scarcely fair to this spearhead to use it as an illustration of Celtic fault ; for it is to be numbered among the finest things that the Celt ever made, and the more important topic that it suggests is the question why, when the Briton could show himself thus capable of so delicate an equipoise of asymmetrical shapes and interior masses, we should nevertheless find ourselves at this late period more commonly confronted by designs of a suave and heavy symmetry.

The coming of the Belgae in the middle of the first century B.C. and their settlement in south-east England may have been a factor of importance, particularly since it is in dispute whether these new-comers were full-blooded Celts in the sense that the earlier invaders of the La Tène Period had been Celts. But it is very difficult to show that their arrival had a noticeable effect on the evolution of style in Britain. We certainly owe to them an amazing development of the enamel industry, and it is true that many of their enamels provide examples of frankly symmetrical patterns ; but there is no reason to suppose that they were uninterested in the ' asymmetrical experiment ',[1] while many symmetrical pieces, including the Birdlip and the Desborough mirrors themselves, are not Belgic at all but belong to the south-western school of Early British art. The Belgae, I think, must be credited with a full share in all that the term Early British art implies, and I have already mentioned their pottery as being typical of the period's feeling for dynamic form. Accordingly, the disturbing influence that brings the asymmetrical experiment to an end must be something greater than that of the Belgic enamels. Only some wildfire fashion spreading suddenly over the whole land could thus strike at the vigorous western scroll-work, and there can be little doubt that Mlle Françoise Henry was right in saying that the new influence was the advent of classical art in its Roman guise.[2] Just as La Tène art began with a ' Greek ' phase, so it ends with a ' Roman ' phase, and all that we need say about the Belgae is that they may have been partly instrumental in this spread of the new style ; for they were in touch with the Continent, now rapidly becoming Romanized, to a far greater degree than were the western or northern Britons.

In a hoard of bronzes found on Polden Hill in Somerset there are two pieces (Pl. 3) that illustrate the change which we must now expect to see becoming general, a change that foreshadows the end of Early British art in southern Britain. The first (Pl. 3, 4) is a splendid example of the western ' mirror ' style at its best ; yet it shows only too plainly how the easily flowing open scroll could be frozen into an almost unctuously symmetrical composition. It is, of course, a fine work, sincerely conceived in form and pattern according to the Celtic principle of the dynamic curves ; but its effect is one of a less subtle and more

---

[1] cf. the mirror from a Belgic grave at Old Warden, Beds. Leeds, *Celtic Ornament*, Oxford, 1933, fig. 14.

[2] F. Henry, *La sculpture irlandaise*, Paris, 1932, I, p. 38 ff.

pompous harmony than work like the spearhead, and this
not merely because it comes from a different hand and a
different province, but because it makes, perhaps unconsciously, some concession to the complacent stateliness of
classical design. Not everybody, perhaps, will feel that
this is so ; but our second piece (Pl. 3, 3), which may
be of rather later manufacture, shows the change in a form
that will be instantly recognizable. Here much of the
swinging lightness of the Early British style is lost and we
are left with what is very little more than a bit of bombastic
Romanizing work by a Celtic designer. It is important,
however, that we should note that outside the sphere of
Roman influence, and this adds force to Mlle Henry's
contention, we are still able even at this late day to find
work that is in the tradition of the ' asymmetrical experiment '. Our example is the undoubtedly late, but nevertheless very charming little bronze mirror (Fig. 2) from
Trelan Bahow, St. Keverne, Cornwall. In the two circles
on the back of this we have a most convincingly un-Roman
design. It is true that the scroll is sadly conventionalized and
the detail so coarse as to be clumsy ; but in their total effect
these roundels are fully representative of the genius of the
British Celt, and reveal the spontaneity and insular originality
which are precisely the qualities that Roman art, either
consciously or unconsciously, now set itself to extinguish.

Perhaps the best known of all the Early British antiquities
of this country is the great bronze shield from Battersea
in the British Museum (Pl. 3). It comes to us appositely
here as an example of the elegant semi-classicism of the
native style in the Belgic east about the time of the Claudian
invasion. In its three large roundels it bears a symmetrical
curvilinear pattern in thin reed-like lines that does not
follow the old foliate theme, but seems rather to approach
the style of Roman volutes and the pelta-type and lotus-
flower arrangement of scrolls. That it is a work in the
Early British manner is, of course, proved by its form and
its rhythm, and by details such as the swellings at the

junctions of the scrolls and at their ends, and the use of the emphatic ornamental nucleus, here the enamelled studs, as a kind of decorative punctuation. But it is a very much altered scroll, very prim, arid, and leafless, and without the abrupt expansions and wandering eccentricity that distinguish earlier forms. The general stylistic change between early and late works is very easily detected by

FIG. 2.—Bronze mirror, Trelan Bahow, St. Keverne, Cornwall (⅓)

comparing this shield and the shield from the Witham (Pl. 1), for the austere proportions of the latter, the tensity of its ornamental spine, and the precise emphatic harmony of its three bosses, are all qualities lacking in the Battersea shield. The one is taut and dynamically vigorous ; the other soft, spreading, and weak.

It is probable that representations of human and animal forms likewise altered as Early British art entered upon its

Roman phase. Here the evidence is inadequate, and the stone head from Gloucester [1] (Pl. 4) is an unexpected warning that even at the beginning of the first century A.D. a resolutely barbaric Celtic style could find expression in sculpture. It is a surprising piece. We do not know that there was ambitious stone-carving in England during prehistoric times, and the appearance of the monumental statue and effigy is generally believed to be the direct result of the influence of Roman art ; yet this little head, though it makes concession to a Roman portrait type, as we see plainly in the treatment of the hair, has more in common with the powerful geometrically conceived abstraction of the Aylesford bucket mask (Pl. 2) than with the urbane Claudian sculpture it was presumably intended to represent. It raises the question whether some allowance should not be made for a lost prehistoric art of the effigy and image, perhaps chiefly expressed in woodwork, whose traditions this carving perpetuates, and we should do well to remember that there are similar stone heads of the La Tène Period in France [2] that are unquestionably Celtic in concept, without even the ' Roman ' hair of the Gloucester sculpture and showing no relation whatever to Roman style. But in England we cannot be sure of the existence of an Early British monumental sculpture,[3] and the Gloucester head

[1] *Journal of Roman Studies*, XXV (1935), p. 218, Pl. XXXVII. The head, which is 8 inches high, still bears traces of a red colouring.

[2] For examples from the sanctuary of Roquepertuse, Bouches-du-Rhône, *XX Bericht R-G Kommission* (1930), p. 116 and Tf. 10.

[3] The interesting thesis of A. Schober, *Jahresheft des österreichischen arch. Inst. in Wien*, XXV (1929), p. 9, to the effect that a pre-Roman sculptural style, including statue-forms, contributes to the development of provincial Roman art obtains, therefore, no corroboration here. But it is not a negligible suggestion. Only as far away as Guernsey there is the prehistoric Gran'mère du Chimquière that combines the rigid menhir-style with a partially plastic treatment (Kendrick, *Archaeology of the Channel Islands*, I, p. 21), and even in this island there are enigmatic carvings that might possibly be prehistoric, for example the menhir with the sculptured head at Laugharne, Carmarthen (*Trans. Carmathen. Ant. Soc.*, Part LXI (1935), Pl., p. 2).

can do no more for the present than bear witness to the Celtic idiosyncrasy of a single artist of western Britain, not to the traditions of an established school.[1] We are on more certain ground in claiming that the kind of change now taking place is illustrated by the minor metal statuette, and here the bronze boar (Pl. 2) from the Lexden tumulus near Colchester, that must have been made very near the year 1 A.D., should be contrasted with my Hounslow example of the boar as interpreted by the earlier Celt. The difference is much the same as that between the two shields, though it is revealed in another manner. The Lexden boar is a sturdy and handsome work, conceived in a friendly naturalistic mood, with a life-like head and body, and faithfully engraved whiskers and dorsal hair ; but compared with his Hounslow progenitor he is a weakling ; for whereas the abstract animal is a supernatural monstrosity of Celtic imagining, this one is a tame reality, a child of nature as the Romans knew her, almost pettable.

So plain an indication of the advent of classicism must be held to have a general value, revealing a trend of fashion that doubtless had a revolutionary effect upon the art of the aristocratic British at the time of the Roman conquest, and in the matter of the animal-figure we may accept the beginning of the first century A.D. as a period of decisive change. Direct survivals of the earlier style are rare after this. The spirited little bronze figure of a horse (Pl. 5) from Silchester is perhaps an example, but we have no information of its date and it might rank as an Early British piece. A more important instance of survival is the remarkable seal-box lid of bronze, found by Professor Newstead in a first-century deposit at Chester, that bears a fine and fantastic enamelled dragon, head turned savagely backwards in the lively manner of the Aylesford bucket beasts (Pl. 2). As La Tène work it is obviously late, because of its drawing and because of its ragged hairy legs ; but

[1] This particular form of the geometrically conceived head is a recurrent phenomenon and finds frequent expression in later European art.

it has nevertheless an authentic wildness, and, like the Hounslow boar, is a fitting inhabitant of that shadow-world of Celtic fantasy now in peril of being left untenanted.

The Early British style very soon came to an end once the Roman Period had begun. There was, however, in northern England a Brigantian school [1] that did keep alive something of the Celtic feeling for eccentric and vivacious ornament until the end of the second century. Its most remarkable product is a fine gold brooch (Pl. 5) that was found at Acsica on the Roman Wall and is now in the

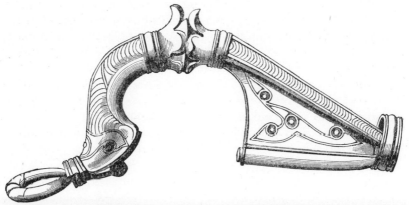

FIG. 3.—Silver-gilt brooch, Backworth, Northumberland (⅓)

Blackgate Museum at Newcastle. Its form is provincial Roman and it is not likely to be earlier than c. A.D. 100 ; but its decoration of embossed scrolls is Early British in style. It is true that this brooch does not really represent a survival of a real ' La Tène ' pattern ; for it is simply a sprawling sequel to the already hybrid work of the Battersea shield, as is shown by the lute- and pelta-motives common to both. Yet there is a certain stubbornly Celtic and flagrantly un-Roman quality about much of the Brigantian work, and on the second-century brooches from Backworth in Northumberland (Fig. 3) there is an engraved scroll on

[1] For this see R. G. Collingwood, *Archaeologia*, LXXX (1930), p. 37.

15

the head and foot-plate that is indubitably a survival from the original and authentic Early British art. Several small enamels dating from the first half of the Roman Period are ornamented with a thin stringy version of the scroll of the same order, for instance the seal-box lid (Pl. 5) from Lincoln, now in the British Museum. But the best examples of the droll Celtic ingenuity of the northern metal-work belonging to the Brigantian school are the delightful ' dragonesque ' brooches (Pl. 5). These have a sinuous double curve, each end of which tapers to a large ' head ' with a curling snout, a big ear, and an eye, the whole looking as though it were made up of the ribbon-like forequarters and neck of the animals on the Aylesford bucket (Pl. 2).[1] There is no evidence, however, that these or any other ornaments in a similar Celtic style were made after the temporary independence of the Brigantian leaders came to an end in the late second century. The time has come, therefore, to interrupt our study of the barbaric tradition by turning aside to consider the significance of the Roman Period in the story of our island's early art.

[1] The origin of the ' animal-head ' on these brooches is probably the plant-scroll ; cf. Leeds, *Celtic Ornament*, p. 107.

II

ROMAN BRITAIN

IN its imperial and official aspect Romano-British art is
not very much more than an unequivocal statement on the
part of the government at Rome of the majestic fact of the
Roman world-empire. It is revealed to us at once as something foreign and imposed ; and this for two main reasons ;
firstly, because the Romans introduced into Britain the
hitherto unacceptable concept of art as a means for the
creation of naturalistic realities by the use of direct visual
observation ; and, secondly, because of the monumental
character of this unfamiliar classicism. Both these revolutionary aspects of the Roman phase in our art-history can
be made self-evident with the aid of a few pictures of surviving sculptures, and I do not intend to do more than
embroider the main lesson by choosing my examples in such
a way that some of them will also reveal the attitude of the
barbarians in this country to works of art that must have
been at first both uncongenial and strange. For we shall
find—and this, I think, is the principal interest of this
chapter—that in addition to those numerous pieces of
indifferent copywork that were dutifully produced by
native artists, there are also rare and precious sculptures
that represent the art of stone-carving under the discipline
of a purely barbaric and un-Roman aesthetic sensibility,
fine and uncompromisingly abstract conceptions that have
not yet received the attention they deserve.

To emphasize first of all the general significance of
Romano-British art in our story I must, however, begin with
a reference to architecture and the monumental sculpture

that is associated with grandiose buildings. The surviving structures, towns, walls, circuses, villas, and forts, need not be described ; for it will be readily conceded that the architecture of our province must have been astonishing in its ubiquity and sudden growth. But we must note that the sculptural accessories of the buildings were, considering the remote position of the island, no less remarkable. It is true that most of the material is from the Roman point of view ordinary, such as cornices and capitals with acanthus foliage and scrolls and geometric ornament, and flutings and mouldings of the common kind ; yet a few architectural fragments still existing are of considerable interest, and one of the most notable of these is the tympanum (Pl. 6) of the temple of Sulis at Bath, a carving that is probably not much later in date than the beginning of the second century.

The tympanum, which is 26 feet long and 8 feet high, is a hard, flat, provincial carving with a marked accent on the linear pattern of its design, witness the ribbed drapery of the Victories that is in the first-century ' Maenad ' style of Germany and Gaul. The bearded Gorgon in the central shield has a matted tangle around the face that fails to achieve the three-dimensional dishevelment of the classical Gorgon head without acquiring any compensating virtues of an abstract or symbolic kind. The face, however, which is treated in a curiously metallic fashion as though copied from bronze, not only preserves the full ferocity of that intent frowning stare so familiar in Graeco-Roman masks, but adds to it an un-Roman quality of menacing divinity. It is here, I think, that we find the focus of such barbaric talent as there is in this sculpture ; but, even so, the carving does not attain the austere geometrical super-realism of the uncontaminated barbaric figure-style. The Gorgon is really no more than a copy of a classical subject,[1] and I see nothing in it that makes me suspect it to be the work

[1] cf., for instance, the bronze Medusa-head from the Nemi ship, *Cambridge Ancient History*, Plate IV, fig. 142*a*.

of a Briton. To appreciate its debased classical character and its lack of decisive barbaric virtues, we cannot do better than compare it with a modest northern version of the same subject (Pl. 7), now in the Blackgate Museum at Newcastle. The second head is tiny, and adorns a shield of only 20 inches in diameter ; but it is interesting because it is conceived geometrically and in abstract terms, and has that hard wedge-shaped nose so often to be found in primitive work. The piece is convincingly powerful and it owes its strength not to the original classical ferocity of the Gorgon, but to the fact that the handling of the subject is now completely and blatantly barbaric.

The barbarian understood and appreciated the acrimonies of expression, the scowl and the frown and the menacing stare, better than the bland gaze of official Roman serenity, and the accomplishment shown by provincial sculptors in carvings of the mask-type is further illustrated by the third-century stone antefix, 22½ inches in height, that comes from Towcester in Northamptonshire and is now in the British Museum (Pl. 7). The head makes obvious concessions to the classical manner, as the dressing of the hair proves ; but the sculptor has had the skill to invest the Roman mask with a strange barbaric tensity, a typically provincial poignancy and dramatic quality. It is as though the mask were no longer conceived as an actor's property, a shield that could be removed from the calm face it covers. The barbarian had identified it with the living countenance behind it, and had invested the person of the player with an indelible imprint of the spiritual tragedy in his part.

One of the most significant contributions of Roman art must have been the appearance in Britain of the sympathetically and naturally drawn human figure. The gods and heroes of early mosaics and paintings, for example, are completely foreign in concept, and so too, in the realm of sculpture, was the free-standing figure or statue proper, such as that most notable advertisement of the Empire, the mighty bronze figure of Hadrian that once stood in Londinium. We can illustrate a normal Roman style by the British Museum Atys (Pl. 8), which was found in London. It is certainly over-heavy and coarse in limb ; but the features are soft and friendly ; the line of the body is graceful ; and the drapery is convincing. It is a poor, modest carving ; but it is humane, and typical of the easy comprehensibility of this kind of Roman figural art. Such free-standing figures are not a part of our subsequent story ; for when the last statue in the Roman towns was overthrown and the last temple figure fallen, this particular form of monumental sculpture passed from the land for so many centuries that we do not find it again until the art of the Gothic Age was already old ; but the example of the Roman statue and of the life-sized bust was copied by native sculptors while it was still before them, and there are several interesting native essays in this ambitious modelling in the round. Thus the large female head at Bath, with hair dressed in the style of the late first century, is a painstaking copy of the official portrait style, as we may see by setting it beside a Roman portrait-bust of the Vespasian Age ; but it has, nevertheless, a definitely provincial mannerism ; it is angular, grim, and hard, and the face, with the wedge-like nose, huge staring eyes, and great square jowl, comes very near to being a complete stylization of the countenance.

I have already mentioned the astonishing Gloucester head (Pl. 4) as an instance of the Celtic handling of sculpture in the round, and we may proceed further with what seems to be an emerging Romano-British style by citing an early head (Pl. 9) from a temple at Benwell in Northumberland.[1] The young solemn face has a classical serenity, but the heavy and geometrically treated eyes and mouth give the countenance divinity that the barbarian could understand, an eerie unworldliness far removed

[1] It is well described by Colonel Spain, *Proc. Soc. Ant. Newcastle-on-Tyne*, 4S, III (1927–8), p. 124.

from human experience. In the same way, the mannered style of the hair, connected perhaps with the ' Antinous ' type of the Hadrianic Age, is proof of the un-Roman aesthetic principles guiding the sculptor ; for it is piled pattern-wise into a heavy ornamental wig and is no natural interpretation of an elaborate coiffure, as in the Flavian busts of women, but a distinct Celtic concept of the hair, both abstract and symbolic.

There seems to have been no immediate sequel to this early work ; but in the second half of the Roman Period the barbaric style in sculpture re-asserts itself in the north in a very remarkable fashion. For example, two stone heads (Pl. 9), both from Corbridge in Northumberland, have a directly stated barbaric tensity and beauty. It may perhaps be true of both of them that they were expected to suggest the ideals of Roman sculpture ; but in performance they show little but a totally un-Roman emotion expressed with a gaunt savage symbolism that entitles them to be respected as particularly valuable examples of our native art. It is a sorry thing that pieces like this should be so rare, for they suggest the existence in the third century of a developing school of northern British sculpture that may have produced many masterpieces illustrating the barbaric interpretation of the human head, plastically conceived. There are not, in truth, many carvings that can be grouped with them. Nevertheless there is one that I cite with unqualified pleasure, the magnificent horned head of red sandstone (Pl. 9) in the Carlisle Museum, which I am inclined to honour as the finest piece of native carving in the whole length of Roman Britain. It is a relentless and implacable Celtic wonder, terrifying in its grimly supernatural power. There is nothing here that is just decadent or unskilled classicism ; on the contrary, the work is conspicuously brilliant in its unimpaired native vigour, and, in fact, gains strength from a courageous and downright renunciation of the classical method.

I am well aware that extravagant praise of this kind

bestowed upon a carving like the Carlisle head may give the impression that I am overanxious to emphasize the excellences of barbaric art ; but the truth is that I have no desire to do more than insist upon the necessity of recognizing the existence of this and other sculptures of an un-Roman sort. For the error that we must avoid above all things is that of confusing these pieces with work that is barbarous simply in the sense that it is a very crude and unskilled copy of a classical original. I admit freely that, as in the other provinces of the Empire, Roman Britain affords numerous instances of figure-work that is either an unhappy compromise between the official classical style and the barbaric style or an unashamed example of awkward bungling in the treatment of a classically conceived theme. We can, in fact, very easily work downwards from tolerable but dull carvings such as the Cirencester Mother-Goddesses (Pl. 8) or the relief on a London sarcophagus (Pl. 8) to grotesque and inexpert figures that possess no single remaining vestige of classical dignity ; but my point is that in the whole series we shall not encounter a single carving that gives rise to such emotions as the Carlisle head. I repeat that this must be valued principally for the reason that it stands outside the long list of degenerate classical sculptures, and I claim that it deliberately conforms to the different ideals of another and opposed variety of aesthetic sensibility.

The monumental effigy in which the figure appears in relief against the background of an architectural niche is a familiar type of the Romano-British memorial. We may have a military or official personage, or a woman of the ruling classes, shown full-length, standing or sitting, or, as in the tombstone of Longinus (Pl. 10) at Colchester, a mounted officer trampling the fallen barbarian foe. My illustration shows a far from negligible piece of sculpture, for there is an obvious sensitiveness in the modelling, and to appreciate its merits as a naturalistic study we have only to compare the detail of the fallen victim, a lively conscious jest of officialdom, with other versions of the same subject, as at Gloucester, where the barbarian is a flat, stylized carving. Occasionally, however, the harsh and abstract treatment of this kind of tombstone at the hands of the provincial sculptor produces a work that, like the Carlisle head, is something more than a pathetic travesty of the Roman original, and in a few such memorials that have positive barbaric virtues we ought perhaps to recognize our own British carvings. An example is the fine slab at Chester commemorating a centurion of the 20th Legion and his wife (Pl. 11). It is, I am sure, a mistake to dismiss this work as a piece of bungling incompetence. One must agree that, according to the Roman standards as expressed in the Colchester monument, the arms of the Chester officer and the legs of his wife are contemptibly silly, and that the details of the costumes are grotesque absurdities. But in spite of this it is really a carving of much dignity and beauty. At least it is genuine, and is barbarously strong and truthful, instead of being a poor classical fake ; and the rigid geometry of the composition gives it an impressive monumental grandeur that many more sculpturesque effigies lack. The figures make no pretence to be living images of Romans ; but in form and pattern they are eloquent and adequate symbols of the stateliness of the Roman officer and the Roman matron. The tombstone is first-century work, and it may be that there was no suitable model of the classical centurial tomb at hand in Chester when the carving was commissioned ; since it is difficult to imagine that the sculptor was seriously attempting to reproduce an official style of which there were examples around him. Indeed the chief interest of the memorial is that it is Roman only in a vague and generalized way ; for in concept and execution it is barbaric, and is much nearer to being an essay in abstract art than a docile study in the classical manner.

The best example that I know in Britain of the completely barbaric version of the effigy is a tombstone (Pl. 11) from

Great Chesters on the Roman Wall, now in the Blackgate Museum at Newcastle-upon-Tyne. It was erected in the third century to the memory of Pervica, whose name suggests that she was a British girl. The figure is a flat silhouetted relief, a geometrically assembled plastic pattern, remote from nature and unsympathetically imagined ; yet it is nevertheless symbolically vital. The sculptor borrowed from classical art nothing more than the fashion of the figured memorial, and he paid no attention to the normal Roman manner for tombstones of this kind. He not only ignored Roman modelling, but also the Roman paraphernalia of drapery and costume-details, and setting himself deliberately to produce a barbaric abstraction, he succeeded in creating a work that must take its place among the greatest of the Romano-British effigies. Pervica's tombstone must not be judged by Roman standards ; for it is consciously a revolt from them and is a part of that extraordinary recrudescence of a frankly barbaric sculpture in the north that we have already noted. But this does not mean that I find it easy to say why this rebellious, beautiful carving should ever have been made. It is obviously inadequate to suppose that so accomplished a sculptor could not have achieved at least a passable imitation of the naturalistic style had he been so minded, and we can only surmise that some surviving prehistoric dread of the living image, a superstitious fear of the likeness as an abode for the ghost, occasioned this astonishing exercise in abstract art.[1]

One of the most interesting effects of provincialism operating upon official Roman sculpture of the ordinary plastic kind is a tendency to convert it into very low reliefs that are handled almost in the manner of a linear drawing. In itself this flat style of carving is by no means a British peculiarity, for it was often used even in Rome, and can be seen on the backs and sides of sarcophagi whose fronts

[1] My colleague, Christopher Hawkes, suggested this explanation to me. It is more reasonable than my own notion that the sculptor was guided by a mixture of aesthetic and political prejudices.

bear sculpture in a deep relief. The point about it is that it provides an obvious opportunity for native talent to emerge in a characteristic way, and I think that in all the provinces work of this kind deserves more study than it has hitherto received. It is not, however, very common outside Italy, where it has a long-established tradition behind it that may reach back as far as the Etruscan stelae. In Britain it is first observable in works that are clearly foreign, for example the admirable mounted warrior, a carving with a relief not more than $\frac{1}{4}$ inch in depth, on the first-century tomb of Sextus at Chester (Pl. 12). This type of monument, and perhaps the sculptor himself, came to us from Noricum or Pannonia, if not from some point farther east in the Greek lands, and one observes how strangely the delicate grace of this faint, lively silhouette is contrasted with the ponderous treatment of the bust of Sextus and of the lions that are carved at the top of the tombstone ; for the sculptor worked with familiar ease at this elegant pattern of the horse, rider, and footman ; but was without experience when it came to honest Roman sculpture in the round.

This flat style did not become fashionable quickly, and in native works it is at first associated with carvings that express in no half-hearted measure the supernatural and symbolic aspect of primitive art. An example is the small relief, 22 inches in length, of Sol Invictus (Pl. 13) from Corbridge, a barbaric drawing that makes very little use of the normal Roman sculptural conception of the image of the god. But in the course of time the style was used in contexts that suggest it could be passed off as standard Roman work, and it can be seen, for instance, in a detail (Pl. 13) of an important carving of the early third century, an ornamental slab set up in honour of Septimius Severus that comes from Risingham and is now at Newcastle-upon-Tyne. It is not surprising, therefore, that at Caerleon there should be memorial slabs (Pl. 13) in which a complete classical apparatus of frame, floral sprays, wreath, and bust, should be treated in this hard low-relief manner.

As a typical example of the style I illustrate a religious carving of the second half of the Roman Period, a plaque from Wellow in Somerset (Pl. 13), now in the British Museum, that shows the three Mother-Goddesses. The figures are cut out silhouette-fashion, and the details are done in a very low relief, for no part of the bodies stands out more than $\frac{3}{8}$ inch from the background.

The most important development of the linear style, and unquestionably a British one, is represented by a carving (Pl. 12) from Netherby, now at Carlisle. Here, on an early third-century slab just over 3 feet in height, is a drawing of a goddess in a relief so low that it is nowhere more than $\frac{1}{2}$ inch in depth. It is startlingly peculiar, because it is fully and frankly Roman in intention, witness the hair, and the fruit, and the splendid couch, and yet it is completely un-Roman in the sculptor's approach to the subject. It is entirely lacking in any sense of plastic solidity, and is bravely conceived as an arrangement of flat masses within borders. The upper parts of the legs, for example, are sunk panels bounded by raised edges, and the whole figure is a balanced pattern-composition of closely defined planes, and not a sculpturesque assembly of modelled forms. It reveals, in short, a concept of the human figure in terms of flat abstract decoration, and the interesting thing is that it is precisely this inorganic decorative quality that adds so much to the charm and interest of figure-drawings in the later barbaric manuscripts (e.g. Pl. 55). It shows that in north Britain at any rate there was a latent native style in monumental figure-drawing capable of breaking with the Roman tradition and of expressing itself in a frankly 'Celtic' manner. It is one of the tragedies of Romano-British art that we should have so few examples of this work and should know so little of its significance.

The classical approach to subjects derived from the world of nature was essentially organic, and decorative themes that include sympathetically realistic animals and plants are common in Roman Britain, not only in the major works of the sculptor, painter, and mosaic-layer, but in the minor products of the metal-worker and potter. A painted basket of purple plums and green leaves from the walls of a villa at Brading in the Isle of Wight is an example of the fashionable still-life group, doubtless the detail of some garden-like decoration, and there are many other fragments of patterned walls over which foliage and gay flowers were spread. On a Silchester wall there were ears of barley. Leafy scrolls appear on the mosaic floors, and trees too, and branches and sprays and flowering plants, even to the end of the Roman Period.

With the animal we come to the first subject in Romano-British art that may be said to have had an already firmly established interest for the native Briton ; but the new menagerie of the mosaics and the sculptures has nothing to do with such essays as the Britons had previously made in modelling or drawing the beasts of the field. Where they had delighted in caricature and fantastic geometrical abstraction, the Roman taste now demanded a recognition of the naturalistic picture, and this not necessarily of the familiar horse or dog or boar, but of the lion and the tiger, the elephant, the panther, the bear, the peacock, the pheasant, the sea-cow, and the gryphon. There are butterflies on the scabbard of a gladius from the Thames that is now in the British Museum. Oceanus, on a pavement, lives in a marine world of dolphins, sea-anemones, and water-plants. Venus, on another pavement, is shown rising from the sea with an encircling company of dolphins, mullet, and limpet-shells. To the last days of Roman Britain the great imperial wild beast show remained with us.

In sculpture there are a number of fine pieces embodying the principles of naturalistic representation in an imposing form, perhaps the best of them being the head and shoulders of a magnificent panther, now in the collection of the Yorkshire Museum. Several of the more important build-

27

ings had elaborate friezes on which there were life-like animal figures. Here again York has the best piece, a fragment showing a dog baiting a horse that stands facing the spectator, his head alone turned towards his aggressor ; but most of this architectural work shows the creatures in profile, and my illustration from Chester (Pl. 14), a detail of the chase, is typical of this series of carvings. The work is not without a certain liveliness ; but most of it is heavily handled and rather unconvincing copy-work, and in few sculptures of the kind do we observe a provincial barbaric quality affecting noticeably the normal dull naturalism of Roman taste ; but the carving at Bath (Pl. 14) is one of the exceptional pieces that reveals a certain barbaric intensification in its gesture and grimness. It was, I think, because this zest for a super-charged violence of expression is Celtic or German, rather than Roman, that the examples of it in Roman Britain are often to be found upon the cheapest and most inconsequential objects. While the Castor ware, for example, cannot be said to illustrate a peculiarly British style, and still less a peculiarly Celtic one, it does preserve in some measure a generalized barbaric ferocity in animal-drawing, almost Scythian in temper. The creatures in the gladiatorial scenes on these cups, and the leaping and racing beasts that hurtle round them, possess a quality that is lacking even in the finest of the purely Roman animals from this country ; a quality of elasticity and ribbon-like corporeal suppleness that one would connect rather with Early British animal-drawing than with the quieter naturalism of official Roman art.

Often, of course, provincialism resulted in merely grotesque misrepresentation, particularly in cases where the subject was unknown to the carver. We see this in sculpture in the free-standing lion-and-his-prey groups, as in the well-known example from Corbridge, and also in those curiously agonized lions, looking a little like ancient Britons, on the Longinus tombstone at Colchester (Pl. 10). In minor pieces of metal-work we observe other ways whereby

the animal lost his Roman naturalism ; thus, on the one
hand, we have that spirited eccentricity seen in the little
horse-shaped brooch (Pl. 15) from Painswick, Gloucestershire, and, on the other hand, the gross linear sketches of
the kind illustrated by a small ornament (Pl. 15) from
Silchester. These two pieces, however, are of early date,
and it is not until the second half of the Roman Period
that such impertinences were permitted as the flagrantly
unnatural distortion of the animal in order that he might
fit a given space. This is, above all, a sign of a truly
barbaric animal-art, which is not only coldly and inorganic-
ally geometrical, but also intolerant of restrictions due to
the necessity of maintaining natural attitudes. The whole
of the later Celtic and Saxon animal-ornament is based
on this release from the control of the life-like and intelligible profile, and it is interesting to discover in Roman
Britain experiments that presage the coming change. My
example is a small copper-gilt pendant (Pl. 15) in Dr.
Oswald's collection from Margidunum in Nottinghamshire.
This is plainly barbaric in a way that the miserable Silchester drawing is not. It represents a new liberty taken,
and is the herald of that accentuated ribbon-like abstraction
of the animal which was subsequently to pass into Saxon art.

Another indication of an increasingly barbaric handling
of the animal that is to be observed in late Romano-British
work is the disintegration of the head, body, and limbs
into, as it were, separate pieces. The first expression of
this tendency is to be seen on carvings such as a Caerleon
slab which shows, in a very low relief, a dog baiting a
lion. Here the lines of the jaw and joints are overemphasized until they seem to divide the dog into his component
parts. In small-scale work, where the effects of a heavy
hand in carving are specially noticeable, this tendency
becomes more and more a characteristic mannerism, and
in such pieces as the knife-handle from Corbridge (Pl. 15)
and the terminal of the silver spoon from Kent (Pl. 15),
we approach, if indeed we do not actually reach, that

Dark Ages style in which the animal really does dissolve into a loose assembly of bits and pieces.

Another contribution of Roman provincial art to the decorative systems of the Dark Ages was the animal-head terminal. The ornamental value of this was already known to the pre-Roman Britons, an obvious example being the bold ox-head finials of the prehistoric iron fire-dogs, and, since lion-masks and the like were used in much the same way in classical decoration, there was no reason why the animal-terminal should not have continued in use. But the sort of Romano-British terminal that I have in mind,

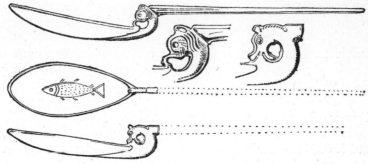

FIG. 4.—Silver spoons from Dorchester ($\frac{1}{2}$: details $\frac{1}{4}$)

a snouted creature with prominent ears, seems to be an expression of native rather than Roman taste. As examples we have the animal-headed pieces of chairs, in wood from Leicester and in shale from Dorset (Pl. 16), which certainly look as though they represent a preponderantly British taste. But more to the point are the Late Roman silver spoons from Dorchester (Fig. 4), for here we come very close indeed to the terminal-types of post-Roman British bronzes (cf. Pl. 33, 2).

The naturalistic foliate scroll of Roman art has nothing to do with the severely abstract version of the scroll that had been perfected in Early British art. It is, on the contrary, sympathetically realistic and organic, and is an importation associated with costly mosaics and fine sculpture that clearly reflects the tastes of rich persons. It occurs, for instance, very frequently on the Samian Ware that was brought over in large quantities from the potteries of Gaul and Germany, and though it is sometimes rather harshly stylized, it retains its classical character to the end. There seem to have been two principal types, one very gay with pretty leaves and flowers, and the other bare and thin, with leaves of the ivy type. I illustrate, however, not one of these, but a less common variety that is to be seen on the handle of a bronze skillet (Pl. 16) from Colchester, now in the British Museum. The pattern is interesting because there is a bird in each of these volutes, and it is therefore one of the earliest examples in Roman Britain of the famous theme of the ' inhabited scroll ', that was later to dominate Western ornament.[1]

In the fourth century we meet for the first time a new type of scroll that is illustrated by a carved stone slab from Corbridge (Pl. 16). It bears a dainty vine that grows out of a vase and spreads in a thin and delicate tracery across the panel. Another slab (Pl. 16), also, in all probability, from Corbridge and now preserved in Hexham Abbey,[2] likewise shows us this new style, this time in its richer ' inhabited ' form, since among the branches of the vine there move the naked figures of fruit-gatherers and a goat and a cock. The work so closely resembles in style the Late Antique designs popular in mosaics that I think these northern sculptures must belong to the late

[1] This motive is also to be found on Samian pottery at Chester, as Professor Newstead has pointed out to me, and also at Wroxeter (*Report*, 1912, fig. 12, p. 38). In Rome it is seen at its finest on early carvings like the Ara Pacis.

[2] cf. the fragments of the same slab at Durham, *Catalogue of the Sculptured and Inscribed Stones in the Cathedral Library*, nos. VIII and IX in the Anglian series, and Collingwood's reconstruction of the whole slab, *Northumbrian Crosses*, fig. 28.

fourth or early fifth century, and it is therefore not likely that this example of the inhabited vine-scroll is in any way connected with the Saxon version of the same theme that we shall next study in sculpture of the second half of the seventh century. The chief value of the two Corbridge pieces is that they provide proof of the far-reaching influences of fashionable classical art in Italy even at the very end of the Roman Period in Britain.[1]

Floral and foliate patterns are not confined to scroll-designs, and on the mosaic pavements they often take the form of roundels, quatrefoils, and crosses. These bold and gaily coloured designs, here illustrated by the second-century pavement from Coombe St. Nicholas in Somerset (Pl. 17), help us to realize a very important characteristic of many mosaics here and in other provinces, and in Italy too, and that is their extraordinary barbaric quality. By this I do not mean that it is un-Roman and against the usage of classical art to design an inorganic geometrical pattern such as forms the background of this pavement, but I say that in this instance the rosettes are tending to become barbaric in manner, and instead of retaining their classical integrity as naturalistic petal-groups, now assume the character of an inorganic abstraction. Indeed, they are such dead and garish patchwork things that, were it not for their static quality and symmetry, they might be introduced without any very violent stylistic impropriety into the pages of a Celtic manuscript. In general terms it would not be overstating this point of view to say that in their usual ornamental type the mosaic pavements, particularly the later ones, betray an attitude to decoration that is definitely not classical. Many of them, of course, are Roman in concept, and contain naturalistic

---

[1] This remark also applies to minor antiquities. Thus a Late Roman silvered buckle-plate bearing a vine-scroll with pecking birds was found in a Saxon grave in Sussex (*Sussex Arch. Coll.*, 57, 1915, Pl. 29, p. 200).

figure-subjects in spacious simple settings of the Pompeiian kind ; but others are in a mixed style in which crude and crowded geometric patterns jostle round and against the classical emblema ; and my contention is that some of them are completely un-Roman, just as the ' Persian ' carpets in our own homes are not European, though perhaps designed and made in Europe.

The interlace-designs on the mosaics, which were used with increasing frequency and emphasis in the second half of the Roman Period, arc characteristically logical,[1] unbroken, smooth-running, and closely knit. The chief patterns are the guilloche or simple twist and, in later work, plaits of three or four strands of equal width. Occasionally, as at a bifurcation of a plait, there are tangled uneven passages looking a little like later knotted interlace ; but the knot itself was never used in these borders ; nor is there any hint of that zoomorphic liveliness, that mesh of wriggling lines, which alters the character of interlace-work when the Dark Ages begin. But the patterns used were nevertheless congenial to barbaric taste, and it is not very surprising that the Roman method of using heavy ostentatious interlace in broad panels and borders, thus established by the mosaics, should reappear in the earliest ornamental system of the Celtic and Hiberno-Saxon manuscripts.

Our early mosaics in Britain do not need description in this book. Thin geometric patterns are common, and in the example (Pl. 17) from Silchester, a whole floor was made up of an assembly of delicately drawn linear figures ; but this was composed in an even smooth-flowing chequer of inset squares in a contained fret-design, and it

---

[1] An apparent exception is the double guilloche that is linked by caliciform or straight cross-pieces, and looks rather like a chain-pattern (Pl. 18). In all probability, however, this pattern is not in origin an interlace. Cf., for instance, the border of the Lion Mosaic at Teramo, *Mem. Amer. Acad. Rome*, VIII (1930), Pl. opp. p. 7, and see R. Hinks, *British Museum Catalogue of Paintings and Mosaics*, p. lvii.

is not really typical of the usual geometric pavement of the ' distributed window ' class, wherein the field is divided by a geometrical framework into a symmetrical system of clearly defined openings that are then filled with figures or busts or rosettes, or some other ornament more prominent than the Silchester squares. The Coombe St. Nicholas pavement (Pl. 17) is an example. But it is the increasing richness of this series that I want to emphasize. A fine example that is dated *c.* 160–90 is illustrated in colour by Dr. Wheeler in his Verulamium report [1] ; but I choose here two even more riotously sumptuous floors (Pl. 19) from Leicestershire—one, of the late second or early third century, from Leicester itself ; and the other, which is probably late third-century work, from Medbourne. The first has a gaily decorated framework with octagonal windows that are filled with brilliant patterns, including intricate designs of overlapping and intersecting circles such as had delighted the continental Celt some centuries earlier, and the second is even more crowded with complicated decoration. They are both exultantly barbaric in temper, and the reason why they are also Roman designs is that they are disciplined and organized in a Roman way. Thus, though they are alive in the whirring ferocity of their pattern, this barbarous tumult is held in check. It is massed, held back, and imprisoned, in its rigid frame. In just the same way certain of the finest decorated pages of the Lindisfarne Gospels owe their splendour to the fact that a similar classical discipline maintains equipoise and order in the arrangement of their intricate ornament (cf. Pl. 40).

A possible immediate connexion between the art of the pavements and the art of the Celtic manuscripts is, as I have hinted, one of the problems that I should like to see studied very seriously. The inquiry would be concerned principally with floors in the south-west of England, and we must notice two of them here that are both notable for

[1] *Soc. Ant., London, Report* XI (1936), Pl. XLII.

the abrupt and jerky emphasis on the joints of the controlling framework. One (Pl. 20) comes from Brislington
in Somerset and is now in the Bristol Museum,[1] and on
this the pattern is a rectangular trellis with large rectangles
marking the intersections of the horizontal and vertical
lines, a decorative scheme that we find again in the very
first manuscript of the Irish series (Pl. 37). The second
pavement (Pl. 20), which is likewise connected with the
ornamental system of the same manuscript (Fig. 21), comes
from Frampton in Dorset. Here the intersections are
marked by large and clearly defined equal-armed crosses.
Furthermore, the scale and type of the curly dolphins in the
inset panels should be observed ; for this is one beginning
of the ribbon-like zoomorphic ornament that is associated
with the heavy geometric patterns of Dark Ages design.

This leads us to another distinguishing feature of the
south-western group of pavements. As an obvious example
of the series I take a better-known Frampton floor (Pl. 21)
which bears the Christian emblem and a portrait of Nep-
tune and an inscription in his honour. Probably Lysons's
engraving is in some respects inaccurate ; but not so
seriously that we are likely to be misled in assessing the
style. Its most striking characteristic is that the pavement
is much more heavily panelled than in earlier designs,
and in the square floor of the main room with the apse the
' windows' containing the figure-subjects have doubled
outlines and are aggressively built together, as though they
were the main structure of the design instead of apertures
in a framework. But that which is much more important
for our special purpose is that the smaller room illustrates
the ornamental system of this group in which two long and
broad panels of equal size containing an unbroken single-
unit figure-design adjoin the main square at each end of
the floor. There is nothing new about such a composition

[1] I have to thank Mr. G. R. Stanton for supplying me with photographs of this pavement and for the help he has given me by studying
and reconstructing the design.

for a rectangular pavement ; but on comparing this with earlier examples it will be seen that the end panels have now a much greater emphasis and function as important figured friezes. In the Frampton example the subjects in these panels are hunting-scenes with large-scale figures that are often the height of the panel itself, and at Wellow in Somerset there are big animals in scroll-like plants, and at Ramsbury in Wiltshire there are confronted animals on either side of a vase. This arrangement of figured friezes seems to be a local one and, so far as I know, peculiar to the pavements of south-western Britain.[1] It seems, therefore, to give an unexpected and significant indication of the source of that early Irish manuscript style in which a carpet-like page of decoration is adorned with friezes of relatively large animals arranged round a square field that contains a central medallion (cf. Pl. 37).[2]

A very interesting study could be made of the history in Roman Britain of that favourite crescentic or shield-shaped decorative form, the pelta. In its classical manner, sometimes with spiral terminals and tails (Pl. 18), it is not of any special significance to us ; but the native variations of the pelta-theme are well worth investigation. At an early period small openwork bronzes that are based on the long-tailed pelta were circulating in the Rhineland and Danube provinces, and a few of these pieces found their way to Britain, for example the Silchester mount (Pl. 22), a flamboyant ornament that contrives to look a

[1] The broad geometric frieze is more common and can be studied in late pavements at Winterton in Lincolnshire. The best example is the mid-third century ' Piaonius ' pavement at Trier.

[2] An alternative source might be provided by certain textiles, and it is clear that portable embroidered cloths of the kind that are so plentiful in Coptic Egypt may have played a part in the formation of the Irish style. The problem of the connexion, if any, between the south-western pavements and the Egyptian textiles has still to be investigated.

little like a plant-scroll design. Of the same date, certainly not later than the second century, are the silver and bronze castings in the form of a sharply broken curve with a heavy trumpet-ridge at the break, and these can be shown on the foreign evidence to be barbaric drolleries in the same pelta-style. Thus the ornament from Icklingham in Suffolk (Pl. 22) is really a whorl of three peltae ; but most of the pieces of this class, for instance the mount from Ashdown in Berkshire (Pl. 22), are asymmetrical S-shaped variants, distorted limbs of peltae so completely barbaric in style that at first glance they do not seem to have anything to do with their classical original. The barbaric tendency, in other words, was to break the pelta, to divide it into two expanding trumpet-shaped scrolls by emphasizing the centre with a ridge or a mouth (as on the second-century Bridgeness building inscription), and also to link it with other peltae into all-over patterns and into spinning forms. In the third and fourth centuries, for instance, we have on our mosaic floors rotating swastikas most cunningly devised from linked peltae,[1] as on the Medbourne pavement (Pl. 19), and another common form of the linked peltae is to be seen on the Frampton pavement in the long strip connecting the two rooms (Pl. 21). A very interesting example, in which the peltae are drawn with large central mouths, will be found in the interior panel of the enamelled altar-shaped plaque (Pl. 23) from the Thames, now in the British Museum. The design in the inner panel is that of an all-over pattern of opposed peltae, as on the late pavements.[2] This has in the field

[1] This is an accurate description of the design as seen in the provinces, but I think it was originally a floral pattern later interpreted as a pelta-group.

[2] Its expanded form has been drawn out by the continental scholar Alois Riegl, *Spät-römische Kunst-Industrie*, Vienna, 1901, p. 192, fig. 87. Lethaby, failing to recognize the peltae, describes the pattern as a La Tène style scroll, *Londinium*, London, 1923, p. 207 ; this, side by side with Riegl's view, is an astonishing tribute to the transforming hand of the native designer.

the trefoil details that adorn the peltae of the late pavements, and such a heavily framed spreading design could
not conceivably be earlier than the fourth century. Moreover, the cantharus-type in the confronted animal-groups,
like that on the Ramsbury pavement, makes the late dating
of the plaque a certainty,[1] and as the piece is unfinished,
and therefore, likely to be Romano-British, it is obviously
an ornament of considerable importance ; for it is thoroughly
barbaric in concept and obviously a precursor of the Dark
Ages trumpet-pattern style.

At this point I may refer, though I do so with some
hesitation, to a small group of embossed brooches (e.g.
Pl. 22, centre left) that is usually assigned to the third or
fourth century. They seem to represent a distinctively
northern [2] version of the linked pelta theme, now reduced
to an almost unrecognizable form as the result of an entirely
insular invention. The design upon them consists of three
S-shaped curves set triskele-wise, each curve having a
thickened trumpet-pattern bend, a long thin curling tail,
and terminals that look like heads of birds. It is an ornament that is purely Celtic in type, and in the lively peaked
terminals we recognize that taste for the bizarre which has
already been manifested in the 'dragonesque' brooches
(Pl. 5). Yet the elements of the pattern are almost
certainly derived from the provincial openwork bronzes of
the first and second century (Pl. 22), for this source, or
some contemporary equivalent, alone explains the heavy
trumpet-pattern head, the dragging tails, the beaked
terminals, and the little curls that project from the edges.
It is possible, therefore, that these brooches may be rather

[1] cf. *Brit. Mus. Cat. Paintings and Mosaics*, no. 49, and the references
there cited.
[2] There are eight of them. Six come from the Brigantian north and
only two from the south. There is, however, a pottery stamp from the
Great Bedwyn villa in Wiltshire (*Proc. Soc. Ant.*, XIX, 1902, p. 188)
that may have been responsible for many repetitions in southern England of an analogous type of ornament.

earlier in date than is commonly supposed ; but they are so fantastically mannered that they are hardly likely to have been made before the third century, and the most remarkable thing about them is that in one detail of their pattern, the long curling tails fining down to thin spirals that encircle the head of another curve, they approach a style of the early Dark Ages that is represented by a charming fifth-century enamelled escutcheon from Kent (Pl. 27), and by various Hiberno-Scottish enamels.[1]

The Thames plaque leads me to the subject of colour. The daily life of the richer sections of the Romano-British community was passed amid surroundings in which colour played a considerable part, and to appreciate this we have only to think of the brilliant polychrome appearance of many mosaics, of the elaborately painted walls, the wide range of colours in the finer ceramic wares, the sumptuous mottled glasses, and the fine enamels. Even sculpture was often painted and there must have been an air of chromatic cheerfulness about Roman Britain that the drab and corroded surviving antiquities do not adequately reflect. In the lesser works, particularly the small enamels, there is, however, a note of such crudely jarring polychromy that it deserves notice as a symptom of provincial barbaric taste. Thus on the bows of some second-century brooches we have a gaudy mosaic of juxtaposed blocks of enamel, red, turquoise blue, and yellow, in the example (Pl. 23) from Chepstow. There is nothing peculiarly British in this violently coloured work, which is, in fact, best seen abroad. But the ' dragonesque ' brooches (Pl. 5) are British, and we must note that they show precisely the same gaiety in colour. The frequent use of millefiori enamel added to this geometric brilliance, and the fine disc-brooch from Chepstow (Pl. 23) with its close-set chequer in red, white, and blue, is the kind of work that inspired many poorer pieces

[1] cf. the Irish latchet, Leeds, *Celtic Ornament*, fig. 36c.

of native manufacture, one of them being illustrated in the top right-hand corner of the same plate. The point that I now wish to emphasize is that this taste for garish polychrome colouring remained with us until the closing days of Roman Britain. The mosaic pavements are the best proof of this, and it is a curious fact that the later they are the more they contain of the minute geometric chequerwork in colour that looks so much like slabs of enlarged millefiori enamel (cf. the narrow strip above the Chi-Rho panel in the Frampton pavement, Pl. 21).[1] But there are enamels that tell the same tale. Our Thames plaque was a gorgeous assembly of blues, reds, and greens, and in this piece we observe of the failings of this violent polychromy, for the hard patchwork effect of the colours results in a serious loss of the pattern-value of the design, the peltae merging, as it were, in an all-over spread of equally high tones. The colour itself ceases to function as a statement of the design, which depends increasingly on a false pattern created by the metal outlines of the coloured fields, and it is just this emphasis on the linear quality of a thin bronze pattern against a brightly coloured field that finds its further expression on the escutcheons of the post-Roman hanging-bowls (cf. Pl. 27). Indeed, it explains why a polychrome background was no longer used when, as on the early bowls, the line-drawing in metal became the principal part of the ornament.

To end this chapter I am going to name a few works that will give us some idea of what official Roman art in this province was like in the late third and early fourth century. It is, I think, a mistake to suppose that the period was one of unrelieved decline in classical impressiveness and grandeur, and, as it happens, it is a carving in stone of great beauty that I select as a first example of

[1] This is better illustrated on the Wellow mosaics and on the Winterton series. It is also to be seen on many late foreign mosaics.

our Late Roman sculpture. This is the Cirencester capital (Pl. 24). It is probably the work of an Asiatic of the Constantian Age and shows busts of Zeus with the bipennis, of Silvanus, and of Bacchus, and of an Amazon,[1] with heads that possess in a marked degree a wild, mournful stare not uncommon in Late Antique portraiture. The eyes are the chief feature. Gloomily gazing, they invest the busts with a dignity that the sculpture itself makes no pretensions to deserve. The heavy line of the nose, deeply carved round the nostrils, and the dark shadow of the mouth, add to the effect of the big troubled eyes, and we feel that in spite of certain crudities in execution the sculptor has given to these countenances a fervent spiritual quality, as though he would reveal to us the soul itself.

There is nothing else in Roman Britain quite like this ; but there are other sculptures of a late date, for instance the vine-scroll panels from Corbridge that I have already noted (Pl. 16). And also from fourth-century Corbridge comes one of the rare carvings with a narrative interest (Pl. 24), the subject being either an imperial apotheosis or an illustration of the solar myth. The slab, now a broken fragment of a longer frieze, shows a crowned figure on a winged horse who approaches the end of a large building in which stands one of the Dioscuri who holds a horse by the bridle. It is really this horse that is in the temple, for the figure, as the cap shows, is just outside it. This very odd spatial arrangement suggests a comparison with Late Antique ivories, and another feature of the panel, the attempt to draw the building in perspective, is also in the manner of the ivory diptychs.

The late mosaics have already been mentioned ; but one of them is remarkable in the contrast that it provides to these sculptures, for it illustrates the grossly uncouth travesties of the official style that were tolerated in the homes of rich persons at this late day in company, presumably,

[1] I have to thank Dr. O. Brendel for advice in the matter of this carving.

with works that still preserved a classical dignity and naturalism. This is the pavement (Pl. 25) from Rudston in Yorkshire, an example of muddled, pathetic conservatism clinging so closely to classical precept that there was little scope for the exercise of barbaric talent. It is doubtful if one could find anywhere a more shocking caricature of classical figural art than in the central roundel. For this wild-haired, thick-armed, steatopygous, weak-kneed creature is Venus stepping from her bath and holding the apple won by her beauty. It would be dishonest to pretend that the figure has acquired new aesthetic values in the course of the deformation it has suffered, and it would be equally misleading to suggest that the drawing has any peculiarly British significance ; for it is a standard and not uncommon decadent classicism of the provinces.[1]

There are a number of minor antiquities illustrating the decorative styles that adorned valuable metal-work at the end of the Roman Period. They can scarcely be said to reflect a popular Romano-British taste, for most of the material is costly silver and elaborate pewter services. But some of the pieces at least may have been made in this country, and there is no doubt that the commoner forms of ornament upon them were widely used. The general style is a close, flat spread of pattern arranged in panels and medallions, rather like some of the pavement designs, and a few of the purely geometric devices of the pavements occur regularly in this metal-work, an example being the familiar interlocking square or triangular frames, here set off against a light background of scrolls or feathery acanthus. Our most elaborate pieces of Late Antique silver are to be found in the wonderful treasure that was discovered in 1919 on Traprain Law, now at Edinburgh. One silver flagon has a plant-scroll with large trefoil leaves (Fig. 5) ;

[1] For another example of this class of mosaic cf. the floor of the Early Christian chapel at Teurina (Schober, *Römerzeit in Österreich*, fig. 36). For the Rudston figure-type cf. the steatite box from Nubia in the Victoria and Albert Museum, Coptic work of the sixth century.

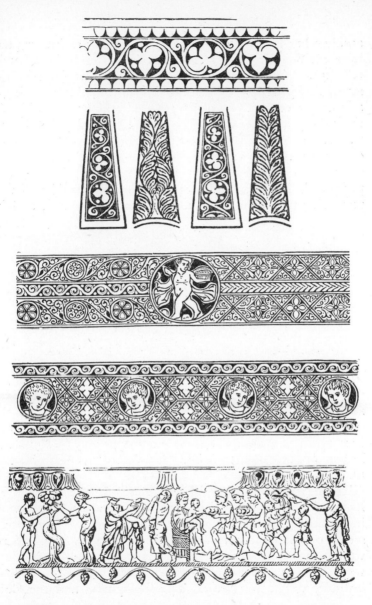

FIG. 5.—Details of ornament on silver vessels in the Treasure
of Traprain

another has lavishly decorated zones that are interrupted by medallions containing figures of genii or human heads (Fig. 5). On both these flagons, which are not necessarily imported pieces, the design is inlaid with niello, and on the edge of one of the spoons in this treasure (Fig. 6) the ornament takes the form of a tiny zigzag border of reserved silver on a narrow niello band, a peculiar and easily recognizable variety of niello-inlay that we shall soon see again on some of our earliest Saxon antiquities (cf. p. 63). It is an important point that we should find this particular type of inlay in a Late Roman context, and in

Fig. 6.—Bowl of silver spoon with niello inlay, Treasure of Traprain (½)

the case of this spoon I think we may claim with some assurance that it is Romano-British work ; for I know no example of this inlay in Late Antique silver abroad, whereas I am able to cite another example of it that may be Romano-British on the bow of a late ' cross-bow ' brooch (Pl. 22) that comes from Bath.[1]

There was no distinguishable Early Christian style in Roman Britain. The Faith was too young and too uncertain in status for us to expect sarcophagi bearing scriptural scenes or other imposing antiquities of the kind, and there were no circumstances attending the change of belief that were likely to cause any appreciable alteration in the ordinary decorative forms. The fish-symbol and the Chi-

[1] It is, however, also to be seen on a similar brooch (Fröhner coll. 273) in the Bibliothèque Nationale at Paris.

44

Rho appear ; but there is not much else to note, though we can be sure that a few small objects bearing Christian figure-subjects were perhaps in circulation. Thus in the Traprain treasure there is a repoussé silver flagon (Fig. 5) that shows the Fall, Moses striking the rock, the Adoration of the Magi, and an unidentified scene, in the form of a continuous frieze without dividing columns. This is the only example of Late Antique Christian art in the country

FIG. 7.—Bronze buckle from Smithfield, London (⅔)

that can be compared with the sculptural style of the western Mediterranean sarcophagi and ivories ; but later came one or two poorer vessels, like the Long Wittenham stoup, with embossed bronze plates bearing Scriptural scenes, probably Gaulish work of the fifth century. These are found not in a Roman context, but in the Saxon graves.

The Traprain find also includes examples of the embossed and strongly faceted metal-work in the ' chip-carving ' style. Such work is best seen on imported German brooches and buckles (Fig. 7) of the fifth century ; but the form

45

of decoration that these continental trinkets bear had been seen in Britain before the Roman Period was over, for example in stone-carving on north country altars, and on minor objects like Late Roman silver vessels and shale patera-handles. On the later German metal-work the ornament is characteristically a close all-over spread of geometric patterns, spiral scrolls, rosettes, and quatrefoil foliate sprays, arranged in panels. These elements are all derived from classical ornament, and the chip-carving panels themselves are sometimes combined with engravings in medallions of classical heads and of naturalistic hunting-scenes. The importance of the style lies in the sharply ridged and heavily faceted treatment of the designs, which results in curiously barbaric mannerisms, as in the case when the background of a spiral scroll is itself raised and faceted, so that it projects itself into the design as a trumpet-shaped shoulder,[1] thus foreshadowing a typical Dark Ages style. The work has an additional interest because of the new fondness shown for flamboyant spirals and tightly curled scrolls. These are drawn with an exuberance and clean precision that must be regarded as factors likely to contribute to the development of curvilinear pattern in post-Roman Britain. The ' equal-armed ' brooches of the invading Saxons (Pl. 29) show that they were no strangers to these rolling spiraliform designs ; and the style was generally common in the German world, for even in such remote places as the Island of Gotland we find at this period remarkable painted stelae bearing roundels in which are tightly curled spiral swastikas of noble and accurate design.

[1] E.g. *Schumacher-Festschrift*, Mainz, 1930, opp. p. 294. Tf. 32, A.

III

ARTHURIAN BRITAIN

IT must have been in the first twilight of the Dark Ages and in the desolation of ruined buildings and broken statuary that the spirit of Romano-British art died. That which had been an era of buildings, an era of towns with fora, baths, and amphitheatres, became an age of wooden halls and mud huts ; and with the passing of architecture, with the passing of even the incentive to build in stone, the essence of the whole unstable provincial classicism that was the result of Roman rule must have been abruptly annihilated. For with architecture went much else, and as the buildings crumbled, so the statues fell, the memorials were broken and neglected, the paintings peeled off the house-walls, and the weeds grew where the pavements had been. And nothing took their place ; not indeed until the days of Paulinus and of Benedict Biscop in the 7th century. Over two hundred years for the beggarly Saxon world of the wooden halls to scorn, to destroy, and to forget that impressive stamp of Roman greatness that had been laid so laboriously upon this far-off province of Britain.

Inevitably, then, since the legacy of Romano-British art cannot amount to more than a trickle of little things, and since the Saxons introduced no ambitious works such as sculptures and pavements, it can only be trifles in the way of personal ornaments and minor property of the individual that 'Arthurian' Britain and Pagan Saxondom offer for our study. Until architecture and its structural and monumental concepts return with the Anglo-Saxon renaissance in the Golden Age of the English Church there is no

47

material that is larger than a bucket or longer than a sword, and the contrast between our Roman and our post-Roman art could scarcely be greater. We have to content ourselves henceforth with bowls and brooches and similar small antiquities ; and though we may find much that is attractive and interesting in the new barbaric styles, I think my first duty is to emphasize the comparative littleness and emptiness of post-Roman archaeology in Britain.

How soon and in what sorry stages Roman art lost its hold on native life we have now no means of telling. It is probable that attempts were made by some of the British princes and invading Teutonic chieftains to foster a Roman tradition, and I am going to suggest that in so far as concerns late Roman craftsmanship this is more noticeable in East Kent than anywhere else (p. 63). And it is possible that even in a purely British context the age of King Arthur was less barbarian than we think ; for we shall find good reason to credit the Britons of the western and midland districts with a lively and inventive civilization that owed much to its Roman foundations. But the fact remains that there is no archaeological evidence of a surviving Roman civilization in town and country, and the most that can be said is that on *a priori* grounds the Britons, however sorely beset by enemies, however crippled by the collapse of the villa-system and the increasing insecurity of the towns, however affected by disastrous economic conditions, are not likely to have reverted suddenly to the squalor of their primordial woad, they who had known and enjoyed for four hundred years the full repertory of Roman arts and life.

So far as style in ornament is concerned, we must, of course, realize that we have now come to the end of the authentic Roman manner ; and even in the British material available for study, which is mostly derived from the Saxon graves in which it was buried as plunder, we cannot expect to find Roman art surviving unchanged. On the contrary, this material suggests that there was a speedy and whole-hearted reversion to a barbaric manner of decoration. The end of Roman rule, in other words, meant the end of an imposed classical fashion ; it meant freedom for the barbaric taste, a licence for those timid native undercurrents in the provincial Roman decorative styles to establish themselves as an ascendant and an aristocratic aesthetic formula.

I have said that the German ' chip-carving ' metal-work, with its intensified use of the tightly curled spiral scroll, is one of the factors controlling the development that we have now to follow. This, no doubt, is a barbarizing influence exerted generally and almost imperceptibly through the agency of Roman life itself in the late fourth and early fifth century, and is not a direct result of the Saxon incursion ; but it is none the less the cause of an appreciable change in style. If we take a typically soft, loose Romano-British curvilinear design, such as the triskeles on the little enamelled disc-brooches (Fig. 8), and compare this with the triskele on the enamelled escutcheon of a post-Roman bronze hanging-bowl from Stoke Golding in Leicestershire (Fig. 9, *b*), the new crisp, closely curled treatment that this piece shows should be attributed not to an automatic British development or to a Celtic revival, but to a German taste that had already made itself felt in the final days of Roman Britain. That this is so can best be demonstrated by a further comparison of both pieces with the painted swastikas of the Gotland stelae which establish beyond dispute the German zest for accurate and involved spiraliform pattern in the fifth century.[1]

But though the Stoke Golding escutcheon may be on this view German in style, it is unquestionably a British piece, and illustrates merely the British counterpart to the German spiraliform designs. It is, in fact, a mount off one of the British series of hanging-bowls that now provide almost our only material for study and represent the continuation of

[1] For these stelae, see Birger Nerman, *Die Volkerwanderungszeit Gotlands*, Stockholm, 1935, pp. 107, 108.

the Romano-British enamel industry in post-Roman times. The hanging-bowl has a long history. In a plain un-enamelled form it was part of the furniture of the Roman household at Pompeii, and it was known in the provincial

Fig. 8.—Designs on Romano-British enamelled brooches and seal-box lid (⅔)

world as early as the second century.[1] It was still used in Germany in the second half of the Roman Period, and escutcheons representing the continental type of this time have been found at Silchester and elsewhere, while two complete bowls from this country seem to be a local variety

[1] An example in the Darmstadt Museum, bearing a maker's stamp, comes from a cremated burial.

50

of the 4th or early 5th century.[1] How soon the bowls with enamelled fittings appear we do not know ; but there is no doubt that some examples, for instance the Baginton bowl (Pl. 26), are ornamented in a fifth-century style and were probably made not very long after the Roman Period was over.

From the fifth to the seventh century enamelled hanging-bowls are found in England alone.[2] The finds represent 18 bowls ; and in 9 instances they are known to come from Saxon graves, as doubtless many others of them do too ; but not a single one has been discovered in a context that can be described as British. Nevertheless, they are undoubtedly present in these burials as loot from the British workshops, or at any rate as a ' foreign ' element in Saxon archaeology.[3] That the Saxons, like the Vikings after them,

[1] Finningley hoard, *Antiquity*, VI (1932), p. 163, fig. 2 ; cf. the escutcheon necks with Romano-British brooches, *Arch. Aeliana*, 3 S., VII (1911), p. 184. Also the Wilton bowl, *Archaeologia*, LVI (1898), p. 40 ; cf. *Richborough Report*, II (1928), fig. 33.

[2] One escutcheon of an early bowl has been found abroad at Mons ; but it is obviously a stray piece, as Mr. Reginald Smith recognized when he reported its existence, *Proc. Soc. Ant.*, XXII (1907–9), p. 82.

[3] Françoise Henry has repeatedly expressed to me her opinion that I am wrong in saying that the bowls are British, for in her view they are of Irish manufacture, and since I wrote this chapter she has published what is undoubtedly the best paper in existence on these hanging-bowls, *Journ. R. Soc. Ant. Ireland*, LXVI, Pt II (1936), p. 209. She knows that I do not agree with her. I think that the distribution of the various types of bowls, as found in England, is much more important than she will admit. If they were really plunder from Ireland the various kinds would be much more evenly scattered. As it is, I claim that my ' developed trumpet-pattern ' class is of south British origin, because it does not occur in the north or north-west, and I infer that the bowls of this class were obtained by the Saxons of the south and the midlands from the adjacent Britons. If they were of Irish make they should be distributed up and down the land. I may add that I attach very little importance to the very interesting point Mlle Henry makes about the colour of our early escutcheons. Why, she asks, are the first escutcheons enamelled in red only, if they are the product of surviving Romano-British enamel-craft, for typical Romano-British enamels are polychrome ? And she answers that the explanation is

were often buried with stolen property, or at least objects that they could not possibly have made themselves, is indisputable, and it is all the more obvious in this case because we find that the Saxon graves frequently contain not complete bowls, but loose escutcheons wrenched off bowls and perforated for suspension on necklaces. There are no less than 9 finds of escutcheons thus mutilated, and I illustrate one of them (Pl. 27) that is believed to come from the Oxford district ; but the best attested discovery occurred in a Saxon grave at Camerton, Somerset, where three escutcheons were found strung together round the neck of a child.[1] This, quite apart from the stylistic reasons in favour of a British origin to which I shall shortly refer, seems to be a decisive point. It is not, of course, necessary to press the theory that the bowls were loot so far that it demands the rigid exclusion of every other view, such as the theory that the production of the bowls may have been partly due to a policy of protection for the native enamel-craft on the part of the admiring Saxon chieftains after their settlement.[2] But though I might agree that one or two of the complete bowls may have been expressly made for Saxon ownership, I think it remains in the highest degree improbable that the Saxons played a really significant part in the furtherance of the British enamel-craft, for the very good reason that this craft seems to have come to an abrupt and unhappy end after the Saxon conquest and settlement were complete. There is, in fact, no enamelling in Saxon

that these escutcheons are really Irish, for Irish work is done at first in red only, and we have here instances of the re-introduction of the enamel-craft, not of its survival. My own view is that our early escutcheons are monochrome for the very good reason that, like the Irish work to which she refers, they were at first line-drawings in reserved metal that demanded a monochrome background. It was only when the pattern-value of the metal line began to be obscured and had become less and less important that the addition of variegated colours in the background was allowed.

[1] *Antiquaries' Journal*, X (1930), p. 292.
[2] *Antiquity*, VI (1932), p. 292.

England after the period of the bowls until we come to the Alfred Jewel in the late ninth century, and this, of course, is in a style that bears no relation to the earlier work. Indeed, so far from protecting the enamel-craft, the Saxons destroyed it ; and in the British Isles it is only in the Hiberno-Scottish area that it survived.

A number of these enamels from the hanging-bowls are in a decorative style that is inspired by and to some extent depends upon the Romano-British tradition. Thus the clumsy Dover escutcheons (Pl. 26) recall by their toothed and jagged patterns earlier Romano-British enamels.[1] The mutilated escutcheon from Eastry, Kent, now in the Maidstone Museum, is an openwork pelta-type ornament (Pl. 26) of Romano-British derivation. So are the enamels of the bowl (Pl. 26) from Baginton, near Coventry,[2] on which the easily rolling spirals are indisputably Late Roman in style, and are, in fact, the enamel counterpart of the ' chip-carving ' scrolls.

But the Baginton bowl, as Mr. Leeds was quick to perceive, represents a dawning native mannerism that is heading away from the urbane regularity of classicizing design. Thus on the ' print ' we find the spiral ends elaborated by a spinning whorl-like treatment and consisting of three members, the third being the terminal of a peaked shoulder that fills the exterior concavities of the S. This shoulder is inherent in the pattern, and it is actually present, as I have already said, in some examples of continental fifth-century ' chip-carving ' metal-work ; but in the mannered use of it here, and in the heavy accent on the three-limbed whorl, I think we have the first signs of the British development of Roman patterns that is shortly to be presented to us as a rich and distinctive barbaric style.

A bowl-escutcheon and ' print ' that were found in the Jutish cemetery at Faversham, Kent, reveal further progress

---

[1] cf. *Antiquity*, VI (1932), p. 170.
[2] *Antiquaries' Journal*, XV (1935), p. 111.

in the development of an idiomatic native style (Pl. 27). On the escutcheon the three terminals, repeating a little drollery that was to be seen in the early Brigantian work of the Roman Period (Pl. 5), are exaggerated and given eyes, so that they look like the heads of birds, and the lines of the scroll have become thin 'hair-spring' coils, set close together, again following a tendency suggested in Brigantian work. It happens that the style of these Kentish enamels finds its counterpart in Hiberno-Scottish work,[1] probably of the fifth and sixth century, so that they might possibly be considered imports from the north ; but the treatment of the scroll-terminals is so very like the Baginton style that one would require a much closer resemblance between the Faversham mounts and the northern work before rejecting the obvious conclusion that the Kentish pieces are also examples of the south English experiment with a pattern that was originally the Roman scroll.

The poor quality of the post-Roman enamel-work of the kind represented by the Dover and Eastry escutcheons [2] shows that the new and more competently handled designs do not represent a general standard of excellence. There is, for instance, an inferior 'northern' variety of the enamelled hanging-bowl that is represented by finds from Barlaston in Staffordshire (Pl. 26) and from an unknown site in Northumberland, and from Barrington in Cambridgeshire. The escutcheons on these bowls bear loose and ragged designs based on the Romano-British swastika- and triskele-patterns. In the Barlaston and Northumberland sets, though not in the Cambridgeshire

---

[1] See Leeds, *Celtic Ornament*, p. 142. The 'hair-spring' coil is well seen on the latchet shown in his Fig. 36, *c* ; but the bird's head terminals in the north have a distinctively ragged and foliate quality that suggests they are not the same as the smooth and inorganic Faversham terminals.

[2] cf. the set from Mildenhall, Suffolk, *Proc. Soc. Ant.*, XXII, pp. 74–5. The escutcheon here bears a feeble pelta-shaped pattern in the form of two large bird-like heads.

example, the craftsmen who made them were doing their best to reproduce the Roman 'millefiori' work, which means that the enamels are probably northern and not southern in origin ; for a series of 'hand-pins' and early penannular brooches from the Hiberno-Scottish world show similar bungled attempts to re-create the sumptuous and exact mosaics of the past. And there is another link with the Hiberno-Scottish school, for a little knife found in Ireland,[1] of a form derived from a Roman claw-like toilet-implement, exactly reproduces the design on the Barlaston escutcheon. Because of its Roman shape we may be tempted to regard it as an English importation ; but the fact that the Barlaston pattern occurs elsewhere in Ireland, and the matter of the millefiori enamelling, should be allowed to emphasize the north-western orientation of the Barlaston school of enamellers.

Decidedly the most important advance made by the British enamellers is that which produced the 'Developed Trumpet-Pattern' style. This was the work of a south English school in the sixth century, and it is a most interesting illustration of the new reassertion of barbaric tendencies, for the series shows not merely the accentuated spiraliform 'spin', but a combination of this with a trumpet-pattern device whereby the junction of pairs of swelling, trumpet-like curves is emphasized by small lenticular 'mouths', a mannerism that occasionally appears in Early British work (e.g. the Desborough mirror, Pl. 3) and is also to be seen in barbaric enamels of the Roman Period, for instance the Lincoln seal-box (Pl. 5) and the Thames plaque (Pl. 23). So far as the hanging-bowl escutcheons are concerned, the development of the ornament is illustrated by comparing an example from Kingston, Kent (Fig. 9, *a*) with the Stoke Golding escutcheon (Fig. 9, *b*) and then with one on a bowl from a Saxon burial on Lowbury Hill, Berkshire (Fig. 9, *c*).

From this last escutcheon there develops a series of

[1] Mahr, *Christian Art in Ancient Ireland*, I, pl. 41, 5.

triskele designs of increasing complexity that lead us to
the final forms of the style as used on the escutcheons of

FIG. 9.—Designs on escutcheons of hanging-bowls from (*a*) Kingston, Kent;
(*b*) Stoke Golding, Leics.; and (*c*) Lowbury, Berks.

the Winchester bowl (Pl. 28), which may be as late as
about A.D. 600. But simultaneously there was another

FIG. 10.—Pelta-designs in rectangular frame (cf. Pl. 23) and in a circle

variety of trumpet-pattern that developed from the whorl
of three peltae. The experiment of adapting the pattern

of the Thames plaque from its rectangular frame in order to fit a roundel provides us with the theme of the new pattern in its first form (Fig. 10). On the escutcheons the pelta-design tends more and more to resolve itself into a thin line-drawing, and in late examples of the period of the Winchester bowl, for instance the escutcheon from the Oxford district (Pl. 27) or the escutcheons in the Victoria and Albert Museum (Pl. 27), the peltae have shrunk to insignificant peaked thickenings of the metal arms proceeding from the central whorl. But examples exist in which the peltae survive as coloured fields, as in an escutcheon

Fig. 11.—Enamelled escutcheon from hanging-bowl, Lullingstone, Kent (⅓)

from Middleton Moor, Derbyshire (now at Sheffield), while on the earlier escutcheons of the bowl in the British Museum from Lullingstone, Kent, we have the design (Pl. 28 and Fig. 11) in a guise that is directly comparable with the pelta source here suggested and is only altered by a few easily comprehended modifications.

The Lullingstone bowl is not typical of British work of the Developed Trumpet-Pattern school, for in many respects it is, like the Dover escutcheons, barbaric more as a result of its debased Roman qualities than because of its native spontaneity and invention. The heavily symmetrical arrangement of its applied ornament has an almost Roman

6

regularity, and details such as the free-style row of stags, the guilloche interlace, the crude geometric devices arranged in short panels, and the key-pattern border of the escutcheons themselves, are all sub-Roman in style and can be connected with types of ornament found on the late mosaic pavements.[1] England, however, produces little of this crude, heavy work of late Roman inspiration. On the contrary, the real development of the trumpet-pattern enamelling coincides, as Mr. Leeds has observed, with a definite rejection of the surviving Roman elements in fifth-century art ; and thus it comes about that in the end the Britons produced vessels of a splendid and wholly barbaric beauty like the magnificent Winchester bowl (Pl. 28) in the British Museum. Such a combination of austerity and ornamental brilliance is a worthy culmination of a native style that had been left to develop in isolation, and it illustrates particularly well the innate genius of the barbarian for using the concentrated ornamental nucleus in adroitly chosen positions without the encumbrance of surrounding or limiting decoration. It was this same genius in the past that gave us the admirable Thames spearhead (Pl. 1), which I have previously described as one of the most un-Roman of our Early British antiquities.

There can be little doubt that the school producing the ' Developed Trumpet-Pattern ' bowls must be assigned in the main to the sixth century, even though its beginnings may take us back into the fifth century and its final work, like the Winchester bowl, may conceivably be a little later than 600. But the problem of the locality of the school is more difficult. Escutcheons representing in all 18 of these trumpet-pattern bowls have been found ; but as 9 of the finds come from Saxon graves and many of the others probably do so too, we cannot be sure that their distribution

[1] I think, however, that this Kentish work is to some extent influenced by a Gaulish or early Merovingian style, for in technique and patterns there are resemblances between the Lullingstone mounts and certain buckles found in France.

gives us more than a vague peripheral indication of the district where the bowls were originally used and made. Nevertheless the map does very strongly suggest that the work was done somewhere in the triangle formed by lines joining Leicester, Bath, and London.[1] It will be observed that when I make the claim that this brilliant ornamental style was evolved in those parts of the southern midlands that were not immediately and fully occupied by the Saxons, I am doing nothing less than force the stylistic evidence to create a British ' Arthurian ' archaeology that was not hitherto known to exist. We must regard it, therefore, as a notable advance if we are able to agree on the testimony of the hanging-bowls that a people completely lost to us archaeologically have in fact left princely and abundant traces of their presence, and can be credited with the invention of a native ornament that is distinguished alike for its intricacy of design and its technical achievement.

The position would be clearer, and the claims on behalf of the Britons better appreciated, if we could rid our minds of the notion that the trumpet-pattern of the bowl-escutcheons is a revival of antique Celtic work. It is this view that has led to unnecessary efforts to account for its advent as an importation from some remote area where the original Celtic style had been fostered during the two centuries in which it is unknown in Roman Britain. But I have tried to make it clear that there is not the slightest reason to suppose that this post-Roman style is anything but a native development of patterns that were a part of Romano-British art. What we have here is not a reversion to a stale prehistoric ornament ; it is not the old ' La Tène ' art introduced a second time ; but a natural resurgence of barbaric tendencies set free by the withdrawal of the Romans and expressed, after observable hesitation and

---

[1] We can certainly rule out the Hiberno-Scottish north, and we can rule out East Kent and Sussex. A Derbyshire and a Lincolnshire find are at present the northernmost. An escutcheon in the British Museum from the Crosthwaite Collection at Keswick is of unknown find-place.

experiment, in a style that is known nowhere else in the British Isles before its appearance on the hanging-bowls. It is, in fact, precisely because of its new stamp, because of the alert invention and vigorous development behind it, that the native inhabitants of the land in which it appears can be regarded as the only people able to have produced it. Nowhere else has it background or history ; nowhere else were its constituent elements already to hand.

The importance of this British development of a new style is considerable, for the achievement of the perfected trumpet-pattern roundel cannot be regarded as anything but one of the major landmarks in our early art. For so completely satisfactory was the final result from the point of view of barbarian aesthetics that in an almost unchanged state this novel and spirited design was destined to sweep victoriously over the whole of the British Isles. Thus, at a later date, it gleams upon the sumptuous metal-work of the Irish and the Scots, decorates the monuments of the Picts, and adorns the pages of the Lindisfarne Gospels, the Canterbury manuscripts, and the Book of Kells. A product of the darkest periods in the history of our country, this surprising British contribution to the northern ornamental style was received with such universal approval in the Hiberno-Saxon world that ultimately we find it nobly and impressively employed as the veritable hall-mark of Early Christian art in the period of its greatest splendour and maximum originality.

IV

PAGAN SAXONS

The Angles and the Saxons at the time of the land-taking in the second half of the fifth century were not, so far as material culture is concerned, impressive peoples, and the average contents of most of their cemeteries, then and later, make a poor display when compared with the normal types of Romano-British antiquities from the towns and villas. Perhaps their hand-made pottery is chiefly responsible for this appearance of inferiority ; for the greater part of it is clumsy stuff that does not stand comparison with the wheel-made Roman wares. But the contrast is generally true, and the long strings of garish nobbly beads, the big fantastically shaped brooches, the exaggerated forms of girdle-hangers, pins, bucket-mounts, and the like, and the sprawling lumpiness of most of the ornamental metal-work, strengthen the total effect of uncouth barbaric craftsmanship that was usually incapable of rising above awkward ostentation and over-elaboration in display. Nevertheless, Saxon metal-work was by no means despicable; for early in the fifth century the invaders had made themselves masters of the chip-carving technique, and at the time of their coming they possessed many 'equal-armed' brooches in the most handsome form of this Late Roman style (Pl. 29), heavily decorated with running scrolls and crouching animals on the margins. In England the pagan Anglo-Saxons made fine 'square-headed' and 'cruciform' brooches that owe much to their own 'invasion period' style, and, technically, these pieces are often of commendable excellence.

61

In the Jutish area, however, there is one district that has an archaeology that is markedly different from the rest of the Teutonic provinces, and that is East Kent. The territory east of the Medway that has Canterbury as its capital and includes the coastal ports between Folkestone and Reculver seems to have enjoyed a cultural richness that was not shared even by other Jutish lands such as the Isle of Wight and the extreme south of Wessex, and there can be little doubt that the quasi-continental character of this district is largely responsible for its greater wealth. The Men of Kent remained in touch with the outside world in a way that other Anglo-Saxons did not ; moreover, they continued to be wealthy. Gold and gems, particularly garnets and amethysts, were imported in large quantities ; lapis lazuli was obtainable ; foreign bronze vessels were in circulation ; glass was plentiful ; and handsome cowrie shells are found.

But more important than this surface-richness is the astonishing fact that the splendour of Kent is to a large extent founded upon local industry. In Kent Roman wheel-made pottery has its Dark Ages counterpart (Pl. 33), and, following first the Roman and then the Frankish fashion, the kilns continued to produce wheel-made wares. Moreover, the craft of the jeweller was here developed to a pitch of excellence that was never attained on the adjacent continent. I illustrate part of a gold cloisonné brooch from Faversham (Pl. 31) that is indubitably Kentish work, and yet so dexterously and delicately made that it easily surpasses the best work in the German world abroad, challenging comparison indeed with the finest cloisonné of the early Byzantine Empire. Kent did not follow in the wake of continental Germanic fashion ; on the contrary it was Kent that decided and moulded fashions for barbarians abroad to copy. Perhaps this is not true of the Merovingian Franks, for Childeric and Clovis were building upon the foundation of Imperial Gaul ; but it is true of most of the west and north Germans, especially in the

Rhineland and on the North Sea littoral. These folk were culturally inferior to the Jutes of Kent and had much to learn from them. It is, for instance, a matter of common knowledge that their famous ' ring-sword ' has its origin as a functioning reality in Kent and nowhere else.[1]

Three factors contributed to the excellence of the material culture of the Jutes in England : firstly, the sustained influence of the provincial crafts of the Late Empire, which in this context means the surviving civilization of Roman Kent ; secondly, the brilliant example of the Merovingian Franks ; and, thirdly, the readiness of the Jutes to adopt British and Frankish fashions. It is the first of these factors that I wish to stress. The Kentish ring-swords, for example, show us a type of niello-ornament that we have seen before, the narrow zigzag of reserved silver against a nielloed ground. It is, it is true, a type of decoration that remained in use throughout the whole of the sixth century, and it is one that is commonly used abroad ; yet there is no difficulty about identifying a very narrow and very neat early version that is derived directly from Late Roman work, as on the spoon from Traprain Law (Fig. 6), in such pieces as the Kentish disc-brooch (Pl. 31, 1). You will look in vain for this finnicky precision on Teutonic pieces that are known to be of late date, for subsequent work of this kind is grossly coarser ; and you will find no evidence that this niello-work comes to Kent from any foreign German source. On the contrary, it is, at first, part of the legacy of provincial Roman craftsmanship. Indeed, so close is the bond with the Roman work that we find the Jutes also had silver spoons bearing this same variety of niello-ornament (Pl. 30).

---

[1] The little movable ring can be seen on swords from Faversham. On the continent the ring is merely a vestigial ornament, a useless and immovable part of the hilt. In this atrophied form the ring-sword is found in Scandinavia and also in the Lombard graves in Italy. It seems to me obvious that the Lombards must have learnt to make swords of this type while they were still dwelling in north Germany and were in contact with the civilization of the North Sea littoral.

When we note it also on buckles that are of fifth-century type (Pl. 30, 4) and as likely to be British as Jutish, we must realize that the case for continuity between Teutonic and Roman work in this country is unassailable.

In the same way that this particular niello-ornament embellishes first of all the costly silver of Roman officials and afterwards the possessions of the Jutish chieftains, so also Jutish fashions represent initially an approximation towards those that were current in the Late Empire. The big thick disc-brooch fastening the chlamys across the shoulder, still in use in the late fourth century and the early fifth, finds an immediate response in Kentish jewellery, giving us those sumptuous ' composite ' disc-brooches (Pl. 31) that are the chief glory of our post-Roman archaeology. No other explanation of the origin of these big drumlike brooches will survive examination, for they have no continental prototype in German archaeology (where they were subsequently imitated) ; and clearly they do not evolve from the Kentish single-plate brooches. Their size and splendour, however, do not in themselves establish the connexion that I believe to exist ; the important thing is, firstly, that their pattern is indubitably based on provincial and probably eastern Roman design, witness our own enamelled brooch from Chester (Fig. 12), and the star-pattern disc-brooches in Palmyrene sculpture (Pl. 32) ; [1] secondly, the jewellery-type is provincial Roman, witness the late jewels that, like these Kentish brooches, have groupings of flat-cut stones with bosses formed of pearls, all in deep box-like settings with openwork curls of gold ribbon in the interspaces (Pl. 32). Here, plainly, is a source of the style of the earliest disc-brooches in Kent more directly relevant than anything in the Germanic series of ' Gothic ' jewels, and though this source is only distantly Roman, since it is not European but a provincial fashion of the eastern Mediterranean area, nevertheless it is a fashion

[1] I would also like to call attention to the central roundel of the pavement from Kabr-Hiram, near Tyre, that is now in the Louvre.

that comes from within the Empire and not from the Teutonic world outside it, and it means that these fine brooches of Kent should properly be appraised as attempts to express in the medium of northern Teutonic craftsmanship the enviable insignia of imperial Rome.

Technically, of course, these brooches represent a surprisingly novel type of jewellery. They are decorated with fine gold cloisonné filled with garnets, lapis lazuli, and glass pastes, and they have rich backgrounds of gold filigree. It is impossible to regard them as a natural development of

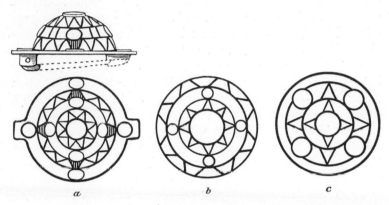

FIG. 12.—Designs on (a) Roman enamelled brooch from Chester, and on Kentish brooches from (b) Sarre and (c) Dover

Romano-British jewellery ; but this does not mean that the earliest of them must be far removed in time from Romano-British work. On the contrary there is every reason to believe that the decisive change in the crafts to which these brooches testify is a result of influences first exerted in the closing days of Roman rule. I have already said that a characteristic type of niello-work is taken from provincial Roman silver, and I will now add that the Kentish gold filigree associated with these jewelled brooches is of Late Roman origin in the same way. For example, that special form in which two pairs of twisted strands of gold wire are laid side by side to imitate a braid (Pl. 32) had already been employed by provincial goldsmiths of the fourth century (Pl. 32).[1] So, too, the beaded gold wires bent into spiral curves had been used on several gold finger-rings from Romano-British sites (Pl. 32), and the peculiar piecework filigree in which short lengths of beaded wire bounded by two thinner beadings are soldered to the background has also its fourth-century beginnings.[2] We may say with every probability that the change in the filigree style of this country is largely due to Germanic influence ; but the point is that the roots of the new fashions reach back into the fourth century, so that the likeliest supposition is that the change began about the same time as the introduction of the Germanic ' chip-carving ' metalwork. There is certainly no need to invoke any foreign influence at an advanced date within the Saxon Period in order to account for the appearance in this period of filigree-work in Kent.

The origins of cloisonné work in this country have not satisfactorily been determined, but I have little doubt that in the first instance the craft was introduced not by the continental Germans, but by way of the Late Empire trade-routes from some far-off source such as Syria or North Africa. This early Mediterranean cloisonné [3] is usually a

[1] It is common on Late Roman jewellery, especially in the Rhineland. In barbarian work of this period we have it in the second Szilagy-Somlyo treasure and in the Sacrau find. In Merovingian jewellery of the fifth century we have it on Childeric's sword. It also occurs on early Danish bracteates.

[2] e.g. in the Sacrau find. It was already used for the composition of highly schematized animals before 500 in Scandinavia, witness the well-known Swedish gold collars.

[3] The type I have in mind is illustrated on the fourth-century Ballana crown from Nubia ; see W. B. Emery, *Ann. du service des antiquités de l'Égypte*, XXXIII (1933), p. 201, Pl. 8. The British Museum has examples from Homs, Syria. Cf. also the Egyptian bracelet, Peirce and Tyler, *L'Art Byzantin*, I, Pl. 91. The work is also represented in South Gaul and in Spain.

coarse inlay of heavy glass pastes in curving cloisons of copper or bronze, and the first signs of a corresponding craft in this country is to be seen on four rather insignificant disc-brooches of the late fourth century that come from

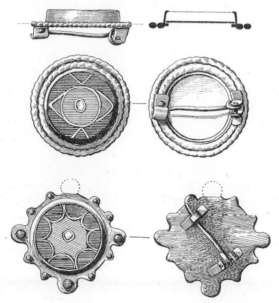

FIG. 13.—Cloisonné enamel brooches from Colchester and London (½)

sites in south-east England [1] (Fig. 13). In the fifth century, however, cloisonné becomes more common throughout western Europe, and there is an instance of the importation into England of an exceptionally fine piece of early gold cloisonné enamel, a gold finger-ring from the Jutish cemetery

[1] Two come from Colchester, one from Ixworth, Suffolk, and one from London. I am not sure that they were originally brooches (cf. the studs on one of the well-known Szilagy-Somlyo brooches). Another form of provincial Roman cloisonné (the 'Drahtemail' or 'running wire' variety) can be seen on the Rhayader bracelet.

67

at Sarre in Kent, now in the collection of Dr. Wacher in Canterbury, which is probably Byzantine or eastern work.[1] But this piece is exceptional, and what we are interested in is the ' Teutonic ' cloisonné which begins with jewellery in the ' Mediterranean Gothic ' style, such as the gilt bronze buckle, inlaid with glass, that comes from Faversham in Kent (Pl. 34), and the heavy gold jewel (Pl. 34) from Milton-next-Sittingbourne, also in Kent, that has very deep straight-edged cells and an inlay of thick garnets, so thick that they need no gold-foil to give them sparkle. This is the earliest type of our garnet-inlay, and it is characterized not only by the depth of the cells, but by the thickness of the garnet slabs that fill them. It is not very common here, and the most important appearance of this type of inlay in the country is on that strange northern jewel that eventually became the pectoral cross of St. Cuthbert.[2] All this, however, provides nothing more than a vague cloisonné background for the Kentish work, a mere acquaintance with the craft ; for the type of inlay that the Jutes of Kent adopted with such enthusiasm is of a different kind and consists of a step-pattern garnet-inlay in which only very thin slabs of the stone were used, these being placed over little pieces of crinkled gold-foil that sparkle through them. Such work was not always done in shallow cells, for the garnets are often bedded on thick fillings of cement in cells of considerable depth ; but the effect is invariably one of a shallow surface-inlay. The work is probably a result of the fashion set by ' Danubian Gothic ' cloisonné, as seen typically in the great fourth-century find at Petrossa, which introduces us to the closely

---

[1] It bears an eagle's head with a ring in the beak and should be compared with a similar design on an Egyptian textile of the fifth century (Peirce and Tyler, *L'Art Byzantin*, I, Pl. 143). A small roundel with a quatrefoil design in the same very fine eastern cloisonné enamel has been used for the central setting of a jewelled Kentish disc-brooch from Ash, now in the Ashmolean Museum.

[2] *Antiquaries Journal*, XVII (1937), p. 283.

patterned field of garnets with a very complicated network of gold cloisons ; but we do not know that our west European 'shallow step-pattern' cloisonné is anywhere earlier than the second half of the fifth century, to which period we must assign the beginnings of the famous Gallo-Frankish school of jewellers that produced the celebrated sword of Childeric (d. 491), now in the Bibliothèque Nationale in Paris.

To this work the earliest 'shallow' cloisonné of Kent is obviously a counterpart ; but it is demonstrably incorrect to say that the Jutish cloisonné is a pale reflection of the Frankish inlay, either in the fifth century or later. No continental piece can be produced that makes any pretensions to being a model for the Kentish jewellers who made the first of our cloisonné brooches, and if the Kentish craftsmen responded to the 'Danubian Gothic' style in the late fifth century, they did so in a way that was peculiarly their own ; for they proceeded immediately to use the new close-set style of inlay for polychrome patterns that only distantly resemble foreign work. They employed it, in fact, regardless of continental precept, for the continued reproduction of provincial Roman designs that were already known to them. Thus it comes about that the enamelled star-pattern of the Chester brooch was translated into the new technique, and the pattern of the Colchester cloisonné roundel (Fig. 13) was transferred to the majestic ensemble of the famous brooch from Kingston, Kent (Pl. 31).

According to orthodox archaeological belief, recently defended with a dour pertinacity by Mr. Leeds,[1] this rich jewellery of Kent is best regarded as a product of the great days at the end of the sixth century and at the beginning of the seventh when, in the reign of King Ethelbert, the political prestige of the Jutes was indeed formidable. But it is a significant fact that the finest jewel that is known to belong to this late period, a brooch (Pl. 31) found with

[1] *Early Anglo-Saxon Art and Archaeology*, Oxford, 1936, p. 41 ff., and p. 115 ff.

coin-pendants in a grave at Sarre, is very different from the better-made and obviously earlier jewellery of the Kingston brooch type (Pl. 31). Both, it is true, are jewelled composite brooches of a single family ; but whereas the Kingston brooch is elegantly thin, the Sarre brooch is clumsily thick. On the one hand, the surface ornament is a brilliant and exact patchwork of garnet, lapis lazuli, and gold filigree ; on the other hand, the sparkle and the polychrome mosaic-effect are gone, and we are left with broad dull zones of lifeless cloisonné and insipid filigree. We can press these differences further, particularly as regards the style of the cloisonné itself, which in the Kingston brooch is thick, crisp, and sturdy, not weak and thin as on the Sarre brooch ; but the striking difference between the backs of the two brooches is perhaps the most obvious index of the serious deterioration in craftsmanship that has taken place. It might, of course, be urged that we should attribute this inferiority of the Sarre brooch merely to the lack of skill of the craftsman concerned ; but here we face the difficulty that these big brooches can be arranged in an evolutionary series (cf. Fig. 12) according to their designs and their ornamental styles and their types of cloison-shape, and an honest observer must concede that archetype forms so different can scarcely have been made in the decades that saw the manufacture of the known late type. We have, indeed, to bear in mind that the complete series of brooches reveals several changes in fashion that are of considerable importance, the introduction of the sixth-century Italian ' honeycomb ' cell, for instance ; so that of necessity the full range of types must represent a long period. Remembering, then, the point I have made concerning the provincial Roman origin of so many of the technical peculiarities of the typologically early brooches, we cannot fail to perceive the unreasonableness of a chronological scheme that makes no allowances for a continuity in the crafts. For if the orthodox view of the late dating of the brooches be accepted, we are to suppose that late in the sixth century there was a sudden and inexplicable revival of the goldsmith's craft in Kent that involved the simultaneous re-invention of a provincial Roman style (gems with wire interspaces), a Roman pattern, a Roman niello-inlay, and a Roman type of filigree. An appeal to some retarded continental influence that may have operated in Kent at this late date is ruled out for the reason that the jewelled disc-brooches that are obviously the earliest have no foreign counterpart at all ; whereas they may be very convincingly claimed as representing an equivalent industry to that which produced in Gaul the sumptuous and beautiful cloisonné of the Gourdon pattern and Childeric's sword. I submit, then, that the proper course is to distribute the jewellery in question over the whole of the sixth century, and to link the earliest pieces to that fifth-century style with which they are so closely in accord.

Side by side with the gold cloisonné jewellery the Teutonic invaders of Kent possessed cheaper ornaments of gilt metal with pastes in cast settings and chip-carving decoration.[1] This we can hardly regard as anything but normal Jutish work that was intended to popularize the fashion of the costlier brooches. The work is technically the same as that used for the big square-headed brooches of the invaders, and, in a sense, it is more obviously Jutish than the gold cloisonné ; for it has been found in the big Jutish cemetery in the Isle of Wight where there is no cloisonné at all. In Kent there is an instance of a Jutish woman being buried with brooches of both types ; so that the two kinds of jewellery were not made for different classes of the community, and the significance of the styles must remain obscure, unless, as I am inclined to think, the true explanation lies in the fact that whereas the cheap ' chip-carving ' brooches are invariably of Jutish manufacture, the cloisonné, on the other hand, was in its beginnings only by adoption Jutish and was really derived first of all

[1] For this see *Antiquity*, VII (1933), p. 431.

from the workshops of surviving British goldsmiths. On this view only can one explain the notable fact that the finest cloisonné brooches are sometimes found in Jutish graves in an unfinished or mutilated state. Thus the superb brooch (Pl. 31, 2) from Faversham, one of the masterpieces of Kentish cloisonné, is completely empty of jewels and shows no signs of ever having had any fillings in its cells. Again, at Aylesford the upper plate only of a cloisonné brooch was found in a grave,[1] and so too, outside Kent, the top of a cloisonné brooch was found at Ixworth in Suffolk under circumstances that led Mr. Roach Smith to observe that 'it was interred in this fragmentary state, and had been separated from the lower portion before it came into the possession of its owner, with whose corpse it had been deposited in the grave'.[2]

It is difficult to resist the impression that in instances such as these the cloisonné jewellery has to a certain extent to be divorced from our Anglo-Saxon archaeology, just as we now set aside the enamelled hanging-bowls of the British, which we have seen (p. 52) are likewise represented in Saxon graves by mutilated pieces. To crystallize this matter I should like to call attention to the fact that each one of the three jewelled pectoral crosses found in this country was found in a seriously mutilated condition (Pl. 34). Thus with the top half of the brooch at Ixworth that I have just mentioned, was a cloisonné pendent cross that had been broken in two and repaired with a binding-plate and rivets. The sixth-century Merovingian pendant from Wilton, Norfolk, has had its original central ornament removed and an ill-fitting seventh-century coin inserted back to front and upside down. St. Cuthbert's pectoral cross had been savagely broken and repaired before it was buried with him in 687. It seems wellnigh incredible that these charming Christian jewels represent ornaments made for seventh-century ecclesiastics, and I prefer as a

[1] *Antiquity*, loc. cit., p. 431.
[2] *Collectanea Antiqua*, IV (1857), p. 163.

better reason for their mutilation the suggestion that they were, when buried, already damaged antiques.[1]

I hasten, however, to explain that in making what now seems to us to be a revolutionary suggestion that our cloisonné jewellery has its British beginnings as well as its Anglo-Saxon development, I do not posit more than a very short-lived phase in which this work can be described as of British manufacture. St. Cuthbert's cross is a lonely phenomenon of the north. In the south I imagine that one of the secrets of Jutish wealth and success is the alacrity with which the new-comers absorbed into their own society the jewellers of the Kent that they had conquered, and I willingly agree that the greater part of the cloisonné in Kent that is now known to us is likely to have been made under Jutish patronage and by Jutish apprentices to the crafts. I agree, furthermore, that cloisonné jewellery remained in use and continued to be made throughout the whole of the Pagan Period, and is to be found, as is natural in many late graves and hoards of treasure ;[2] but again I insist that the late Sarre brooch (Pl. 31), which may have been made about 600, shows us that the jewellery that was actually made at this late date was woefully inferior stuff and is itself a guarantee of the much earlier date of the finer work.

I turn now to a brief study of the development of animal-pattern in Anglo-Saxon England. In the sense in which

[1] For an account of these crosses see *Antiquaries Journal*, XVII (1937), p. 283.

[2] A good idea of the later jewellery can be obtained from the seventh-century Wieuverd hoard at Leyden : the two cloisonné pieces here are considerably older than the date of deposit, for not only are they both sadly damaged, but one of them has been laboriously repaired. They do very well, however, to illustrate the comparatively poor work of the second half of the sixth century. The suggestion, apparently still endorsed by continental archaeologists, that this hoard proves the late date of pieces like our Kingston brooch, is so silly that it needs no refuting.

we use the term here, that is to say with the meaning customarily attached to it by students of European archaeology ever since the distinguished Swede, Bernhard Salin, wrote his famous book,[1] animal-pattern is a new form of ornament that we have not yet encountered. For up to the end of the Roman Period, here and on the adjacent continent, the animal, though often strangely distorted, generally [2] preserves its identity as a recognizable version of the living form. It may be stylized, as on the Witham shield (Fig. 1), into a mannered travesty ; it may be bent and shrivelled, contorted and crippled, and elongated or compressed ; but it remains steadfastly an animal. The little Romano-British mount from Margidunum (Pl. 15) will illustrate the maximum maltreatment of the creature in the days before it ceased to be a reasonable representation of itself and dissolved into abstract animal-ornament. For that is the change that now takes place under the influence of Anglo-Saxon designers. Henceforward the creature loses its zoological reality and is converted into mere pattern.

This dissolution is achieved by two main stylistic processes, the first of which (here called the Helmet Style) turns the animal into a discordant mosaic of little bits and pieces without regard to the natural rhythm of the animal-form ; while the second (here called the Ribbon Style) over-emphasizes this form, turning it into a curvilinear S-like statement that has the smooth quality of easy-flowing interlace. These are the famous Styles I and II of Salin. They are simply two different ways of achieving an abstract pattern, and though their development and their import

---

[1] *Die Altgermanische Thierornamentik*, Stockholm, 1904. Animal-pattern in this country is further discussed by N. Åberg, *The Anglo-Saxons in England*, Upsala, 1926 ; by the present author, *IPEK*, IX (1934), p. 66 ; and by Leeds, *Early Anglo-Saxon Art and Archaeology*, Oxford, 1936.

[2] The complete disintegration of the animal on the Gaulish and British coins is an exception to this rule.

may not be the same, they represent together a single Germanic aesthetic tendency. Emphatically they are not different arts (as is so often believed), nor do they represent different people and different ages, and in no wise are they irreconcilable or mutually exclusive. Indeed, though their extreme forms are stylistically dissimilar, they nevertheless shade off into one another, presenting us with obvious fusions of themselves ; and even in their extreme forms they are able to appear side by side, as we shall see, incontestably contemporary and incontestably the work of the same designer.

A tendency to carve an animal-form in such a way that it begins to look as though it were made up of sharply accentuated separate pieces can be traced far back into the fifth century, and, indeed, into the Roman Period itself. The knife-handle from Corbridge (Pl. 15) and the Barham spoon (Pl. 15) have already shown us the beginnings of the process ; but the principal victim of the Saxon experiment is undoubtedly the crouching quadruped that appears on the margin of the equal-armed brooches (Pl. 29). These examples are in themselves almost a sufficient preparation for the break-up of the creature that is to be seen on later Saxon work, for instance on the sixth-century mounts here illustrated (Pl. 29) or on the foot-plate of the fine brooch from Soham, Cambridgeshire (Pl. 30). But if we look carefully at the animals on this last example we see that they show with particular prominence a feature that does demand further explanation, namely a large and massive 'helmet' with a curly crest. At first glance we might take this to be an over-emphasized mane and ear ; but this obviously will not do for the even more emphatic form of the animal heads at the top of the Soham brooch. Helmet is the only word.

This it is that gives the name to the style, and its continual appearance as the head-dress of an animal is one of the distinguishing marks of Anglo-Saxon zoomorphic design. To discover its significance we must look at the

75

finest and the earliest examples of the Helmet Style that we possess, for instance, one of the metal mouth-pieces

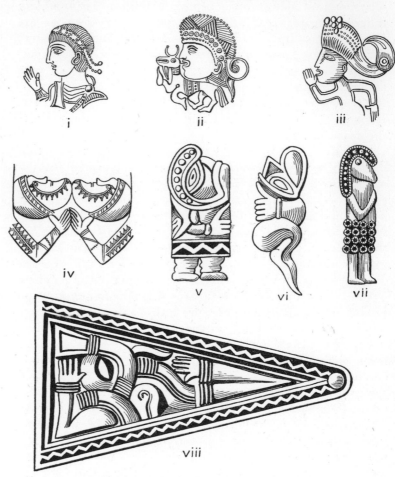

FIG. 14.—The 'Helmet and hand' motive in early German art on the Continent (i–vii) and in Anglo-Saxon art (viii)

of a pair of drinking-horns (Pl. 35) that were found in the grave of an early sixth-century Teutonic chieftain at Taplow, probably the Taeppa whose barrow or 'low' is commemorated in the name of this Thames-side town. In the design here (Fig. 15, viii) the subject is not an animal, but a man. It is typical patchwork composition, and the human form is not recognizable ; but we are still left with two arms that end in lifelike little hands, each with four fingers and a thumb, and there is a head, shown in profile, wearing a helmet with a clearly defined brim and a curly appendage that looks like a crest of some kind.

Those who know the barbarian arts of the Dark Ages will realize that this pattern has a history behind it, and the truth is that in origin it is less an ' animal-art ' than an ' emperor-art ' ; for it is ultimately to be traced back to such Late Roman presentations of the emperor as the medal of Constantius II (337–61) that is illustrated here (Pl. 35). The fifth-century continental German bracteates, which are imitations in embossed gold of the coins and medals of the late Empire, show the manner in which this portrait-bust with elaborate head-dress and raised hand was converted into the barbaric travesty that we see on the Taplow horn (Fig. 14). This, however, represents an advance on the continental stage of the design and is an English achievement of the beginning of the sixth century. It is, indeed, to some extent an animal-pattern ; for parts of the horse that often appears in the original designs as the emperor's mount are to be recognized here in the form of a distinct thigh, leg, and foot on the panels of the terminal of the horn (Pl. 35) and on the horizontal panels of the rim. Thus the Taplow style is really an amalgamation of the emperor and his horse, and as a rough generalization it may be said that what we are now witnessing is the Anglo-Saxon absurdity of crowning the Teutonic animal with an Emperor's hat. It is this continual insistence upon the ' helmet ' form of the head that distinguishes the English variety of Salin's first style, and as the head-dress of an animal even the early Taplow-type helmet can be seen on numerous examples of Saxon metal-work. We have already seen it on the marginal beasts of the Soham

77

brooch (Pl. 30) where 'Taplow' ornament is added to the otherwise plain Anglian 'long' brooch, and there was certainly a vigorous Anglian school in the sixth century that produced many fine pieces of this sort. On the other hand, in Jutish Kent, where the style probably originated and the Taplow horns were made,[1] we have fewer examples of the best varieties of the Helmet Style, for here in the workshops of the finest jewellers the Ribbon

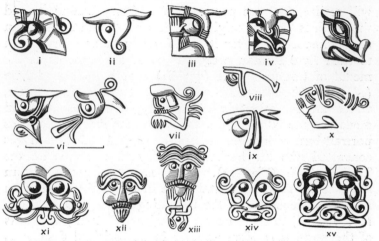

Fig. 15.—Heads and masks in the Anglo-Saxon Helmet Style

Style quickly ousted it from favour; but it is to be seen on one or two notable objects—for instance, the magnificent buckle and plate from Howletts (detail: Fig. 16, v), now in the British Museum.

The Helmet Style is, of course, something more than the insistent use of a particular type of animal-ornament. It is plainly an altered expression of the Late Roman chip-carving varieties of pattern, and adheres to these in the

---

[1] The Taplow burial has an admittedly Kentish character; the niello-work on the horns is perhaps the strongest proof of Kentish origin of these pieces.

panelled arrangement of its elements and in the use of the
marginal animal. It is, in fact, a natural Teutonic development of the style of the equal-armed brooches (Pl. 29)
of the fifth century, and even the later and highly mannered
pieces of the sixth century often contain modest versions
of the running scrolls that are the dominant ornament of
the earlier metal-work (Pl. 30, 1 head-plate). So, too,
the Helmet Style includes the use of the quatrefoil and the
rosette, as on the mouth-piece of the Taplow horn. But
the clearest proof of the classical roots of this German work
is supplied by the repeated use of the mask. Just as the

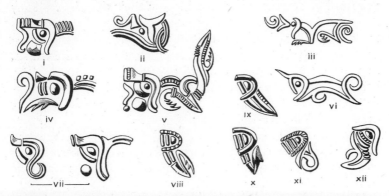

Fig. 16.—Animal-patterns in the Kentish variety of the Helmet Style

Taplow find presents us with the initial stage of the Helmet
theme proper, so also it provides us with the most spirited
and the most Roman-looking version of the mask (Pl. 35),
and it is clear that the vigour and coherence of the design
grows less and less as the quality of the helmet-patterns
diminishes and the ' Taplow stage ' is left behind. The
tendency is, of course, towards the same kind of loosening
and break-up as is experienced by the animal, and the
stages in the dissolution of the mask can be very easily
followed, the final result being an even and meaningless
spread of details (Fig. 15, xi, xiv, xv), the faint *modelled*
quality of the Taplow version very quickly disappearing.

It is only rarely in Helmet Style pieces that one finds animals without the characteristic ' helmet ', but one unusual example of the versatility and adventurous exuberance of some of the Anglo-Saxon craftsmen is supplied by the shield-boss (Pl. 29) from Bidford-on-Avon, Warwickshire. On the stud, encircling a central rosette, is a ring of dissolved and grossly stylized helmet-pattern, illustrating the restless and crowded mosaic effect of this type of work ; but on the flange of the boss there are plates made up of a panel containing a smooth linked-loop device and two terminal animal-heads in the form of open-jawed creatures that surprise us by the power and precision of their drawing. They owe much, of course, to the space available for them and to their scale ; but the truth is that they represent an emergence of that other tendency of the Saxon artist which, as we shall see, provides us with the Ribbon Style. The boss is, indeed, a most fortunate illustration of the persistence of certain elements in Anglo-Saxon art in the very hour of the failure of others ; for on the stud we witness the inevitable decline of the artificial Taplow style, while on the flange we catch a glimpse of that vigorous rhythmic work that was responsible for one of the major barbaric contributions to later Christian art.

Much Saxon work in the Helmet Style is of a decidedly inferior quality,[1] but following upon the ' Taplow ' phase at the beginning of the sixth century, there is a period before the middle of the century in which we find numerous highly ornate and clever designs, as the ' square-headed ' brooches show. We can accept these as representatives of a recognizable culminating-point of the Helmet Style, and I select the fine brooch (Pl. 30) from Chessel Down in the Isle of Wight as typical of them. It shows that by this time the pattern, as we see in the inner field of the head-plate, had broken violently into a chaotic mosaic of fragments that include recognizable heads and limbs and

[1] For the ' Common Style ' see my paper in *IPEK*, loc. cit., p. 74.

lengths of body, signalling the disruption (one might almost say the *explosion*) of the Helmet Style animal into a meaningless litter of bits ; but in spite of this the general design of the brooch retains the clean, though crowded, precision of the earlier work, such as the Taplow horn or the equal-armed brooch from Germany (Pl. 29), and in fact includes scroll-pattern, niello-details, and masks that provide close links with the style as first expressed.

Nevertheless the real tendency of the Helmet Style towards an ever-increasing dissolution of its component details could only lead to the complete decay of the manner, and, though unskilled craftsmanship must share the responsibility for the downfall with the passage of time, in the later sixth and early seventh century we are left with nothing but flabby travesties of the original work. The collapse can be seen in its most shocking form in a series of late Anglian brooches,[1] and it seems that the final phase of the Helmet Style is to be found in the northern and eastern districts of Saxon England, rather than in the south where it first took shape. This is because it was in the south, particularly in Kent, that the more coherent Ribbon Style had from the very beginning been available as an alternative variety of abstract ornament and was in a position to usurp the attention of the designer so successfully that the Helmet Style formula has a shorter life here than in any other part of Saxon England.

In England, I think, there can be no doubt that the Ribbon Style (Salin's Style II) is founded on the half-Roman half-Germanic free-style animal art of the fifth century.[2] Late Roman art in this country includes examples of the form of animal out of which the Ribbon Style developed, little creatures that already show a tendency to loosen into soft ribbon-like curls or spirals, the trick of turning the head to look backwards over the body making a dominant

---

[1] For the Degenerate Style, see *IPEK*, loc. cit., p. 75.

[2] For continental forms of this, see J. Bröndsted, *Nordisk Kultur : Kunst.*, Oslo, 1931, p. 102 ff.

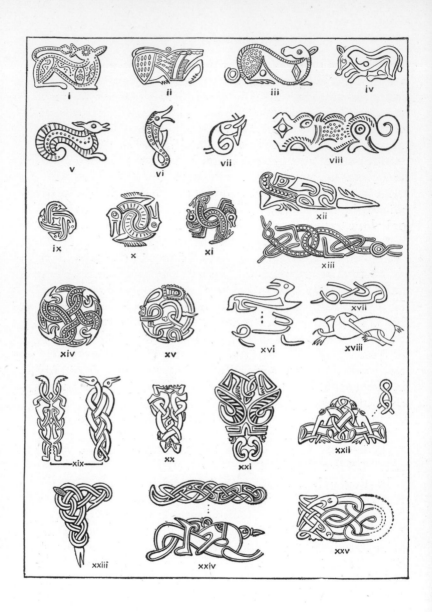

FIG. 17.—Evolution of the Anglo-Saxon Ribbon Style animal

S-curve of the design. The fallen stag [1] on a silver finger-ring from Amesbury, part of a hoard buried *circa* A.D. 400, illustrates the type well, and it is a perhaps not very much later stage of this free-style animal from which the English Ribbon Style develops, a stage that belongs to the years of the Saxon settlement in the second half of the fifth and early years of the sixth century. Most of the work that shows this particular phase is British ; for example, the animals on the silver penannular brooches [2] from the Saxon graves of Sussex and Kent (Pl. 33 ; Fig. 17, ii, iii, v) and those on the enamelled escutcheons of hanging-bowls from Kent (Pl. 33 ; Fig. 17, vi) and Derbyshire (Fig. 17, vii).[3] If we compare the silver Romano-British brooch in the form of a dolphin (Pl. 33) with one of the animal-sketches on the inner ring of a penannular brooch from the Jutish cemetery at Howletts in Kent (Fig. 17, viii ; and Pl. 33) we shall see that the stylistic bond between the design of the Roman Period and that of the post-Roman period is indeed a close one ; but a more important point is that the British animal-style was one entirely congenial to the northern Germans, as the Danish bracteates show, and in an example like that on the sword-chape from the Brighthampton cemetery in Oxfordshire [4] we may well have a Saxon version of the same theme.

The stylistic advance that now takes place in England seems to have been at first almost entirely a Kentish development.[5] The principal factors that occasioned the rapid

---

[1] The animal is a quadruped and not, as one thinks at first glance, a sea-cow. For the Amesbury hoard see *Proc. Soc. Ant. I S. IV* (1859), 27 ; *B.M. Catalogue of Finger Rings, Greek, etc.*, 1205–7.

[2] These have been admirably described recently by Mr. Leeds, *Early Anglo-Saxon Art and Arch.*, p. 3 ff. It is not, however, made properly clear that this south-eastern work is British work in an obviously German mood, as comparison with a famous Danish bracteate will show.

[3] cf. Leeds, op. cit., fig. 40.

[4] *Archaeologia*, XXXVIII (1860), Pl. II, p. 96.

[5] There is no evidence abroad of an orderly continental development of the Ribbon Style from its late Roman beginnings. As in the case of

flowering of the Ribbon Style in this area were (i) the use
made by the Kentish jeweller of piece-work filigree as a
method of ornamenting metal surfaces, and (ii) the designer's
practice of severing, as it were, existing ribbon-patterns,
such as plaits, twists, and linked loops, and providing them
with movement and life by the addition of animal-heads
at the loose ends. One of a pair of hanging-bowl prints
from Faversham (Fig. 18) illustrates the processes at work,
for it bears an example of the familiar linked-loop pattern
of the Roman mosaic pavements (cf. Pl. 19) that has now
acquired a zoomorphic liveliness by the severing of its

Fig. 18.—Enamelled escutcheons from a hanging-bowl, Faversham,
Kent (¼)

strands and the adding of animal-heads. Thus we see
that even in the fifth century, for there can be no doubt
of the date of the bowl from which this print comes, the
Ribbon Style is already a part of the inherent barbarism
of an age that in other metal-work turns the pelta into
British trumpet-pattern and the emperor's bust into the
Saxon travesty of the early Helmet Style. There is nothing
alien or foreign in the Ribbon Style, which, as far as its
history in England is concerned, is merely a symptom,
at first localized, of the general swing-over to barbaric
ornament. Indeed, again and again in the centuries that

the ring-sword, which is only to be found in its original stage in England,
the initial stages are to be found here alone, and must be the source of
types of pattern that by the end of VI had been incorporated in the
designs of continental Germans.

follow we find examples of this conversion of authentic ribbon-patterns into the zoomorphic Ribbon Style (e.g. Fig. 17, xiv, xxiii, xxv), for the trick is nothing more nor less than the expression of a universal barbaric instinct, common to the Celt and German alike.

The fellow to the Faversham print with the linked loops bears four typical and early free-style animals (Fig. 18), and we can use one of them to illustrate the astonishing effect of the transformation of a familiar creature into filigree-work (Fig. 17, xvi, xvii). We obtain by a straightforward jeweller's technique the grotesque little sketch of an animal that is to be seen on the superb brooch (Pl. 31) from Kingston, Kent ; for we have simply taken the piece-work filigree version of the animal (Fig. 17, xvi) and twisted him so that he fits into the rather awkward panel that has to be filled (Fig. 17, xvii ; cf. Pl. 31). His tail and leg are tucked into one corner and his head is forced back so that the jaws bite the body. This gives us a very common form of the Ribbon Style animal in filigree (e.g. Fig. 17, xiii), and we can see that stylistically these designs closely resemble some that are to be seen in embossed metal-work in the Taplow find. One of these examples (Pl. 35), a triangular mount on the horn at the inner end of the terminal, actually occurs on the very horn that provides us with our standard example of the Helmet Style work ; so we have proof that both styles are included in a single form of barbaric aesthetic expression. Moreover, we have proof that the Ribbon Style cannot reasonably be divorced chronologically from the early work in the Helmet Style.[1]

[1] Mr. Leeds, struggling with an obtuseness most unusual on his part to defend the old and absurd late dating of this Taplow grave, now claims that the mount bearing the Ribbon Style pattern is a subsequent addition to the ornament of the horn (op. cit., p. 76). I am afraid he is wrong here ; for it is demonstrably part of the original fittings. But even if it were not present, my claim that the two styles are contemporary holds good ; for the panels above it are decorated in the ' Fusion ' style (see p. 87 here) which implies knowledge of the Ribbon Style formula.

The filigree version is, of course, highly schematized; but this extreme form is only one aspect of the Ribbon Style animal. We can, indeed, demonstrate that it is only a changed contemporary form of the more easily recognizable ' ribbon ' animal by the example of the Jutish sword-pommel from Crundale, Kent (Pl. 33 ; Fig. 17,

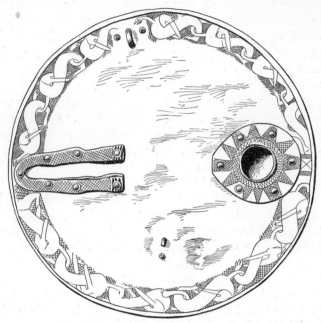

FIG. 19.—Engraved silver back-plate of jewelled brooch from Faversham, Kent (¼)

xxii), for this bears on the face a pair of full-bodied creatures as *drawn*, and on the flanks a copy of the *filigree sketch*, both presented to us here in cast metal. On a handsome jewelled buckle, believed to be from the same grave as the sword, we have the beginnings of an *engraving* of the creature,[1] and there is a complete marginal procession of these creatures engraved on the back of a big jewelled brooch (Fig. 19)

[1] *IPEK*, IX (1934), Tf. 28, 12.

from Faversham, Kent. This, together with the sword-pommel, gives us the style as it had been perfected in Kent before the middle of the sixth century, by which time we have the first sign of the barbaric *linking* of the procession of creatures; and nothing is gained here by a detailed examination of the other variants that we encounter then and later in the Kentish area and elsewhere.[1]

It was almost inevitable that the more coherent and rhythmic Ribbon Style should leave its mark upon some of the uncomfortable mosaic-compositions in the Helmet Style. There is, in fact, a recognizable Fusion Style, and there are examples of it a date very early in the sixth century. It is not necessary to describe the mixed style here [2]; but I must mention a significant occurrence of it in the Taplow barrow, the famous Saxon burial of which I have already spoken. On the terminals of the larger pair of horns (Pl. 35) there is a typical piece of Fusion Style design, an ingeniously entangled pattern in which biting jaws and a bold ribbon-interlace do their best to transform a design of obvious 'Helmet' parentage (cf. the 'head and hand' at the base of the larger of the two connected panels with the same detail on the mouth-piece of this horn, Pl. 35; Fig. 15, iii). This piece of decoration occurs on the very horn that bears the archetype pattern of the Helmet Style, and above the terminal, as I have said (p. 85), is an embossed triangular mount that is decorated in the Ribbon Style proper (Pl. 35). Thus on a single object of early sixth-century date we have examples of both animal-patterns, in their characteristic forms and also a pattern that is a mixture of them both, all three plainly done simultaneously by a single designer. Nothing could expose

---

[1] For these see *IPEK*, loc. cit. Illustrations of some typical Ribbon Style designs will be found in Fig. 17. The rare bracteate type (xv) may be imported, and in any case it is a 'ribbon' adaptation of a pattern in the Helmet Style. The buckle-patterns (xix, xx) are probably due to foreign influence.

[2] For an account of it see *IPEK*, loc. cit., p. 73.

more clearly the futility of the current archaeological belief that the Ribbon Style in England is a separate and later manifestation of barbaric art.

The handsome gold buckle (Pl. 34) in the Taplow barrow bears a version in filigree of the design on the embossed triangular mount that adorns the horn. It is clearly of the same early date as the horns, and indeed corresponds to them not merely in this detail of pattern but in the general richness of its style. It is interesting, therefore, to discover upon it a somewhat rough and unpractised Jutish experiment in cloisonné, exactly simulating the fine Kentish work, but not equalling it in daintiness and precision. We could scarcely expect, I think, any plainer declaration that I am right in saying that some at least of this Kentish cloisonné-work was made at a date even earlier than that of this buckle, nor a happier corroboration of the view that in origin this cloisonné is not Jutish work. I say this because I am now informed that it is no longer necessary to combat the old view that the Taplow barrow is a seventh-century burial, the proper placing of it at the beginning of the sixth having found favour even in the world of academic archaeology.[1]

I do not think that the removal of the best of the cloisonné jewellery, or for that matter of the best of the square-headed and cruciform brooches and other ornaments, to a considerably earlier stage in Anglo-Saxon archaeology than has been hitherto thought possible leaves us with any uncomfortable lacunae. On the contrary, it enables us to draw a more convincing picture of the material that,

[1] I fear, however, that since I wrote the above sentence my informant has changed his mind again. I should like to point out that the Taplow chieftain had a small and early type of shield-boss, an angon (an early Saxon weapon copying the Roman pilum), a set of four glasses made *circa* 500 (not just *one* glass, but a *set* of them), and horns, almost brand new when they were buried, that bear the Anglo-Saxon archetype pattern of the Helmet Style, and drinking-cups that bear human masks that are nearer than any other Saxon masks to the classical original.

starting with the rich and exuberant forms of the 'invasion style' equal-armed brooches (Pl. 29), so soon develops into the 'Baroque' richness of the mature Anglo-Saxon style and then slowly but surely passes into decline. As a measure of the mature style I should like to cite a grave-group from Chessel Down that provides us with a silver spoon, a fine crystal sphere mounted as a pendant, and a set of three square-headed brooches (Pl. 30) ; for the archaeologist knows that the spoon and the sphere are early pieces [1] and the grave is not likely to be later than 525. Yet we see that we have already arrived at an elaborate type of square-headed brooch,[2] behind which there must lie a considerable activity in morphological development and in experiment with animal-pattern. What, I think, we have to realize is that the invader arrived attuned to the Baroque, to preposterous shapes, and to rich ornament. It is natural that the most extravagant and fanciful works should follow quickly upon his settlement, and natural that this pristine vigour should soon exhaust itself, leaving us with a series of brooches and other ornaments that represent stage after stage of increasingly weak and increasingly muddle-headed copywork.

This palpably inferior craftsmanship of the second half of the sixth century and the first part of the seventh does not require illustration here ; but some reference is necessary to the occasional survival of the fine style, for nothing, I think, better demonstrates the reasonableness of the chronological system that I am advocating. In Kent we have already found a very useful indication of the late decorative style in the sadly degenerate Sarre brooch (Pl. 31), but we may take as further guide the bronze-gilt mounts from Faversham (Pl. 36). They possess a typically Kentish richness and ornate quality, but they are florid and

[1] Such spheres occur abroad in a fourth-century find (Szilagy-Somlyo I) and in a fifth-century find (Childeric's grave).

[2] Mr. Leeds most correctly observes that ' none of the Kentish square-heads can be late ', op. cit., p. 47.

weak. The crispness of the early work and the purposeful handling of the pattern have gone. Where there was once control and systematized decoration, we have here an insipid spread of plait-like ornament containing vestigial zoomorphic details.[1] This is what Kentish art was really like in the days of St. Augustine, a mere degradation of the pagan animal-pattern into a meaningless and tightly-knit jumble of interlacing lines used recklessly as a complete surface-covering.

North of the Thames a comparable style had appeared at the same late date, and this I have called the 'Anglian Development' of the ribbon-pattern work. It has a special importance because it carries Pagan Saxon design forward in time until it is within measurable distance of eighth-century Northumbrian art, represented by the Lindisfarne Gospels, in which the Ribbon Animal is one of the principal elements. Whether we are really entitled to say that the Anglian Development is either partly or wholly responsible for the appearance of the lacertine animal in the later Northumbrian school I take leave to doubt ; but at least we can say here and now that the style was known in eastern England in the seventh century and therefore *might* have been adopted into the Christian art of the north in the next century without the agency of any exterior influence. Two examples of this later Anglian work will suffice. The first (Pl. 36) is one of two richly ornamented discs from Allington Hill, Cambridgeshire, whereon we see the Crundale-type creature (Fig. 17, xxiv ; cf. xxii) in a handsome low-relief design that is enclosed in a ring of advanced

---

[1] It is worth noting that in the Kentish jewellery the animal, as drawn in wire-work, began to turn, as time passed, into designs that are almost pure interlace ; thus on late cloisonné brooches, like those from Abingdon, the animal is represented by a little piece of wire interlace that is only with difficulty recognized as being a zoomorphic pattern. There was a general tendency in the late Pagan Period to make a much greater use of simple interlace designs than in the early part of the period, when there was a movement away from Roman plaits and braids.

zoomorphic interlacing, this pattern being a version in chased metal of a design that is really the converted plait. The plait is, in fact, a dominating feature of the Anglian group of Ribbon Style ornaments,[1] and we have it again on our second example, a jewelled mount from Hardingstone, Northamptonshire (Pl. 36; Fig. 17, xxiii). The two pieces may be taken together as illustrations of the final expression of the taste for the sumptuous jewelled roundel that begins with the Kentish brooches, and we have still the same system of bosses, one in the centre and four in the field, and, in the Hardingstone disc, the familiar star-like pattern in the centre. But the cloisonné decoration is gone, the boss is now an ugly white lump, and the ornament is an evenly spread close interlace in low relief that completely covers and entirely dominates the roundel. The Kentish ribbon-animal of the Crundale pommel (Pl. 33) is here seen to be sinking back into a cold, flat, lifeless mesh. The design has still considerable cunning, but it lacks the authentic stamp of original barbaric vigour, and it would only be with very great reluctance that I should suggest we have in this Anglian Development the source of that new and important flowering of the barbaric style that we are soon to encounter in the arts of Christian England.

[1] It is well seen on two bronze mounts at Moyses Hall, Bury St. Edmunds, *V.C.H. Suffolk*, I, p. 338, and also on the Castle Bytham brooch from Lincolnshire, *Burlington Fine Arts Club Exhibition Catalogue* 19, Pl. I, A 12.

V

THE EARLY CHURCH

The history of art in this island scarcely pauses to consider the subject of Christianity in Roman Britain. Apart from the foundations of the church at Silchester, little is known of the new Faith archaeologically, and there is nothing at all that we can regard as representing a distinctive ecclesiastical art of the period. The occurrence of a gold finger-ring inscribed *Vivas in Deo* and of others in silver bearing the Chi-Rho, and of this emblem as the focal-point of an elaborate mosaic pavement (Pl. 21), may perhaps be taken as showing that Christianity was not exclusively confined to the poorer classes ; but we have no evidence that the Church in the closing days of Roman Britain had more than a modest share in the vernacular art of the time.

We know even less, archaeologically, of the post-Roman British Church in the fifth and sixth century. But that it survived and was important as a creative force, offering new ideals, new courage, and spiritual calm in the face of danger and oppression, this much at least can be inferred.[1] It is reasonable to assume, therefore, that the bishops and clergy must have endorsed and shared in the new decorative style that was then emerging in the lands not immediately taken by the Saxons. There are not, of course, adequate grounds for attributing the development of the trumpet-pattern on our ornamental hanging-bowls to ecclesiastical

[1] cf. R. H. Hodgkin, *History of the Anglo-Saxons*, Oxford, 1935, I, pp. 60–73.

patronage of the enamellers ; but other writers have noticed the ' Christian ' appearance of the earliest British bowls, for instance the openwork Faversham escutcheons with their ' cross ' flanked by ' fishes ' (Pl. 33) and the Lullingstone bowl with its fish-symbols, so the possibility that the whole sub-Roman series is really a set of church-lamps may yet prove to be by no means negligible. Without, however, entering seriously into such speculation, the significant probability is that in Christian centres of the midlands and south-western England the rich but barbaric trumpet-pattern style (p. 55) in its most resplendent and developed forms must have been a device frequently seen and persistently practised.

Christianity was eventually blotted out by the pagan invaders in the lands held by them, and after the middle of the sixth century the British Church survived only in the south-west of England, in Wales, and in Strathclyde Britain. Probably Glastonbury was the chief stronghold of British Christians on the borders of pagan England just before the time of the arrival of St. Augustine in Kent ; but even Glastonbury may have been in jeopardy for a while, and St. David's removal from Caerleon to a remote western peninsula suggests that the early monasteries on the frontier may have been at one time in extreme danger. But the British Church did survive. St. David, we know, built an addition to the Vetusta Ecclesia at Glastonbury in the late sixth century, and in 603 the bishops and clergy of Britain in a stubborn and unconciliatory mood were ready to challenge St. Augustine and his Roman order.

In the meantime the Church in Ireland had become the principal home of Celtic Christianity. St. Patrick had begun his mission there in 432. He was a Briton of the post-Roman period, probably from the Clyde neighbourhood, and the Church he established, subsequently developed on a monastic basis largely under the influence of southern Gaul and of Wales, was in origin, as Dr. Flower has observed, the fifth century British Church. But later on the tide began to flow in a reverse direction. From the Church of Ireland in the year 563 came St. Columba, to found the monastery on Iona, a small island off the coast of Mull. And from Iona two great adventures were undertaken by the Columban Church, the first being the mission to the Picts and the second being the mission to pagan England. It is this last activity that completes the cycle. With Patrick the British Church had gone to Ireland ; with Columba it recrossed the Irish Sea ; and with St. Aidan, who left Iona in 635 to found the Lindisfarne monastery, this ancient Church returns to the land of its origin with new strength and new sanctity to do battle with the pagans who had driven it into exile.

It is not, of course, true that the Columban mission to Northumbria represents the sole contact between the Irish and the English at that time. Glastonbury, an Hiberno-British monastery, was already in the position of a frontier-post and is not likely to have been backward in missionary endeavour in a field then being explored by Augustine and his disciples. Indeed, we know that an Irishman founded Malmesbury about 640. Moreover, the English themselves after the Augustinian conversion were willing to be taught in the Celtic schools, and the Gaul Agilbercht, who was Bishop of Wessex about 650, came to his see direct from his training in Ireland. But the fact remains that after the establishment of the Lindisfarne monastery the closest bond between England and Ireland was the unremitting activity of the Columban Church in the north.

It is in this period of the return of Celtic Christianity into England, and probably as much as twenty years after the beginning of the Columban mission to Northumbria, that the earliest known example of the new Christian art was given to the world. This is the Book of Durrow, now in Trinity College Library at Dublin, an illuminated copy of the Gospels in Latin that has pages measuring about 9¾ inches by 6 inches and is named after the monastery in Co. Offaly where it is said to have been written.[1] It is the earliest of a series of pre-Carolingian English and Irish manuscripts. This the ornament establishes beyond all possible doubt, as we shall see ; but we can obtain corroboration by an examination of the ' Great Monogram ' page in the single-column illuminated Gospels of the Irish and Lindisfarne groups, the page, that is to say, on which the 18th verse of Matthew I is to be found. The opening of this verse ' Now the birth of Jesus Christ was on this wise ' comes as the grand climax to the seventeen verses of genealogy, and it was heralded by an emphatic illumination of the sacred monogram at the point where the scribe came to the words ' CHRISTI autem generatio sic erat '. In the later single-column Gospels of this group the emphasis by ornament becomes so gloriously and extravagantly a salutation that the monogram dominates the entire page. Thus in the Lindisfarne Gospels, which we know to have been written *c.* 700, there are only four lines of text below the Great Monogram, while in the Book of Kells (*c.* 800) we reach a climax in a monogram so magnificently monstrous that it leaves room for no more than two other words ' autem generatio '. But if we look at the relatively unpretentious corresponding page (also single-column) in the Book of Durrow (Fig. 20) we see that this manuscript lies typologically far behind the other Gospels and must be dated at least some way back into the seventh century ; for it is incredible that a scribe so diligent and so expert in the most elaborate forms of ornament would have rejected the noble device of the Great Monogram had it been already conceived in his day. This argument will have even more force when we realize that in spite of a total ignorance of a naturalistic figural style he did not neglect to insert the appropriate figures of the Evangelists and their symbols.

[1] For literature and description see H. Zimmermann, *Vorkarolingische Miniaturen*, Berlin, 1916. Text, p. 231, cf. p. 92 ; Pls. 160–5. E. A. Lowe, *Codices Latini Antiquiores*, II, Oxford, 1935, No. 273 and pp. xiv, xv.

Fig. 20.—Evolution of the Great Monogram page in early Celtic
manuscripts
(Top : *Book of Durrow, Lindisfarne Gospels.* Bottom : *St. Gall MS.* 51, *Book
of Kells*)

He was working to a rule ; but to a rule that did not yet include the giant Monogram.

The Book of Durrow is in its ornament the only manuscript in the early Irish and English group that is wholly and relentlessly barbaric in concept from beginning to end. Unlike the others, it makes no concession whatsoever in the representations of the Evangelists and their symbols to the classical figure-style, either in drawing or in modelling. The figure of St. Matthew (Pl. 38) is simply a long chequered plate in red, yellow and green, that looks like a panel of millefiori enamel ; it has feet at one end, and a head at the other ; but the face is coloured by red dots instead of a tint, and there is neither shading nor naturalism of any kind. The symbols of the Evangelists on the folio on which all four appear together are equally grotesque and unreal. We are as yet completely outside the stage in which copies of classical paintings, or obvious adaptions or translations of them, interrupt the sequences of barbaric ornament. In fact we see here an unashamed expression of an ancient barbarian style, occasionally discernible in Gallo-Roman sculpture,[1] in which the human figure is represented simply as a menhir with a head on it. This is not to say that the Durrow form of figure is weak and unskilled ; for there is cunning and adroit symbolism in this bold conceit of an anthropomorphic plate of metalwork. And as for the principal pages of Celtic ornament, there can be no question whatever about their magnificent design and brilliant execution. They are plainly the work of one of the master-illuminators of the age. The trumpet-pattern, for instance, a bold red and yellow with occasional green set off against a black ground, is beyond doubt to be seen here in the most sumptuous and the most expert form it ever assumed (Pl. 37), and we can feel certain that a considerable period of apprenticeship lies behind this amazingly clever page. So, too, the animal folio

---

[1] e.g. Le Comminges, *Esperandieu*, Recueil, II, 883, 888–9, where it is associated with geometric compass-patterns.

(Pl. 37), which has red and yellow, and green and yellow creatures on a black field, is distinguished for the sureness and the hard metallic quality of its design. In general the Durrow style is characterized by a bold spreading rhythm that brings the intricate patterns up on a large scale to usurp the page and lessen the effect of the heavy panelling, and in this respect it is unlike the subsequent manuscripts of the Hiberno-Saxon school in which the equivalent designs are like a small-mesh net (cf. Pl. 41) that makes a relatively unobtrusive filling of its frame.

The origin of this style is no easy matter to determine. It is commonly admitted that it has no adequate pedigree in Ireland, and though it may be Irish in the sense that it is a purely insular version of an imported style, we must look for the source of the decoration elsewhere. When we remember that the Book of Durrow is the first of the manuscripts illuminated in the Celtic style, the arrangement and set-out of the ornamental pages obviously need some explanation and, in fact, provide an important clue to the origin of Durrow art ; for whence came, we may ask, this curious system of a carpet-like spread of decoration with heavy borders and ostentatious panelling and its persistent space-filling interlace, and why is it that the panels contain complicated geometric panels and large-scale rows of animals ? It is not possible to derive an ornamental page thus arranged in a single framed composition from any foreign manuscript source, for this Durrow type of illumination is new, and unquestionably an insular development. Perhaps a vague approximation to the style is to be found in certain Coptic texiles from Egypt ; but such likenesses as there are do not seem to be sufficiently close for the connexion to be significant, and I am convinced that our question is best answered from the archaeology of Britain itself. Accordingly, I suggest that what we have before us here in the ornamental scheme of the Durrow pages is nothing more nor less than a developed barbaric version of the Roman decorative schemes so well established by our late mosaic pavements of the west country type (p. 35). Allowing for a measurable degree of Celticization of the elements in these floors, or perhaps in their equivalent textiles which are more likely to have been the source of the Irish style, the similarity in plan and concept is too close to be without significance. Indeed, a comparison of the decorative plan of the Durrow cruciform page (Pl. 37) and those of late Roman pavements in Dorset and Somerset (Fig. 21, Pl. 20) provides almost conclusive proof that we are dealing with one and the same decorative system.

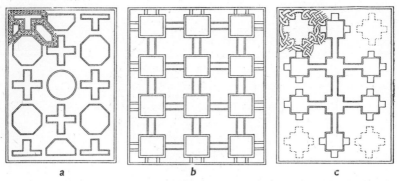

FIG. 21.—Designs on Romano–British pavements (*a* and *b*), and in the Book of Durrow (*c*)

Moreover, not merely the geometric type, but also the panel type of pavement finds its counter-part in the Book of Durrow ; for the animal folio (Pl. 37) with its framework of panels surrounding a free central medallion is as closely connected with the pavement style (cf. Pl. 21) as is the cruciform page, and the continued use of the animal as a large-size filling of these panels is thereby explained. The conclusion seems to be irresistible. The Durrow style is basically a continuation of a Romano-British decorative scheme that in one of its manifestations is represented by the art of the mosaic pavements. Nowhere else do we find this fusion of hard geometric patterns and a flowing interlace background ; nowhere else this system of horizontal and vertical panels containing heavy ornament and arranged in an unmistakably carpet-like form.

But the Durrow style is not wholly derived from a texile or mosaic original, for one of its immediate sources seems to have been metal-work, above all enamelled ornaments.[1] We have already noticed the millefiori panel that does duty for the body of St. Matthew ; but the metallic character of the animals is even more remarkable, and this not only in the isolated figures, such as the bull of St. Luke, but also in the Ribbon Style animal in the

Fig. 22.—Enamelled escutcheon of hanging-bowl from Benty Grange, Derbyshire

vertical panels of the best-known folio (Pl. 37), where the yellow-painted creatures with their sharp metallic edge reproduce the enamel style of the Benty Grange bowl-escutcheon from Derbyshire (Fig. 22) which also bears a linked pattern of yellow beasts. From the point of view of the development of the Ribbon Pattern animal, the Durrow type as exemplified in these same vertical panels most closely resembles the style of the Kentish sword-pommel from Crundale (Pl. 33), and as the later Saxon work that is closer to Durrow in date tends to become increasingly dissimilar in style (cf. Pl. 36), we have here another clue

[1] See J. M. Doran, *Burlington Magazine*, XIII (1908), p. 138.

to the origin of Durrow art. For the Crundale pommel represents an early sixth-century development of the Late Roman free-style animal (Fig. 17), and the fact that a nearly equivalent stage occurs in British enamel, actually in the yellow colour that is reproduced in the Book of Durrow, suggests very forcibly that the Christian painting perpetuates in the seventh century a stage of animal-art that had already been achieved in Britain and is, in fact, the source of the Durrow type. Thus not only in the lay-out of the ornamental pages, but also in the Ribbon Style itself we see in the Book of Durrow a natural Irish sequel to that post-Roman British art that must have found its way into the island at the time of the westerly retreat of the British Church.

It is a further strengthening of this view that I have been able to assign a relatively early date to the Crundale pommel. For if this be Jutish work, as it well may be, it would be a violation of all historical probability that the seventh-century Kent of Ethelbert should contribute one lonely element to the Irish style, which in other respects is totally unlike the later Kentish ornament (cf. Pl. 36). Indeed, it cannot be too strongly insisted that the tendency of the Anglo-Saxon Ribbon Style is to move away from the Durrow open manner in the direction of a close interlace, as is to be seen in the work of the Anglian Development (Pl. 36). But at an early period it is reasonable that a style in its initial stages British (Fig. 17) should lead us rapidly to a Kentish version that is wholly dissimilar from any continental German form of the Ribbon Pattern animal and at the same time closely allied to the Irish form that was evolved from the same British beginnings.

It would be a mistake, I think, to contend that the Durrow style is throughout an insular invention. Celtic monasticism in Ireland owed much to its Egyptian origin, and I see no reason to suppose that there are not strongly characterized Coptic elements in this Irish ornament, though this is recognizable for the most part in details, as for instance, in the type and handling of the Eagle of St. John.[1] I think, too, that something more than an inevitable Celticization of the plaits and twists of our Roman pavements is required to explain the open and irregular type of Durrow interlace, and this something is almost certainly Coptic or Syrian influence.[2] But we are still free to accept the knot itself as part of the local ornamental repertory, because this had already occurred in Kentish ornament by the early sixth century and may have been included in the Ribbon Style formulae when they were introduced into Ireland. In Kent the invention of the knot was probably the result of a technical process of the jewellers who translated the plait into their favourite piece-work filigree ; for Romilly Allen showed many years ago that the ' Stafford ' knot is a simple development of the double plait and can be easily produced by setting out the plait-design in a series of short disconnected lengths of wire.[3] The knot was certainly adopted into the general Kentish style without any accompanying signs of a disturbing foreign influence, for it is sometimes to be seen in cast metal on the Jutish key-stone brooches ; and if it could enter naturally into the developing Ribbon Style of Kent, I do not see any reason why it should

[1] See W. R. Hovey, *Art Studies*, VI (1928), p. 116 for this and other evidences of the influence of Coptic art in Ireland.

[2] See F. Henry, op. cit., p. 92 ff.

[3] On the edge of the Crundale buckle, which was probably found with the sword that I have just mentioned, there is an interesting example of the ' Stafford ' knot in piece-work filigree, and I think that the pattern was certainly derived from a plait in this case. The buckle bears the fish-symbol and a fine piece of minute scale-pattern cloisonné of a type that can only be matched in very early work (Petrossa treasure, Concesti treasure, Childeric's grave). Judging by its form this buckle should be sixth-century work and Jutish in make ; but its decoration is certainly not Jutish in style, and Crundale itself lies outside the principal area of the Jutish settlement. It is possible, therefore, that we should reckon with some surviving British element in the craftsmanship of this piece and of the accompanying sword. I am convinced that this is the real explanation of the resemblance between the animal-pattern of the sword and that of the Book of Durrow.

not find its way in a similarly unobtrusive and natural manner into early Irish interlaces.[1]

Another metallic element in the Book of Durrow is the trumpet-pattern. This is not precisely of the same form as the patterns on our hanging-bowls, for it shows variations probably derived from Irish metalwork of the kind in which the bird's head terminal and the closely coiled ' hair-spring ' spiral are used.[2] But that it is a loosened and adapted version of the principal theme of the enamelled roundels on the finer British hanging-bowls can scarcely be denied, and was, in fact, recognized long ago. And here again we have another clue to the origin of Durrow art that points to British sources ; for the pattern, so I have claimed (p. 59), was a British invention of the midlands and the south. It cannot be shown to be a virile Saxon style of the seventh century, and is unknown north of the Humber in enamel versions, so that it is less likely to have been discovered by the Irish when they reached Northumbria than to have been introduced into that area by the Columban missionaries. The trumpet-pattern in the Lindisfarne Gospels (Pl. 39) is on this view a return of an originally British art to the country of its origin, and my suggestion is that it found its way to Ireland during the westerly retreat of the British Church in the sixth century, like the Ribbon Style and the ' carpet ' plan of the ornamental pages.

The most important metallic element in Durrow is the millefiori pattern. This is probably a local contribution of the Irish, for enamel of this kind was being made in Ireland at the time the Book of Durrow was illuminated and had been made there for some time before. The ' enamelled '

---

[1] Mr. Doran has made an ingenious suggestion that would account for the local origin of the ' stopped knot ' type of interlace, *Burlington Magazine*, loc. cit., p. 144.

[2] e.g. the latchet, A. Mahr, *Christian Art in Ancient Ireland*, I (1932), Pl. I, 8. This design is perhaps a legacy of the antique Celtic style (see p. 54) ; it is without robustness or dynamic qualities and contributed little to the Christian style, even though it is the source of the Durrow ' hair-spring ' spiral and the ' bird's head ' terminal.

character of the manuscript is sufficiently obvious to demand an immediate source in metal-work, and if this be so, then the source must be Irish ; for millefiori enamel was not made in these islands outside the Hiberno-Scottish world during the seventh century. The style, of course, can be traced back to Romano-British enamel-work (Pl. 23) and minute chequer-patterns are to be found in our late west country pavements (Pl. 21) ; but here the connexion does not commend itself as one made directly without the intervention of an Irish school of enamellers. It is, however, probable that we should seek in the geometric repertory of the pavement style the source of the step-pattern devices and the fret, as seen in the Book of Durrow, though the inevitable Celticization of these themes lead to elaborately changed forms, such as the typically barbaric conversion of the square fret into the diagonal fret.

My survey, therefore, leads me to the conclusion that the Book of Durrow is the work of an illuminator inexperienced in Late Antique or Gaulish painting and dependent largely upon patterns derived from his own metal-work and that of the British Church. No doubt continental fashion, and perhaps also contact with the Roman mission in England, may have been responsible for the principal manuscript conventions to be seen in the disciplined and standard use of ornament as a means of illuminating a text ; but the fact remains that the earliest Irish Christian style, with its flat carpet-like spread of ornament, and metallic treatment of the figures, is an insular development of an art that has no continental roots, but is basically the art of the British Church, introduced into Ireland, perhaps by way of the Dee or the Bristol Channel, at the time of the flight to the west before the advancing Saxons. At the period of Aidan's mission to Lindisfarne this Irish decorative system must have been in existence as the established method of illumination of the Columban Church, a noble and homogeneous Irish style, frank in its barbarism and total rejection of a classical figural style. It is, therefore, natural enough that it should contribute substantially to the decoration of the famous Northumbrian text that was written after the arrival of the Irish in Lindisfarne.[1]

Of Northumbrian art as expressed in the illumination of manuscripts we know nothing until we come to a period long after the Synod of Whitby (664), which marks the beginning of the ascendancy of the Roman Church in the north ; for the Lindisfarne Gospels, now in the British Museum, were written about A.D. 700. This noble manuscript[2] is much bigger and more imposing than the Book of Durrow, as it has leaves measuring $13\frac{1}{2}$ in. by $9\frac{3}{4}$ in. It is a Latin text glossed in Anglo-Saxon in the tenth century by a priest of the name of Aldred who stated in a colophon that the book was written by Eadfrith, a bishop of Lindisfarne who died in 721. Aldred also tells us that the manuscript was bound by Bishop Aethelwald (724–40), and further embellished with jewels and metal-work by an anchorite named Billfrith. All this, including the writing, took place over thirty years after the Synod, at a time when the Celtic Church had long since ceased to be influential in Northumbria, and no Celtic person, on Aldred's evidence, had anything to do with the making of the book. It is clearly a monument of the Roman, not the Celtic,

[1] The text of the Book of Durrow is said on palaeographical grounds to be Northumbrian. Lowe, op. cit. ; F. C. Burkitt, *Antiquity*, IX (1935), p. 33. Mr. A. W. Clapham, arguing that Irish art before the mission to Lindisfarne in 635 cannot be shown to have possessed its subsequent ' Celtic ' character, has suggested that the decoration of the Book of Durrow is likewise of Northumbrian origin, *Antiquity*, VIII (1934), p. 43. This seems to me improbable. If my date for the manuscript (*c.* 650) is correct, the maturity and idiosyncratic accomplishment of its style are almost sufficient to exclude the possibility that it is a mere borrowing or adaptation of an English art unknown to Irish scribes ten or twenty years before the manuscript was written. Moreover, the requisite English art of that period in Northumbria is purely hypothetical. If the Book of Durrow be dated later, its abrupt stylistic divorce from the known Northumbrian style of *c.* 700 makes a derivation from the art of the Lindisfarne Gospels out of the question.

[2] The Lindisfarne Gospels, with introduction by E. G. Millar, British Museum, 1923.

Church in England, and its text depends, through the Codex Amiatinus (p. 113), on an Italian original, and the tables of feast days follow the use of Naples. The four miniatures of the Evangelists are versions of Italian pictorial compositions, and though they reveal an insular hardening in style [1] and colouring, and are to a certain extent geometrically conceived (observe especially the treatment of the nose), nevertheless they betray a sympathy with the art of the Roman world that the illuminator of the Book of Durrow did not share (Pl. 38). The occasional use of gold leaf in the colouring is another indication of foreign influence unknown to the Durrow school.

But even if the Lindisfarne Gospels are thus a product of the great days of the Anglo-Saxon renaissance in Northumbria, which we are presently to study, its principal ornamental system is in the northern barbaric tradition, and, though almost violently changed in style, it is in essence a direct development of that Irish art that we have seen established in the Book of Durrow. It is richer and more sumptuous, and contains a remarkable new element in its numerous bird figures ; the Irish millefiori work has disappeared, and there is less accent on the trumpet-pattern motive ; but in concept and intention the ornament is a continuation of the earlier Celtic style.

We can take as a measure of the much-increased grandeur the celebrated Monogram folio (Pl. 39) and one of the cruciform pages (Pl. 40). We see at once on comparing the cruciform page with that of the Book of Durrow (Pl. 37) that the bond uniting the two manuscripts is unmistakable ; but we also note the remarkable stylistic change due to the alteration in the scale of the pattern. In the Lindisfarne Gospels the ornament is now reduced to a small tightly woven web, a subordinate and systematized background of space-filling devices, wholly unlike the loose, flaunting patterns in the Durrow book, which stand out from the page with the emphasis of principal themes, boldly stated.

[1] cf. Roger Hinks, *Carolingian Art*, London, 1935, p. 90.

The treatment of the interlace backgrounds in the two cruciform pages illustrated makes this vital stylistic change very conspicuous ; in the Book of Durrow it is a heavy and ostentatious large-scale pattern ; in the Lindisfarne Gospels it is reduced to a light, closely woven haze.

In some respects, therefore, the Northumbrian manuscript represents a further progress in the direction of a barbarian taste. The way in which the Monogram, itself bearing elaborate decoration, is set off against a background that has the same prominent ornamental value is an instance of this ; so is the trick of separating heads and hind-quarters by long lengths of borders that thus form amusingly distorted bodies ; but above all the tendency towards barbarian over-elaboration is to be observed in the crowded and multitudinous array of intricate details with which the Lindisfarne illuminator filled his pages. This is done according to the system so splendidly exploited by the Irish in contemporary metal-work such as the Tara brooch, and to be seen in even more stupendous exuberance in the century-later Book of Kells. The Lindisfarne Gospels undoubtedly represent an approach to this highly developed style. Of many of the pages in the Gospels we may truly say that they are a veritable Celtic bewilderment in which pattern and background spread themselves in a rich and almost endless parade of dexterous designs, a perpetual challenge to the eye and a perpetual delight.

Nevertheless, in certain details of the Lindisfarne ornament there are indications of an intrusive taste that was not thus barbaric. The animal-ornament, for instance, is plainly a continuation of our familiar Ribbon Style ; but a very short inspection will show that it is not an uncontaminated development from the Durrow stage. The double metallic contours remain and joint-spirals at the spring of the forelegs are still used ; but an entirely new note is struck by the surprising naturalism of the heads of the typical Lindisfarne beasts (Pl. 38, 3). They have alert sensitive ears, a life-like snout with nostrils, powerful jaws,

107

and a general canine perkiness that is a complete novelty in our Ribbon Style series. They have four legs, not two only as in the Book of Durrow, and they have convincing paws with carefully drawn heel and claws. In the same way the birds have a big hooked bill, a gaily feathered body, and a foot with three powerful claws.

An outstanding characteristic of the Lindisfarne stage of animal-ornament is that the creatures, both birds and beasts, are to a notable extent enmeshed in, or set off against, an interlaced background formed out of their own necks, limbs, and tails. Sometimes the Celtic animal is involved in a tracery of such a highly complicated nature that it has the appearance of a quasi-vegetable thicket. The great page of interlaced animals and birds (Pl. 41) well illustrates this new Lindisfarne manner. It is an amazing piece of illumination, intricately and ingeniously designed, that looks at first glance less like an arrangement of birds and beasts than a maze of writhing and climbing plants, the bodies of the animals themselves contriving to resemble the main stems of a vine-scroll. Taking into account the increased naturalism of certain details of the Lindisfarne Ribbon Style creatures, and noting in particular the tendril-like background and alternating birds and beasts in such a passage as the centre panel of the Q on folio 139 (Pl. 38), we see that there is good reason for agreeing with Mlle Françoise Henry, who claimed for these peculiarities, when calling attention to them for the first time, an origin in the semi-naturalistic vine-scroll of the Northumbrian crosses [1] that I shall presently cite as the sculptural representatives of the late seventh-century renaissance, for which the travelled ecclesiastics of the Roman Church were responsible. Thus, for a second time, we are reminded that the Lindisfarne Gospels were written long after the Synod of Whitby, which marks the beginning of the decline of the Columban Church in Northumbria, and after the beginning of the new era that dawns in 669 with the arrival

[1] *La Sculpture irlandaise*, Paris, 1932, I, p. 61 ff.

FIG. 23.—Cruciform designs in Celtic manuscripts and on Northumbrian grave-stones

in England of Theodore, a Greek of Tarsus, as Archbishop of Canterbury. Indeed it is likely that an influence responsible for such a direct intrusion into Northumbrian art as the classical type of Evangelist portrait must also have been the cause of this obvious modification of purely Celtic design, which now shows the marked effect of the well-known classical type of the vine-scroll with birds and beasts climbing in the foliage (Pl. 38).

In the Celtic world in which the Durrow style had been perfected a controlling cruciform lay-out had been used as a basis of a patterned page (Fig. 21), and we find that this cruciform theme is further elaborated in the Lindisfarne Gospels. It is not surprising, therefore, that there should be variations of this cross-pattern as the principal ornament of the small and generally rectangular stone slabs that formed the head-stones of seventh- and eighth-century graves in the monastic cemeteries of Columban foundations in Northumbria, such as Lindisfarne and Hartlepool.[1] These simple, charming memorials are undoubtedly Celtic, and a recent attempt to derive them from Teutonic designs as seen on jewellery and coins cannot be seriously entertained. They are, on the contrary, an off-spring of the distributed geometrical style that, having its origin in the Roman pavements (Pl. 20), receives its Celtic impress in the Book of Durrow. A small group of drawings (Fig. 23) will make this relationship so clear that further comment is not required. Moreover, as Sir Charles Peers has wisely observed, these memorials are known in England only in the area of the strongest Columban influence, and they were in use there for only a short space of time ; whereas in Ireland, at such cemeteries as Clonmacnoise, similar or related designs were still employed for the decoration of small grave-stones long after the type had vanished from the Northumbrian graveyards.

[1] The series has been described by Baldwin Brown, *Arts in Early England*, V, p. 58 ff. and by Sir Charles Peers, *Archaeologia*, LXXIV (1925), p. 254.

VI

THE ANGLO-SAXON RENAISSANCE

ROMAN architecture, which in this context is the building art of Roman Britain and of Gaul, had had little, if any, influence on the development of the Celtic monastery, and was in no sense fostered or further developed by the early Irish Church. St. Ninian in the fifth century and St. David in the sixth may have done something towards perpetuating a building tradition in Britain ; but there can hardly have been any serious or significant attempt to express Celtic Christianity in the terms of an inspiring Roman or Romanesque architecture and monumental art, even in this island where the ruins of towns and temples were still standing. In the Saxon world of the sixth and the early seventh century life was passed in wooden halls and rude huts, and the Celts in this same period, so far as record goes, were content in their monastic buildings with a scattering of modest cells and oratories within the area of a dry-built boundary wall. The refectory was probably the largest building in these kraal-like enclosures ; but even this does not seem to have had any architectural pretensions, and was probably constructed of rough dry-walling, if not of wood.

There can be no doubt, then, that the English church-building of the seventh century is a result of the new influence and example of the Roman Church, operating first in the days of St. Augustine and Paulinus, and afterwards, with much increased vigour, in the decade following the Synod of Whitby. With this sudden and pregnant happening, which is nothing less than the reappearance of the greatest of the arts, we are here only momentarily concerned.[1] But a related phenomenon, the return of an impressive monumental sculpture, is of immediate importance for our story. That it would thus return might indeed be surmised. But it happens that we have direct evidence on this point, for when the church at Monkwearmouth was built about 675, its builder, Benedict Biscop, placed a sculptured standing figure, some 6 feet in height, in the gable of the porch, where its weathered and sadly mutilated remains can still be seen. It is now scarcely recognizable as a figure-carving ; but it probably represented Christ, or St. Peter, to whom the church is dedicated, and its original size and impressive character can be inferred. Thus, since there is no reason to doubt that the porch up to the top of the gable is a part of Benedict's original church, we have here at Monkwearmouth a most notable illustration not merely of the kind of building, but also of the grandiose sort of sculpture that now astonished a native world accustomed only to the intricacies and littleness of ordinary barbaric decoration.

Nor was this all. When Benedict came back from his repeated visits to Rome, he brought with him for the enrichment of the two monasteries at Monkwearmouth and Jarrow a number of pictures, doubtless of Italian work. The paintings were on boards and were a carefully selected series that was intended to have teaching value, setting forth the Christian story in an understandable form, whether the beholder could read or no. Thus at Monkwearmouth there were scenes from the Gospels, figures of the Virgin and of the Apostles, and a representation of the Last Judgement ; while at Jarrow was a set of types and antitypes in which scenes from the Old and the New Testament were juxtaposed, such as Isaac bearing the wood for his sacrifice and Christ carrying the cross.

And with the pictures came books ; for instance, the Codex Laudianus in the Bodleian Library, a Greek and

[1] The early churches are particularly well described by Mr. A. W. Clapham, *English Romanesque Architecture before the Conquest*, Oxford, 1930.

Latin version of the Acts, which is believed to have been one of the manuscripts brought to this country by Benedict himself. The outstanding testimony, however, to the new activity in the Anglo-Saxon libraries is the huge Codex Amiatinus, now in the Laurentian Library at Florence, which was written in the monastery of Jarrow at the order of the first abbot, Ceolfrid (d. 716). This celebrated manuscript was one of three complete copies of the Vulgate made under his direction, and it was the chosen volume that he took to Italy as a gift to the Pope himself, though its delivery was prevented by the death of Ceolfrid at Langres. The book is almost entirely Italian in style and shows no weakening whatsoever in the direction of a barbaric Celtic or English ornamental apparatus such as is seen in the Book of Durrow and the Lindisfarne Gospels.[1] It is, in truth, a most astonishing production for an English monastery of this period and illustrates the extraordinary and uncompromising allegiance of certain ecclesiastics to the Italian manner at a time when purely native styles and mixed Italo-Saxon styles were being vigorously developed in England. Benedict, we know, built Monkwearmouth Church according to the Roman manner which, so Bede tells us, he had always admired, and Ceolfrid undoubtedly shared the tastes of his famous contemporary. I illustrate here (Pl. 42) the Christ Majesty folio of the Codex, for it is certainly a Jarrow illumination, whereas the better-known folio showing Ezra as a scribe may not be part of the original Anglo-Saxon book and is probably an Italian painting. It is clearly by a different artist, and is generally softer and more impressionistic in manner, and in many details, for instance the treatment of the sandal-straps on the feet, it reveals a much greater feeling for naturalism. The Majesty

[1] In the whole of this vast book there is only one initial with interlace embellishment (folio. 805*b*) and even this is much more Italian in style than northern ; it should be compared with some of the seventh-century gold-foil crosses from the Lombard graves.

folio is, of course, in intention whole-heartedly faithful to the continental style of painting and it has carefully modelled Romanesque figures ; but it reveals nevertheless certain characteristics that betray its provincial origin, such as the use of black outlines for the figures, the definitely barbaric treatment of the feet, the lack of experience suggested by the awkward stiffness of the Evangelists' symbols, and the method of drawing the eagle's eye. Moreover, the colouring, a rich assembly of orange, blues, crimson, brown, and gold, shows more violent contrasts and is much harsher in tone than that of the Ezra folio. Thus we find on the Majesty page a very broad border of vivid orange jarring in a disturbing way with the bright crimson of the second ring of the central medallion ; but on the Ezra page the orange border is narrow, and is pleasantly and quietly absorbed into the composition by the warm browns of the furniture.

Even in the lesser crafts the new influence of the Saxon renaissance is observable. There is, for example, the coffin of St. Cuthbert (Pl. 43). The Saint had died at Lindisfarne in 687 and had been buried in a stone coffin ; but in 698 his body was disinterred and placed in a wooden coffin intended to be kept above ground, and this, perhaps the least pretentious and yet the most affecting relic of the early Northumbrian Church, is now to be seen in the Cathedral Library at Durham. It is elaborately ornamented, but not in the Columban or barbaric style, such as might have been appropriate in a memorial of this period at Lindisfarne. On the contrary, it is purely a renaissance piece, and its decoration consists of incised full-length drawings of Christ surrounded by the symbols of the Evangelists, a seated figure of the Virgin and Child, and half-length figures of Archangels and Apostles. These drawings have a conscious Romanesque dignity, though they are crude and show few signs of a practised manner ; but the craftsman was trying to portray the figures sympathetically, and to recognize the significance of the drapery and of the positional character of the effigies. There is, moreover, considerable attention to detail. The hair, with its curls and parting, is carefully treated, and St. Paul has a fine spiky beard ; the slightly turned head with the single-stroke ' profile ' nose is used in addition to the directly frontal face ; the ridging of the upper lip is shown, and wing-feathers and drapery-folds have character and a certain rough accuracy. In some passages, for instance the lower drapery of the Christ and of the Matthew-symbol, and in the long light fingers of the hands, there is an airy vivacious quality betraying not merely a native zest for the new figure-style, but the beginnings of that calligraphic adaptation of it best exemplified in the contemporary drawings of the Evangelists in the Lindisfarne Gospels. In short, the work is young and enthusiastic. And it shows no sign of that kind of provincialism which we associate with the bungling and uninspired copywork of a decaying art.[1]

Just as church-building in the north was accompanied by the appearance of major works of sculpture, like the figure on Benedict's porch, so in the south the early Augustinian buildings may have contained, or at least have been associated with, carvings of equal importance. The evidence is not absolutely decisive ; but the probability that the pieces of a round-shaft cross at Reculver, in Kent, published by Sir Charles Peers,[2] dates from the seventh century is so strong that it is almost a certainty. What is left of this richly figured pillar is in fragments,[3] but they are all of the same stone and bear every appearance of being part of a single monument ; and no fragments of any other early cross have been found on the site. They are likely, therefore, to be pieces of a sculptured round-shaft cross

---

[1] This point is best appreciated by comparing the coffin with the stone sarcophagus-cover in the Hypogeum (c. 600) at Poitiers ; see Clapham, op. cit., p. 43.

[2] *Archaeologia*, LXXVII (1927), p. 241.

[3] With the exception of one fragment in private possession at Canterbury, these are at present housed in the new church at Reculver.

with many figure-subjects thereon that Leland, the sixteenth-century antiquary, saw when it stood in front of the chancel arch of Reculver Church. When, on excavation, the base of this cross was located, it was found to be contemporary with or earlier than the late seventh-century Saxon church, because the original *opus signinum* pavement is stopped against it on two sides ; there is, accordingly, little room for doubt that the surviving fragments belong to a cross that was either set up when the church was built, or was in existence when the church was erected, as it were, to enshrine it. If this be so, we have in these few broken carvings nothing less than a unique and precious example of Kentish sculpture at the first blossoming of the renaissance, either in the days of Archbishop Theodore or perhaps even in the time of St. Augustine himself.

The carvings, which still bear abundant traces of their original colouring, are so unlike anything else in England, or for that matter abroad, that we could scarcely hope to establish their early date without this corroborative evidence. But one of the fragments (Pl. 46) bears a heavy foliate scroll of the Italian type that we also see in the south on the Britford panels [1] (Pl. 76), and in the roundels made by its stem there are human busts. Here we may at least suspect that we have very early work, because the free-style bust in a plant-scroll is a very rare decorative theme that in this instance looks as though it must have been directly derived from Late Antique art [2] ; but I do not feel that this is a decisive point, for it is possible that the Reculver design is, after all, merely a version of the more common classical theme of the peopled plant. But the fact that this scroll-

---

[1] Note the lobed arrangement of rather fat leaves on the inner side of the volutes which occurs both at Britford and at Reculver.

[2] I am thinking of a well-known mosaic at Sta. Constanza in Rome, and I may also mention the Romano-British pavement from Thruxton, Hants. The Reculver design should, however, be contrasted with that of the ' Angel Cross ' at Otley, a later Northumbrian carving (p. 194) ; for there the busts stand on plinths and are flanked by sprays instead of being enmeshed in a scroll.

pattern is itself framed and then surrounded by a heavy interlace border may be significant, for the complete design has
quite clearly that mosaic-floor or carpet-like quality of panels
in interlace fields that I have also claimed to be a contribution from Late Antique art (p. 98) ; and it may, therefore,
perhaps be possible to detect in this fragment of the Reculver
pillar the English counterpart of that stage of Celtic design
represented by the ornamental system of the Book of
Durrow. That is to say, the Reculver cross may owe the
arrangement of this particular panel to a fashion that was
most of all important in the earliest stages of the development of Christian art in the British Isles.

The really astonishing thing about the Reculver carvings is the sensitive and vivacious treatment of the larger
figures, for no Golden Age sculpture in England comes
near to being their equal in this soft classical grace. The
best-known fragment (Pl. 46) is 13½ inches high and is
part of a circular shaft divided by vertical ribs into panels,
each of which was occupied by a draped figure. It bears
the lower halves of two of these. Both have cloaks the
edges of which swing in narrow folds against the right
leg and fan out into long zigzag frills, sometimes of as many
as twelve angles ; in each case this cloak is lifted on the
left side of the body so that the zigzag edges divide over
the left knee, and both have an under-skirt of which the
front is raised slightly. The gentler creases and ripples
of the textile are indicated by grooves, and there is a sense
of pleasant and easy naturalism about the work, which
has not as yet hardened into a rigid schematic style. We
know nothing about the origins and affinities of this sculpture. By hypothesis it should be an obvious reflection
of a continental or eastern style ; but the source cannot
be found, and so far from showing itself to be immediately
connected with any known Italian, Gaulish, or Syrian sculpture of the Late Antique schools, the Reculver figural style
differs markedly from anything abroad. Moreover, its
iconography is as startling as its figure-style, and as difficult

to explain.[1]   The truth is that the Kentish sculpture stands alone, and its peculiarity and precociousness can only be accounted for on the grounds that it is already English and representative of a vigorously experimental insular art. It remains the most baffling and incomprehensible carving in the country, and it is in the highest degree unsatisfactory that we should have so little to say about it ; but we may agree that by assigning it, as Sir Charles Peers has done, to the early days of the Kentish renaissance, at least we place this unique monument in the one context in which the naïve enthusiasm of the sculpture and its iconographical invention may be reasonably expected as a natural off-spring of the age itself.

The revolution caused by the intense and undisguised Italian taste of the leading ecclesiastics of the Roman Church in England during the late seventh century was destined to be profound, and that we should speak of a ' renaissance ' when confronted by this sudden return of a humanistic art is no more than the event deserves.   For the main fact is the reappearance in this country of monu-mental sculpture and the concept of the plastic figure in scene and effigy, which, having been known before in its Romano-British guise, now astonishes us as a phenomenon of Anglo-Saxon art.   That there is no direct continuity does not invalidate a relationship such as the term renais-sance implies ; for the circuitous process whereby an altered and quasi-oriental Late Antique art, introduced by St. Augustine and Archbishop Theodore and Adrian of Naples and Benedict Biscop, blossoms in the land of its adoption into a specifically English and premature variety of Romanesque art does not lessen the significance of the underlying Roman classicism in the foreign taste which was the essential stimulus of the change that is now observ-able in England.

[1] On one fragment (Pl. 46) there is a figure hastening up a rocky slope towards a second figure who holds a long and narrow rope-like object that curls across the composition scroll-fashion.

The result is a commonplace of our history-books. For now dawns the Golden Age of the English Church wherein learning and the arts prospered to such an extent that during the sixty-six years between the arrival of Theodore (669) and the death of Bede (735) the remote province of England, happily aloof from a continent made miserable by barbarian wars and the Arab invasion, achieved a position that without exaggeration may be described as supreme in western civilization. It is not always easy to appreciate the intensity and the rapidity of the movement, but of the intellectual brilliance of its leaders there can be no doubt, and it is no small thing that in a Saxon world only just emerging from the darkness of paganism, the English Church could give to the world a man who ' stands out without possible rival as the foremost scholar of the west '.[1] For such, beyond cavil, was the Venerable Bede.

In the arts the attainment of this country in the Golden Age is no less remarkable than that made in the world of learning. For England was not merely a convert to the classical tradition, but actually its guardian and foremost promoter. If from our distant standpoint we seek the lineage of Anglo-Saxon renaissance drawing and sculpture, we have to look either back or forward in the direct pedigree of the great classical tradition. The work stands alone in Europe, not the contemporary version of a continental art, but a sudden and unique revelation of the mainstream itself. It is perhaps one of the most remarkable events in the whole art-history of England. For a brief moment this country, rousing itself from its obsession with barbaric ornament, stands out bravely and is illumined in the sight of all Europe as the principal custodian of that immense and potent tradition that had found expression in Greek and Roman and Late Antique art and was to become in the western world Carolingian and Ottonian art. This is the phenomenon that we now witness, an English

[1] H. St. L. B. Moss, *The Birth of the Middle Ages*, Oxford, 1935, p. 181.

anticipation of the great Carolingian renaissance ; for in the late seventh and early eighth century, before the age of Charlemagne had dawned, a noble Romanesque art had already flowered. And this, let it be remembered, in a country that for three hundred years had not only denied its principles, but had forgotten even its existence.

It is not, of course, to be expected that the more fashionable and foreign-looking forms of English renaissance art should alone represent the early decades of the Golden Age, nor that a homogeneous Anglo-Saxon style, based on humanistic themes, should have been evolved rapidly. Great though the enthusiasm of the spiritual leaders may have been, and boldly experimental though the designers were, the time itself was one of conflicting tendencies so seriously opposed that confusion and uncertainty did undoubtedly prevail. The Celtic tradition in manuscript-illumination was too well-grounded, too vigorous and successfully splendid in its brilliant ornament, for such a style to fade instantly at the touch of classicism. Indeed, in this branch of decorative art the battle went at first to the barbarians, and the Lindisfarne style, made famous in the Gospels and subsequently perpetuated in other manuscripts of the same school, is, apart from the notable concession in the matter of the Evangelist drawings, an unmistakable triumph of the barbaric tradition. The style was too strong to be extinguished ; nor, indeed, is it to be supposed that the leaders of the new movement desired its suppression. Even Benedict Biscop, the foremost exponent of classicism, saw nothing incongruous in adorning the plinths of his porch at Monkwearmouth with snake-like animal-carvings in the barbaric Ribbon Style, and it is not hard to find other examples of a juxtaposition of elements derived from classical and barbaric art.

There is, for instance, the late seventh-century leather binding (Pl. 43) of a Gospel of St. John taken out of the coffin of St. Cuthbert in the year 1104 and now in the keeping of Stonyhurst College.[1] The manuscript is Italian, or an English text of a markedly Italian character ; but the binding is local Northumbrian work. The rectangular panel on the front is framed by narrow margins containing a two-strand twist, like the panels of the contemporary Franks Casket (see below), and there are two lengths of a more complicated interlace within it that are in the Lindisfarne manner ; while the step-pattern on the back of the cover might almost have been copied directly out of the Gospels.[2] But in the middle of the panel on the front there is a fleshy symmetrical version of the foliate fruit-bearing scroll in high relief that is a testimony to the new foreign taste of the age, for its heavy vase-like trunk and ostentatiously balanced arrangement around a central heart-shaped leaf has nothing to do with native Northumbrian scroll-work. The repoussé silver covering of the little portable altar of oak, also found in St. Cuthbert's coffin, reveals, though it is perhaps a century later, a similar mixture of the foreign and the native styles,[3] so that we are bound to make allowance for a certain hesitancy and duality of purpose in Saxon work of the Golden Age. It is perhaps the strength rather than the weakness of the English renaissance that this should be so, and much of the beauty and virility of our early art is due to the freedom of the artist to make the best of both worlds and to experiment with combinations of graceful foliate themes of a classical order and rich barbaric patterns in a manner that has never been attempted in this country before or since.

The age, however, was witness not only of a conflict between two opposed artistic traditions. In England Christianity itself was new ; for the conversion had been a slow process, and even in Bede's day cannot be said to

[1] G. Baldwin Brown, *Arts in Early England*, VI, Pt. I, p. 1 ; Victoria and Albert Museum, *Exhibn. English Medieval Art*, 1930, No. I, Pl. I.
[2] cf. folio 94*b*, centre, and folio 2*b*.
[3] Baldwin Brown, op. cit., p. 10.

have been complete. In the art of the time this meant that the struggle widened into a clash between Christian and pagan themes, and we have the Franks Casket as an illustration of that further confusion in which subjects derived from entirely different religious backgrounds appeared side by side. The casket (Pls. 44, 45) is made of whale's bone and is now in the British Museum.[1] It is Northumbrian work, probably contemporary with the Lindisfarne Gospels and the Stonyhurst binding, and the first thing that is remarkable about it is that it introduces us to narrative scenes composed of groups of figures, a form of pictorial art of which we have seen nothing since the day of such rare pieces of fifth-century ecclesiastical metalwork as the Long Wittenham stoup (p. 45). But it is the choice of subjects that now claims our attention, for the carver, while primarily interested in scenes from northern mythology, has nevertheless included and given great importance to a scene from the story of the Nativity, and he has also selected for illustration scenes from the history of the Jews and of the Romans. Probably, as Mr. Dalton has suggested, he was working from some illustrated Chronicle of the World ; but it is doubtful if he had any intention of expressing an intelligible sequence of events, and the extraordinary and apparently arbitrary jumble of the pictures on this small box is in fact typical of the heterogeneous interests of the age. Instead of labouring to produce a coherent religious or historical statement, the artist, on the contrary, attempted to please pagan and Christian alike with a joyous and inconsequential parade of scenes that were probably intended to have more ornamental than didactic value.

[1] *British Museum Ivory Cat.*, no. 30 ; Baldwin Brown, op. cit., p. 18 ; A. Goldschmidt, *Elfenbeinskulpturen*, II, 186–7 ; M. Longhurst, *English Ivories*, London, 1926, pp. 1, 65. The name by which the casket is known is a tribute to Sir Augustus Franks, Keeper of British Antiquities, who was responsible for the acquisition of the casket in 1867. Note that one panel, represented in the British Museum by a cast, is in the Bargello Museum at Florence.

The subjects are as follows : on the top of the casket is Egil the Archer defending his home, with the explanatory label ' Egil ' in the picture-space ; on the right of the front panel is the Adoration of the Magi, with the label ' Magi ', and to the left of this on the same panel is Wayland the Smith in his forge ; on the right end of the box is a scene from the Siegfried saga,[1] and on the left end are Romulus and Remus and the wolf, and on the back is the capture of Jerusalem by Titus.

Stylistically the scenes are crowded and chaotic, and are far from being immediate copies of an Italian or other foreign-type composition. It is difficult to believe that there is not a strong northern element in the Franks Casket, and we may perhaps trace its more violently barbaric features to a native style of carving such as is to be seen in the primitive figure-groups of the middle Pictish area. These have nothing to do with the Northumbrian renaissance, but they may have had some influence upon Northumbrian art ; for they are part of the adjacent archaeology and may reflect tendencies in design that were operative over a large area. The Pictish carvings in question are found in Forfar and Perthshire, and their chronology is uncertain ; but it is reasonable to suppose that some of them may be within a decade or so the contemporary of the Franks Casket. They bear an assembly of free-style figures without logical spatial arrangement, but presumably possessing some sort of narrative significance ; and there is no doubt that in the flat treatment of the picture and in various matters of detail they help toward the creation of a northern background for the Casket style.[2]

[1] For a recent interpretation of this difficult panel, see Karl Spiess, *Josef Strzygowski-Festschrift*, Klagenfurt, 1932, p. 160.

[2] cf., for instance, the Inchbraybech stone (Romilly Allen, *Early Christian Monuments of Scotland*, Fig. 235A and B) ; note the animal-headed human beings (*casket*, right side ; *stone*, front, right corner) ; the treatment of human legs and feet (*casket*, right side, right-hand group ; *stone*, front, right corner) ; the warrior's shield (*casket*, right side ; *stone*, back) ; the sword (*casket*, top, left ; *stone*, back) ; the

The sculptural style of the Franks Casket does not represent any very considerable advance on this barbaric work; for the work is both arid and incompetent. The relief is little more than a straight-sided fretwork or 'silhouette' treatment that leaves the component figures and details uneasily distinct, looking like the loose pieces of a jig-saw puzzle. Except for the slanting gashes that give some slight modelling to the folds of a cloak, or the cupping of the undersurface of the shields or the faint rounding of the body in the hollow of an arm-joint, there is little that is sculpturesque about the presentation of the scenes on the box. And just as the artist ignored the classicizing tendencies in this respect, so he likewise rejected a classical discipline and simplicity in composition. True to the northern barbaric tradition he preferred a restless and crowded design for his panels, using runes, pellets, foliage, and interlace to fill up every gap in the pictures, and, aided by the dissolving quality of his figures, he achieves an effect of complicated abstract surface-pattern directly comparable with that of the pages of the Lindisfarne Gospels. In this respect the left side of the casket (Pl. 44) is perhaps the most significant. And this similarity in general result is made the stronger by certain details in the carving. There can be no mistake about the pair of bird's heads protruding from a piece of interlace that occupies the top of the arch in the centre of the back panel, for this comes straight out of Lindisfarne art.[1] The interlace between the legs of the horse on the right side of the casket is another link with the Lindisfarne manner, and the central portion of the Romulus and Remus face is wholly barbaric in concept. Moreover, the little animals in the

pointed hood (*casket*, right, right-hand group; *stone*, back, bottom left); the triple-furrow carving of the human bust (*casket*, front; *stone*, back, bottom right). The Murthly stone (Romilly Allen, op. cit., p. 306) has the figures arranged in a frieze, which is an advance on the 'scattered' style, and this, too, bears an animal-headed human being.

[1] cf. folio 2*b*.

corner-spaces of the front are a direct contribution from the old northern repertory of patterns and recall the Durrow stage of animal-drawing (cf. Pl. 37).

In short the Franks Casket reveals only a partial acceptance of the great art of the renaissance, and to a certain extent may be said to offer a resistance to it. It is a strange, hesitant, and experimental work that most appropriately illustrates the aesthetic disorder of the age. But, this much said, the fact remains that the outstanding characteristic of the carving is its vitality. Its uncertainty is not that of weakness, but of a too exuberant strength, and there can be no doubt of the ingenuity of the designer or of the ambitious enthusiasm with which he addressed himself to his task. A confusion in purpose and manner is more than counter-balanced by this undeniable quality of nascent power. It is in an atmosphere, therefore, of vigorous local experiment that the young art of the renaissance was nurtured, and the rapidity and manifold developments of its subsequent growth are no more than a natural result of the zealous native invention that at the bidding of the Church was now largely directed to the propagation of the foreign style.

VII

EARLY NORTHUMBRIAN CROSSES

IT is on the sculptured standing crosses of stone, noblest of the surviving antiquities of the Golden Age of the Church, that the flowering of the Saxon renaissance is to be seen in its most impressive form. As a type of monument these crosses represent insular, probably Irish, invention ;[1] indeed, it is not impossible that they are to be connected with the ancient menhir-cult of the Celtic world [2] and first appear as the result of a deliberate policy whereby the public and easily comprehended testimony of the native menhir or menhir-like memorial, or of the wooden idol, became a part of the missionary apparatus of the Church itself. There are, it is true, no transitional forms between the menhir and the high cross ; for in the post Roman civilization the memorial had not progressed beyond the stage of the tall rough-hewn stone bearing an incised chrism, and the new architectural and sculptural grandeur of the Golden Age cross is of a revolutionary kind ; but the abruptness of the change is in keeping with the astonishing suddenness of the renaissance, and at least we may say it would be characteristic of the leaders of the Anglo-Saxon Church in the seventh century that they should appreciate immediately the advantages of developing for their own purposes the Celtic type of publicly exhibited memorial.

No department of our national antiquities is more

---

[1] I have in mind early Irish crosses like that of Carndonagh and the cross-bearing slab of Fahan Mura (F. Henry, *La Sculpture irlandaise*, II, Pl. 14).

[2] cf. R. G. Collingwood, *Cumberland and Westmorland Ant. and Arch. Soc. Trans.*, XXXV (1935), p. 3 ff.

urgently in need of organized study than the English crosses,[1] and for my present purpose I find it an excessively embarrassing fact that the principal problems of chronology and stylistic development are not likely to be solved before a complete survey of the material has been accomplished. Until this has been done,[2] and until the results have been fully discussed, I am unable to do more than call attention by means of a few examples chosen from among the more important crosses to certain salient points that seem to have a bearing on the main story of the development of the arts in England, and in this chapter I cannot promise to come to grips, as Mr. W. G. Collingwood alone in this country has done, with the whole huge series of the Northumbrian crosses, arranging them into schools and period-groups.

It is well that we should realize at the outset that though the early English crosses, by which I mean those commonly assigned to the late seventh or early eighth century, undoubtedly reflect the renaissance, they are not so ostentatiously foreign in style as is sometimes assumed. No existing cross looks as though it bears the same relation to continental work as does the 'Majesty' folio of the Codex Amiatinus ; and though the themes used, particularly the vine-scroll and the figures, have their origin abroad, it may be truly said that no cross in these islands is without its idiomatic insular stamp. In the matter of the vine-scroll types Dr. Kitzinger has demonstrated how difficult it is to produce anything that looks in the least like being an immediate foreign model,[3] and the same thing may be

---

[1] For general accounts see A. W. Clapham, *English Romanesque Architecture before the Conquest*, Oxford, 1930, and J. Bröndsted, *Early English Ornament*, London, 1924 ; for a detailed study of those in the north, W. G. Collingwood, *Northumbrian Crosses of the, Pre-Norman Age*, London, 1927. Also G. Baldwin Brown, *Arts in Early England*, VI, Pt. 2, London, 1937.

[2] The survey is now being carried out in the Department of British Antiquities in the British Museum.

[3] *Antiquity*, X (1936), p. 61.

said of most of the figure-types. The crosses represent a frankly English application of the continental or eastern sculptural method to a local form of monument. They are a vehicle for the popularization of the new art of the Church, and therefore in concept and design they necessarily make many concessions to native taste.

This does not mean that the crosses present us immediately with barbarous travesties of the foreign sculptural forms. Their very purpose as significant monuments of Christianity demanded some measure of resistance to the in-born aesthetic tendencies of the northerner whose artistic traditions were in concept and practice totally incapable of providing a medium for such public declarations of the Faith as naturalistic figure-carving and ornament could provide.[1] Thus it comes about that the early Golden Age enjoyed side by side with the bright-patterned abstract nonsense of the 'Celtic' Manuscripts a conscientiously humane and classical sculpture ; and of this we may take as the principal examples those two noble crosses of Ruthwell and Bewcastle (Pls. 47 and 48).

Of these even the Ruthwell cross, which is the earlier of the two, represents only an acclimatized classicism and has peculiarly English mannerisms ; but of its inspiring Romanesque nobility, strongly contrasting with the flashy inorganic surface-decoration of later and more barbaric types of cross (cf. Pl. 51), there can be no possible doubt. Ruthwell is in Dumfriesshire, and the great cross, now in the church, is a tapering two-piece shaft of red sandstone a little over 17 feet in height. Its ornament consists of figure-subjects in a series of close-set panels and of full-length vine-scrolls containing birds and animals ; there is no interlace or any other contribution from the northern repertory of patterns, in which respect the Ruthwell cross differs from that of Bewcastle. The figures are in deep relief and are plastically conceived, even though the drapery is heavy

[1] The vine-scroll itself may have had symbolical significance ; but cf. Dr. Kitzinger's remarks, op. cit., p. 62.

and the postures rigid. On the remaining fragments of the head are panels representing St. John and St. Matthew with their symbols, and also a perched eagle and a half-figure of an archer. On one face of the shaft we have St. John the Baptist with the Lamb, a Christ Majesty, St. Paul and St. Anthony, the Flight into Egypt, and a panel now obliterated ; on the opposite face are the Visitation, an imposing scene usually described as Mary Magdalene wiping the feet of Christ with her hair, the healing of the blind man, the Annunciation, and the Crucifixion.

The heaviness of the Ruthwell style, especially notice-able in the thick ponderous drapery that has nothing of the easy swing and light movement of the Reculver work, is above all exemplified in the carving of the Christ with the Mary Magdalene (Pl. 47). Here the coarse over-weighted folds of the skirt and the lower part of the cloak, and the astonishing rendering of the bent figure with its gross arm and huge long-fingered hand, are clumsier than any passage in the rest of the figure-carving on the cross, and they are, therefore, typical of the aesthetic unsteadiness of the age. Thanks to lack of training, or to the lack of a suitable foreign model, we see in this powerful detail of the woman's arm a sudden irresponsible abandonment of the naturalistic sculpturesque manner in favour of a purely barbarous emphasis of gesture. It is a toppling backwards from the serenity of the general Ruthwell figure-style in the direction of the violent mannerisms of the Franks Casket. To see the real renaissance manner of early Northumbria we must look at the Christ Majesty of the opposite face. Though it has faults of stiffness, and though there are pitiful infelicities such as the treatment of the lower edge of the skirt and of the feet, and of the animal-heads upon which they stand, yet there is a combination of real monumental serenity and humane dignity in this fine work. The head is of natural proportions, measuring one-seventh of the total length of the body ; but when we look at the equivalent figure on the Bewcastle cross (Pl. 48)

[Handwritten annotation in top margin: Here is a lovely example of "pure form" analysis. He does nothing with the inscriptions or with the Cont. sources. He thus fails to see imp. of the connection with Ravenna & misidentifies the X⁵ figure as a "majesty". I think we can safely say that he fails to see the connection because he looks only for formal similarities & not for similarities of thought.]

we find a Christ more noticeably gaunt in quality, the head being only one-ninth of the full height, while the sculptural style is here in general effect weaker and flatter, and in detail rather more heavy-handed and uncouth, witness the deep and weighty central loop of the cloak. This famous cross, a Strathclyde neighbour of Ruthwell, is now a headless shaft of grey sandstone 14½ feet in height. Only one face bears figure-carvings, and these are not arranged in close-set panels, as at Ruthwell, but are separated by spaces left blank for the inscription, which here consists of runes only, instead of mixed Latin letters and runes as at Ruthwell. And there are no longer graceful narrative groups, but three lean ill-proportioned figures, in descending order, St. John the Baptist, Christ Majesty, and St. John the Evangelist.

There is a full-length vine-scroll containing birds and beasts on the back of the Bewcastle cross, but the sides are now broken up into panels of ornament, some bearing vine-scrolls without living creatures, and others framing purely abstract patterns such as elaborate interlaces and lengths of chequer-work. This cross is, therefore, frankly more barbaric in its decorative system than the Ruthwell cross, which shows no trace of this typical Northumbrian art, but adheres to the foreign concept of the storied page and the flowing scroll. The inhabited vine-scrolls of both the crosses are of the same type, but that of the Bewcastle cross shows a harder and more conventional treatment of the theme, both as regards the plant and the creatures in it. The Ruthwell scroll is, of course, far from being an original and unchanged imported pattern, for the heavy emphasis on the thick pipe-like line of the running spirals of the principal ascending stem, and the economy in the use of leaves and fruit, and the transformation of the vine into a mongrel creeper of dubious botanical origin, are all signs of English development; and the animals are English inventions too; for they have lost their hind legs and have acquired long coiling tails with fan-like terminals so that they seem to be related partly to the sea-cow or hippocamp series and partly to the gryphon genus,[1] though they still possess some climbing ability and are able to grip with their fore-paws and bite with their mouths in an attractively vivacious manner. On the Bewcastle cross, as though suiting its texture to the panels of interlace and chequer, the scroll is flatter and less lifelike, and noticeably more abstract in quality. In fact, it is so far removed from being a refreshing glimpse of plant and animal life that it may be said to represent an almost complete translation of a sensitive organic ornament into a dead and over-crowded surface-pattern. As regards the living creatures, which here include stiff and uncomfortable little quadru-peds in addition to the bipeds with fins and fish-like tails, there is a more pronounced rigidity of the attitudes and an increase in size in relation to the containing volute. And the background becomes less and less a part of the picture. It is no longer a mysterious space against which, as some creeper straying across a window, the scroll is set off, but is now the mere machinery of relief, a means of accentuating the edges of the design.

Yet there is still a considerable richness in the Bewcastle stage of ornament, as the shorter panels of the vine-scroll testify. The symmetrical double scroll with the little rectangular tie,[2] and the figure of eight with its interlace-ments of small branches, are spirited designs that still show the complicated ' activity ' of the plant to which Dr. Kitzinger, in making a comparison with Coptic sculpture, most aptly refers.[3] The Bewcastle cross, therefore, must not be written off simply as an inferior and more barbaric version of Ruthwell, for, in addition to the obvious signs

---

[1] A real gryphon with wings appears on the Jedburgh slab, a carving of about the same date as the Ruthwell cross. The tail, however, is that of the sea-cow of late classical art.

[2] This panel is illustrated by Dr. Kitzinger, op. cit., Pl. III, B (opp. p. 64).

[3] op. cit., p. 65.

of its derived Anglo-Saxon character, there is also evidence of the operation of a new and to some extent independent stimulus from outside.[1] Though it is in part a copy of Ruthwell, it nevertheless comes very near to being a new type of cross as a result of this response to tastes and fashions that were unknown to the Ruthwell sculptor, and it is precisely this dual operation, here detected, of changing exterior influences and changing interior style that makes the general sequence of the Anglo-Saxon crosses so hard to follow. We see that in this aesthetically restless and persistently experimental age there was no such thing, even within the narrow limits of a local school, as a constant type of cross ; and no such thing as a single evolutionary pedigree, based on the test of complexity of design and degree of naturalism, for the vine-scroll, or for the birds and beasts, or for the figure-sculpture ; and even if we are as yet unable to establish satisfactorily the main stylistic phases, at least it will be a welcome advance if we determine to rid ourselves of misconceptions that are the result of a too facile simplification of this most embarrassingly complex series of Saxon carvings.

From this it follows that unless crosses are very closely connected in their general ornamental system it is very nearly a waste of time to try to assess their relative chronology at sight and on grounds of minor typological alterations. One would, in particular, distrust any reasoning of this sort that attempts to establish the Bewcastle cross as earlier or later in date than the Acca cross (Pl. 49), which we suppose to have been carved *c.* 740 (see p. 134). The crosses are not sufficiently alike for the purpose. They do not belong to the same aesthetic complex ; and that being so, it may not be a decisive point that on the Acca cross we have a more stylized, more English, version of the symmetrical double scroll than on the Bewcastle cross. Yet there are two factors that ought at least to

[1] The short panelled scroll may itself be due to Coptic influence, as Dr. Kitzinger shows.

help us to decide the date of the last-named monument, and the first is that it undoubtedly represents a group of tendencies marked enough to possess a period-value. The fact that it so closely resembles a great cross like that at Ruthwell which is purely Romanesque in concept, and yet differs from it by the introduction of a new ornamental system of panelled abstract ornament in a vertical row, can only be interpreted as a sign that it was erected at an early date in the eighth century. For it must be obvious that the stylistic change between two crosses so closely connected is of a peculiar kind, a kind that cannot belong to any other age than that which produced the Lindisfarne Gospels ; for I am not thinking simply of the sudden conjunction of plant-scroll and an interlace of a mannered northern type, but of the use of a nearly classical scroll and an early variety of interlace in a carefully organized close-textured carpet-like spread.[1] The second point I have to make concerns the character of the interlace itself, since on the north side of the cross below the chequer panel there is a panel bearing a distinctive assymetrical interlace with bold lateral curves in the ' hollow line ' manner as opposed to the ' solid line ' type also used on the cross ;[2] and the importance of this is that it has its direct counterpart in the Lindisfarne Gospels (folio 211*a*), and does not occur in this form in later English work.[3] To those familiar with the Northumbrian styles it must be evident that we have here two reasons for dating Bewcastle *c.* 700 that are as convincing as any arguments yet advanced ; and we

[1] cf. Lindisfarne Gospels, folio 27, initials LIB, and contrast later interlace-scroll combinations as on the Hackness and Easby crosses and on the cross at Rothley, Leics.

[2] The combination of these two types, following manuscript designs, is rare on English crosses. In itself, however, it is not a proof of early date, for though it occurs in the Lindisfarne Gospels, it remained in use in Irish MSS. throughout the eighth century.

[3] The Durham Cassiodorus (folio 172*b*), a later manuscript of the Lindisfarne group, dated by Zimmerman *c.* 750, shows how this crisp lop-sided design subsequently weakens.

should not lose sight of Mr. Hodgkin's pertinent remark that a monument commemorating, as does the Bewcastle Cross, Alcfrith, son of King Oswy, is not likely to have been set up later than the death of Wilfred (709), whose patron this unfortunate and rather unimportant royalty had been.[1]

The Bewcastle cross heralds a stylistic change that is more easily discernible in the art of Northumbria at about the time of the death of Bede (735). In the direct tradition of the quasi-classical carvings this took the form of a definite swinging away from the humane Romanesque modelling of the Ruthwell work in the direction of a cold and characteristically northern interpretation of the imported ornamental motives, and this particular aspect of the altered manner is well illustrated by the celebrated ' Acca ' cross which can be dated on external evidence *c.* 740.[2] It comes from Hexham and is now preserved in the Abbey there, though for a long time it was kept in Durham Cathedral Library. It has a tapering shaft 11 feet in height, of which three faces are decorated by elaborate vine-scrolls, all alike in being thin and flat in appearance, their rich effect being less that of a luxurious vegetable curtain than that

---

[1] Hodgkin, *History of the Anglo-Saxons*, I, p. 363.

[2] Acca, who was bishop of Hexham from 709 to 732, died in 740, and Symeon of Durham, writing in the early twelfth century, says (*Historia Regum*, s.a. 740) that Acca was buried outside the east wall of Hexham church, two wonderfully carved stone crosses being set up, one at his head and one at his feet, the cross at the head bearing an inscription to the effect that Acca was buried there. The present ' Acca ' cross is in fragments which had been scattered ; but one portion of it was found in 1858 during the building of the new east end of Hexham Abbey, i.e. close to the site of Acca's grave. The cross is inscribed, but illegibly. Two other sculptured crosses, both uninscribed, come from Hexham, the best-known of these (*Durham Cat.*, IV) being found, as was a part of the ' Acca ' cross itself, on the site of St. Mary's Church, and as this bears a vine-scroll of the same order as that on the ' Acca ' cross, it has been supposed to be the cross that stood at the foot of the grave. It is, however, an inferior and rather different carving, and was probably the head-stone of another grave.

of confused and intricate surface-ornament of an abstract kind. The designer, indeed, has frankly abandoned his nature-theme in the case of the single vine in order to experiment with the branch as a vehicle for the introduction of purely abstract interlace ; and even on the principal broad face the inanimate interlace intrudes into the plant-motif, while the heavy symmetrically arranged leaves and bunches do not conceal the fact that the two vines, as organic growths, are not really the main interest of the sculpture.

The use of short panels of purely abstract ornament, as seen on the Bewcastle cross, started a fashion in the decoration of Northumbrian crosses that reaches its peak in the small and slender fragment of a shaft, 2 feet in height, from Aberlady, East Lothian, now at Carlowrie Castle in West Lothian (Pl. 51). This has a long scroll on the edges, but the front and the back are divided into short panels that contain ornament chosen from the repertory of the native designer. Even the figure of the angel on the front is separated by only a narrow bar from a panel of northern animal-ornament ; and on the back are four birds with their necks and legs interlaced, above an area filled by a diagonal key-pattern. Nothing could be more openly barbaric in concept. The animal panel, indeed, in which the elongated necks of the two beasts form parallel diagonals that are locked together by the legs, is a design of markedly Irish quality, and in this particular design it is not to be found in England, though, as a class, such compositions are to be seen in the Lindisfarne Gospels [1] and in sculpture.[2] The birds are certainly in the Lindisfarne manner, as Sir Charles Peers has pointed out ; but the design is seen here in a debased form, witness the draggled tails and long intercrossing legs without claws, and the lack of the large scale-like body-feathers.[3] On

[1] e.g. folios 138b and 139.

[2] e.g. at Lindisfarne (*Archaeologia*, LXXIV, Pl. LII, i).

[3] cf. the Lindisfarne Gospels type and also the St. Andrew Auckland cross.

the sides of the Aberlady cross are two vine-scrolls, both of the same type, a rather hard open pattern that has suggested comparison with a Syrian form of the scroll, as seen in the late seventh-century mosaics in the Dome of the Rock, Jerusalem.[1] As this same type of scroll makes a brief and hesitating appearance in the manuscript art of southern England in the middle of the eighth century,[2] and as the general style of the Aberlady cross and the details of its barbaric ornament is suitably placed, both as regards earlier and later Northumbrian work and in relation to Irish ornament, at this period, we may reasonably assign the carving to the decades close to the year 750.

The intrusion of an openly provincial form of ornament in the decorative scheme of the crosses is perhaps better exemplified by the back of the Abercorn cross (Pl. 50) in Co. Linlithgow, where we have an arrangement of panels containing a diagonal key-pattern, an interlace, and a whorl-like Ribbon Animal that is a deliberate representation in stone of a manuscript style (c. 750) used in the Irish Gospels at St. Gall (MS. 51) ;[3] moreover, the interlace panel of the folio of this manuscript that I have in mind is almost exactly reproduced in the stone-carving. We are beyond a doubt at this point in the history of Anglo-Saxon sculpture very near the middle of the eighth century,[4] and the tortuously ornamental, but rather schematized plant-scroll of the period, represented in three different versions on this one shaft, is conceived in an abstract mood that is in accord with the avowedly barbarizing tendencies of the age There are several other crosses belonging to this definitely Irish-looking phase of

[1] Kitzinger, op. cit., p. 68.

[2] Zimmermann pointed this out ; see *Vorkarolingische Miniaturen,* Text, p. 132. The manuscript in question is the Codex Aureus, Plate IV, Tf. 284.

[3] cf. Zimmermann, III, Tf. 186.

[4] The interlace type survives in manuscripts until c. 800, cf. the MacRegol Gospels in the Bodleian Library (Zimmermann, III, Tf. 199), which are dated by an inscription.

Anglo-Saxon sculpture in the second half of the eighth century that is characterized by panelled interlace and flowing Ribbon Style animal-ornament as a principal method of ornamentation. A good example is the shaft from St. Oswald's, Durham, now in the Cathedral Library,[1] which shows very well this barbarous backsliding in a district south of the Border.

A similar tendency towards a barbaric hardening in style can be observed in the English manuscripts that followed the Lindisfarne Gospels. The style becomes much more Irish in character, and approaches the manner of the mid-eighth-century Gospels of St. Chad, now at Lichfield, that were illuminated by an Irish monk. In them, when we look to see how the human figure is portrayed, we find that there has been no perseverance with the copying of the ' painterly ' Italian style, for the illuminator has employed a type of figure-drawing that is a purely schematic characterization, a symbolic pattern-composition and not the recognizable likeness of a man. The picture of St. Luke (Pl. 53) is a bold assembly of hard metallic ribbons with those flaunting mockeries of natural detail, such as the fold between the feet, that were the delight of insular draughtsmanship. The magnificent face with its geometrically conceived nose and delicate pelta-shaped ears is a notable example of the calligraphic interpretation of the countenance such as we find in other Irish manuscripts, for instance the contemporary St. Gall Gospels that I have recently mentioned.[2] The flowering staff that the figure holds is important as a further instance of the barbaric style, for it shows that spiraliform volute with the ' tailed ' end that makes its first appearance in Anglo-Saxon art in a scroll-panel on the north face of the Bewcastle cross ; but here it is stiffened and wiry, a bristling

---

[1] *Durham Cat.*, XV.

[2] A fine study of this manuscript (St. Gall, 51) has lately been published by Mlle G. L. Micheli, *Revue Archéologique*, Avril-Juin, 1936, p. 192 ff.

affair of menacing spikes that has little in common with the sagging naturalism of the sculptured version. Yet this is an intrusive detail, and the greater part of the ornament of the Gospels adheres to the forms already established in the Durrow style. It is true that the Lindisfarne bird appears ; but Northumbrian ' naturalism ' and ' scroll ' passages are not found, and the trumpet-pattern panel in the Quoniam folio is entirely Durrowesque.

The Durham Cassiodorus (Pl. 54) illustrates the contemporary English work. The figure of King David is a remarkable mixture of two styles, for it is neither plain pattern-work nor corporeally solid. There is a purplish red cloak with very stiff pipe-like rolls and a little shading ; but the king himself is a delicately penned Hiberno-Saxon fantasy, non-plastic and unreal, a fay creature with brilliant blue-green eyes, and a throne, a vermilion-bordered frame with cross-pieces, that is furniture appropriate to this spectral person. We have here an English attempt, not made by the Irish illuminator of the St. Chad Gospels, to conform to a classical type of subject, and it is because of the urgent barbaric mood of the age that the result is a striking schematic abstraction of the original design. But in spite of the barbaric character of the manuscript the painter of the Cassiodorus did not use the accustomed ornaments of the Celtic school in the traditional manner or with the dexterity that is to be seen in the St. Chad Gospels. The Ribbon Style animals in the panelled borders have lost much of their earlier spring and vigour, and their untidy background of very thin interlace adds to, rather than disguises, the feebleness of the design. It is further indication of the weakening of the Lindisfarne style that we should meet an intruder here, a leaping leonine beast whose form, though it is caught up in a whirling mass of interlace, is ostentatiously different from the ribbon-pattern animals. It is as though the lion of St. Mark had been absorbed into the repertory of stock patterns of Anglo-Saxon ornament, and the appearance of this beast in a marginal array of barbaric designs is typical of the age, for he is the northern counterpart of the Merovingian lion of the eighth-century Frankish manuscripts.[1]

This Cassiodorus lion is of a metallic hardness and is sharply contoured like the St. Mark's lion in the Book of Durrow. He represents, as does the other figure of David in the same manuscript (Pl. 54),[2] that distinctive hard-edged clarity, that scrupulous tidiness of outline, which makes the pages of Durrow so attractive ; and it is precisely this quality that we find in the Northumbrian manuscripts of the same age that belong to the Echternach group. The name for this series was bestowed by Zimmermann and is taken from Willibrord's foundation at Echternach in Luxembourg, whence comes the most famous manuscript of the type, the Gospels (Lat. 9389) in the Bibliothèque Nationale at Paris. The Echternach style has to a great extent a foreign, Frankish feel ; but it is nevertheless a magnificent recrudescence of the Celtic aspect of Northumbrian art, and it really owes more to the foundation-principles of the Durrow style than to anything else, though it is an advance upon the Durrow manner that is inspired by continental illumination. Once more the figure-style, as seen in the symbol of St. Matthew (Pl. 55), is purely an ornamental composition ; but the Echternach work differs because of the astonishing ' bull's eye ' effect of the design, the figure-pattern shrinking and withdrawing into the centre of the page where it shines with jewel-like brilliance as the centre-point of a spacious frame. It is the most grimly splendid of the barbaric manuscript styles, and it is doubtful if any English illumination excels the Echternach Gospels in meticulous draughtsmanship and cunningly displayed richness. Yet the Echternach style belongs to the resolutely barbaric phase of Northumbrian

[1] cf. the Codex Aureus (p. 159 below), folio 6a top, for one of the stages whereby the lion enters into the northern network of interlace.
[2] The hair is a pale straw colour ; the halo is straw colour and light red ; the face a whitish buff, and the cloak pinkish red.

art in the middle of the eighth century, and it is only divorced from the Lindisfarne style and the Cassiodorus style because it is to an appreciable degree affected by Frankish influence, or by the oriental influence that was responsible for the manifestation of a similar taste in France.[1] That which is new is the felicitous and spacious organization of the design. The ornamental pages become a framework, like the skeletons of elaborate kites, in which the principal pattern shines with a kaleidoscopic and closely organized brilliance. The copious ragged muddle into which the Lindisfarne style showed signs of sinking is now crystallized and disciplined. The tumultuous riot of barbaric ornament is abandoned, and the boldly illuminated initials and symbols flaunt themselves grandly without the challenge of a copiously ornamental background (Pl. 55 ; cf. Pls. 39–41).

Such was the barbaric mood in the Northumbrian illumination of the second half of the eighth century. No direct counterpart to this exists in sculpture, but the magnificent cross (Pl. 52) at South Church, St. Andrew, Auckland, in Co. Durham, is a carving of this period that also reflects the hard and violent barbarism of the age. We see it in the treatment of the scroll. The theme is that of the jungle-like plant in which birds and beasts disport themselves and are pursued by hunters ; but there is none of the early naturalism and daintiness left, and we are left with an economically rigid version that is purely abstract in concept. It is a hard, unfriendly invention of the north ; a simple running spiral without branches and interconnecting tendrils and with a minimum of foliage and fruit. Yet it does not lack spring and rhythm. It coils without the inert rope-like deadness of many more naturalistic Anglo-Saxon vine-scrolls, and its lines balance and frame the contained animals and birds with a nicely adjusted emphasis. There is nothing here of that narrow strangle-

[1] cf. Zimmermann, *Vorkarolingische Miniaturen*, Text, p. 81. The author has in mind the influence of oriental textiles.

hold of overpowering branches that oppresses the fauna of many other vine-scrolls, and though the pattern is barbarically changed, it is also barbarically elegant and courageous, showing no insipid degeneration due to uninspired copying. The birds and the beasts enforce this point. They are distorted grotesques ; yet they are all alive with a savage schematic vigour. They are derived, it is true, from Lindisfarne types ; for the beasts have huge eyes and thin lower jaws ; the birds have large-feathered bodies, great hooked bills, wings and tails that interlock with the scrolls, and enormous claws ; and all this we can find in Lindisfarne work.[1] But they have at the same time a monstrous gauntness and emphasis that make them different. They are barbarically absurd in their rejection of the earlier naturalism. For the first time in sculpture we see here the curious and characteristically Anglo-Saxon mannerism of bringing the far leg of the animal over the front of the containing scroll, the near leg being tucked behind it. Such awkwardness of stance would have seemed ridiculous and disturbing on the Ruthwell and Bewcastle crosses. Here it is an acceptable eccentricity of barbaric design.[2]

The figure-carvings on the cross differ totally from the modelled work of Ruthwell and Bewcastle. Here sculpturesque treatment is reduced to a minimum, and the artist gains his ends by a silhouette emphasis of the outline of the head and body, the maximum depth of relief being not more than half an inch. The strength of the compositions lies in the brilliant staring rigidity of the surface-patterns and the clear-cut precision of the linear forms. There is an ' Echternach ' hardness about the work, and a suggestion of that orientalizing style that had already

[1] cf. Lindisfarne Gospels, folio 2b (corners) and folio 10.
[2] I call this the Anglo-Saxon ' lock '. It occurs in many later carvings (cf. p. 200). If we substitute the tail or lappet of the animal for the bough, we can trace the origin of the mannerism back to the Lindisfarne Gospels (e.g. folio 14, top of columns).

contributed to the manuscripts of the Durrow and Echternach tradition. There is no doubt, for instance, that the iconography of the cross owes something to eastern invention, for the remarkable rope-bound Christ comes to us from a distant, perhaps Syrian, source,[1] and only the vigorous calligraphic intensity of the figures and the treatment of faces and hair, which recalls a style established in manuscripts and St. Cuthbert's coffin, give these fine groups their unquestionable northern stamp.

[1] cf. the bound bodies of the crucified thieves in the sixth-century Rabula Gospels at Florence, or the silver plate from Perm (Smirnov, *Oriental Silver*, Pl. 15).

VIII

CAROLINGIAN INFLUENCES

How long this admirable barbaric work of the Echternach-Auckland style continued in Northumbria we do not know ; but it is likely that it was short-lived, not lasting many years after Alcuin, the Francophile, had become head of the school of York (776). For in the closing decades of the century we encounter a marked stylistic change that may have been partly due to the influence of Alcuin himself and partly to the classicizing tastes of Mercia during the supremacy of Offa. The new ' Carolingian ' style, as first seen in English manuscripts, is illustrated by the Cuthbert Gospels at Vienna. This is probably York or Mercian work and is known to be not later than 800.[1] The illumination is more Frankish in type than anything we have yet examined, more conscientious in its adherence to a Carolingian form of decoration, and more classically serious in the impressionist and dramatic style of painting used for the figures.[2] These Gospels make no use whatsoever of trumpet-pattern, and there are few of the whirling spiraliform designs still to be found in northern work of the second half of the eighth century ; in fact, the manuscript is connected only in details with the older forms of Northumbrian art, witness (Pl. 58) the bird-pattern of folio 166a,[3] the Saxon ' lock '

---

[1] Zimmermann, *Vorkarolingische Miniaturen*, Text, p. 137.

[2] For an interesting comparison between the figure-style of the Cuthbert Gospels and the frescoes at Tarrasa in north-east Spain, see *Art Studies*, VI (1928), p. 124.

[3] In the N of IN (Zimmermann, Tf. 312) ; cf. similar designs in the Lindisfarne Gospels and on the Aberlady cross (Pl. 51).

of the animals' legs at the bottom of the Cannon Tables,[1] and a number of peculiarities in the interlace, for instance the stringy asymmetrical pattern in the frame surrounding St. Matthew.[2] That which is new in the repertory of minor ornaments may perhaps be taken as showing the influence of Mercian art, for instance the unusual treatment of the theme of the inhabited vine-scroll on the Monogram folio,[3] which belongs to a heavily ornamental type of decoration that also finds expression in the Canterbury illumination of the south, though its details are not southern, nor done in the Northumbrian manner of the days before the Mercian supremacy. A most important novelty is that in the panel below the Monogram the letters A and M of the word AVTEM have animal-headed serifs, thus heralding a distinctive ornamental style that we shall find further developed in Mercian manuscripts. In the Cuthbert Gospels these serifs do not achieve the full turbulence of the Mercian ' biting beast ' style, such as we shall presently see in the Rome Gospels (Pl. 57), and they still have some of the restraint of the animal-heads on letters of the Lindisfarne Gospels, that look longingly at the adjacent letters without daring actually to bite them ;[4] but they are different in manner from this Lindisfarne work and undoubtedly approach the style of the Mercian majuscules that so soon afterwards are converted into writhing, biting fantasies of the most extravagant kind.

The nature of the stylistic change that was taking place in the Mercian-Northumbrian area about 800 is illustrated in a more startling fashion by the Rome Gospels to which I have just referred.[5] In the arrangement of its ornamental

---

[1] Folios 21a and 21b (Zimmermann, Tf. 307–8).

[2] Folio 17b, left side, top of upper panel (Zimmermann, Tf. 297).

[3] Folio 22a (Zimmermann, Tf. 309).

[4] e.g. folio 27. On folio 3 are birds' heads that bite the initials of which they form part. cf. also Gospels of St. Chad, folio 221.

[5] Vatican, Barb. lat. 570. Note that Zimmermann assigns this manuscript to southern England (Text, p. 140).

pages this depends to some extent on the Lindisfarne tradition, and the Monogram folio (Pl. 56) is of the familiar Hiberno-Saxon plan, showing a restraint in the use of background that suggests the influence of the Echternach style. Yet the manuscript is transformed. The austerity, the hardness, and the prim mannerisms of the middle eighth century are banished, and the illuminator indulges in every sort of untidy prettiness and all those frivolous comicalities that make barbaric work of the early ninth century so enchanting. The ludicrous zoomorphic trumpet-pattern is typical of this sudden gaiety, and so is the sprightly little stiff-stemmed plant with the pecking birds and winged leonine bipeds, and also the animal-headed interlace,[1] a significant detail that has its origin, if not in Mercia, in south English art. Another curious innovation that we see here for the first time is the device known as ' penetration ' that makes an interlacing ribbon or limb pass directly *through*, and not over or under, the ribbon limb, or body whose path it crosses. This we shall see again in ninth-century work in England, in sculpture on the Croft shaft, on a shaft in St. Peter's, Northampton, and on a tombstone at Ramsbury in Wiltshire (p. 214). It also occurs in West Saxon metal-work, for example the Wallingford sword (p. 184), and is common in foreign metal-work of the Carolingian age, both Frankish and Scandinavian.[2]

The colouring, too, in these Gospels is alive with a new and cheerful exuberance ; for the panels of the Monogram folio are brightly bordered in purple, orange-red, yellow, and light blue and blue-green, and they have a surcharged ornament of dots in red or in white, that looks like a form

[1] Folio 1*a*, bottom of second column from right (Zimmermann, Tf. 317).

[2] It is very rare in Irish art, though there are occasional instances of ' penetration ' in the Book of Kells. I do not know the origin of this mannerism, but I should like to suggest that it is a Carolingian, and not a barbaric, invention. Cf. the climbing plants that grow through the columns of the calendar-tables in the ninth-century Gospels in the Pierpont Morgan collection (MS. 728, fol. 13).

of embellishment borrowed from a southern school. The little scroll is especially characteristic of the new style, for its birds and animals are in gaily variegated tints and it has prettily shaded and spotted leaves and fruit. Elsewhere in the book we find a similar brightness and increased vivacity in design. The majuscules with animal-headed appendages that fill the panelled lines in the text are now astir and writhing. The letters twist and turn in lively confusion, and they grip and bite and snarl and snap, and sometimes tail off unexpectedly into waving flowers and leaves. In the illustrated panel (Pl. 57) these letters are coloured a pale grey and they have yellow heads with red mouths and white tongues and lappets, and they are set off against a light purple background that is dotted in white and dark purple.

The animal-ornament betrays an increasing preference for the biped with the long curly tail, and this creature, foreshadowing the style that was to become more and more common in Mercia, has often a vigorously drawn heraldic body that is set off against the light lacy intertwinings of the tail. The intricate confusions of animal-pattern in the Lindisfarne style is disappearing ; the ' ribbon ' formulae are less and less used, and we now come upon our first example in minor manuscript ornament of the enclosed ' portrait ' method of presenting a single animal as a complete little picture in its own frame,[1] this being one of the very clear signs of the foreign influences now operating upon English art. But the most obvious examples in the book of a new continental manner and of the rich prettiness of the general style of the Rome Gospels are the portraits of the Evangelists (Pl. 57) with their dainty flowered backgrounds. These figures have elaborately modelled faces with white high-lights and carefully controlled natural shading, and in this respect they differ markedly from the mannered figural style that we have recently examined. Moreover, they are far gentler folk than the gigantic and formidable figures of the Cuthbert Gospels, and they are more

[1] Folio 18a, centre of X in Monogram.

amusingly and more gaily coloured ; thus St. Matthew in our illustration has light-blue hair, a yellow halo, a green dress with red and yellow lines, and a purple cloak, while the background is light blue and light green with scrolls in dark red.

It is no coincidence that the lavish and amusing prettiness which is the keynote of the decorated pages in the Rome Gospels finds a simultaneous expression in Irish art ; for that supreme masterpiece of the Celtic illuminator, the Book of Kells, can be shown on many counts to be a greater and more magnificent response to the same impulse to transform the barbaric style. And herein lies a clue to the origin of the Rome Gospels, for it may be truly said that the central panel of the Canon Tables (Pl. 57) [1] is a fantastic design of such flippant and whimsical impertinence that it is without rival outside the Book of Kells, and most plainly stamps the manuscript in which it is found as the work of no other region than the Hiberno-Saxon area, which at this period (c. 800) can scarcely be held to extend southwards beyond Mercia. It is the authentic surrealism of the Celtic world that is now freed from the exact discipline of an established system of ornament and is able to expand unfettered into its own extravagant imaginative style. The face at the top of the centre column is, in particular, a remarkable piece of painting that illustrates the process whereby a naturalistic countenance was converted into an abstract barbaric monstrosity. For, though it is seriously and effectively modelled with white high-lights and blue shadows, very well done, it is nevertheless rendered inhuman and unearthly by the brilliant orange-red lines used for the eyelids and the nostrils, and by the great staring black eyes and the blue beard.

The Rome Gospels are to be attributed to Mercia with some hesitation, for a slightly later manuscript that is certainly Mercian represents a further change in style, and only the supposition that this later work, the Book of Cerne (p. 165), represents the West Saxon ascendancy, beginning

[1] Folio 1a (Zimmermann, Tf. 317).

147

in 825, whereas the Rome Gospels belong to the age of Offa, gives plausibility to an otherwise unexplained alteration in taste. There is one other manuscript, however, that mirrors north English art within a few years of the death of Offa (796) and gives us a further example of the highly ornate style that we have just been studying, namely the Leningrad Gospels.[1] That the illumination in this manuscript shows certain signs of southern influence is incontestable, and there is no doubt that the structure of the Canon Tables and the small-scale geometric panelling of their columns suggests some close connexion with the style of the Canterbury Gospels.[2] But this much is to be expected at a time when southern influence was so rapidly gaining ground in the north and, as we have seen, the older varieties of the Northumbrian Ribbon Style animal were giving place to heraldic bipeds and foreign leonine forms. There are not wanting, however, proofs that we are still in the Hiberno-Saxon world, and one of them is supplied by the interlace panels that have small cruciform insets, a typical Irish convention of the Kells period,[3] and another is the flat and characteristically metallic treatment of the animal-forms ; but the decisive point is that the Leningrad Gospels are northern in their principal ornamental compositions and are properly to be counted as fantastic elaborations of the Echternach style. To the earlier formulae they add a rich sprinkling of pretty ornament of the fashion set by the Rome Gospels, and a finicky surcharged decoration in the Canterbury manner ;[4] but they are nevertheless founded solidly upon the earlier Northumbrian art. A

[1] Again note that Zimmermann attributes these to south England (Text, p. 143 ff., p. 304).

[2] Royal I.E., VI (p. 162).

[3] e.g. Book of Kells, folio 292a, bottom right corner, and the Mac Regol Gospels, folio 52a. The type makes a brief and hesitating appearance in early Canterbury work (Codex Aureus, folio 6a).

[4] e.g. folio 18a, the over-painted yellow design of dots, lines, and spirals, on the animal between the L and I of LIBER ; cf. the Canterbury Gospels, Royal I.E., VI, folio 4a, borders of panels.

comparison between the opening page of St. Matthew's Gospel in this work, and in the Lindisfarne Gospels and in the Echternach Gospels, will make the close bond that exists within this northern group plainly recognizable (Pl. 59). Moreover, these three pages summarize for us the ' grand style ' of *c.* 700, the hard barbaric Echternach style of *c.* 750, and the luscious northern Baroque of *c.* 800.

Northumbrian sculpture likewise reflects this sumptuous ornamental style of the end of the eighth and the beginning of the ninth century, as we may see by the example of the tiny fragment of a cross-shaft at Croft in Yorkshire (Pl. 61). The scroll on the edge is still the Abercorn type of design and calls for no comment ; but on the front and back are two scroll-compositions containing birds and beasts of a new kind ; and the change in style that these designs represent is indeed remarkable. The plant has turned into a thin wiry pattern and is a tumultuous array of fantastically shaped decorative elements. The details are exaggerated and intensely vivid ; they have a novel and undisciplined zest ; there are mannerisms hitherto unknown in sculpture ; for example, in the groups of leaves there are instances of ' penetration ' (p. 145), the volute of the scrolls passing not over nor under, but *through* the blades. The birds and the beasts are gay barbaric sketches that respond in quality to the type of scroll that surrounds them ; unusual oddities in their form are permitted, and the central figure on the left side of the long panel is a mere wisp of a thing, as slender and as symbolic as the White Horse of Uffington itself. This animal enters into the scroll-composition to the extent of providing a leaf at the end of its tail and by the lock of its legs over the stem ; but this willingness to force the animal into the intricacies of the main pattern of the panel is better illustrated at the bottom of the other face of the stone where we have a composition that jettisons the controlling scroll-theme, and yet simulates it by forcing the curling winged bodies of the creatures to provide a scroll-like appearance.

As an illustration of the new and astonishing types of design that were now beginning to make a profound impression upon Northumbrian art, and as proof of the extraordinary versatility and catholicity of the northern artist of this period, nothing could be more instructive than the little bowl of embossed metal (Pl. 60) from Ormside, Westmorland, that is now in the museum at York.[1] Whereas the Croft stone has shown us sculpture in which a traditional theme interpreted the new mood for rich ornamental effects, in the Ormside bowl we have, as it were, an essay that deserts antique Northumbrian arrangements in favour of a completely novel decorative theme (Fig. 24). It is true that the plant-scrolls in the four panels are versions of a type used on the Croft carving and have unmistakable Northumbrian characteristics;[2] but they represent a flagrantly un-English use of this type, inasmuch as there is here no suggestion of the rhythm of the creeping or climbing plant. And the fauna almost defies description. The birds are in the highest degree fantastic; many of the animals are new and nameless curiosities. We recognize two lions with shaggy manes and big ears and furrowed brows, heads bent down. There are creatures of the same kind with monstrously elongated necks, biting at branches.

[1] For this bowl see Baldwin Brown, V, p. 318 ff., and *Cumberland and Westmorland Ant. Arch. Soc.*, Extra Series, XI (1899), with coloured illustrations, p. 297, and ib., XV (1899), p. 381; also *Reliquary and Ill. Arch.*, N.S., XIII (1907), p. 200. The bowl probably comes from a viking's grave and it bears additions that are as late as 900; see E. T. Leeds, *Liverpool Annals of Archaeology*, IV, p. 8. It has an outer bowl of embossed silver and a lining of gilt copper, with two jewelled discs of the same material, one inside and one outside the hollowed base of the cup. The inner disc bears interlace work in applied milled wire, and the outer one interlace ornament in repoussé. The rim is decorated with glass pastes in rectangular settings, an embossed metal ribbon, and applied twisted wires.

[2] I am thinking of the familiar pointed leaves with two or four berries at the base, the character of the budding leaves, and the flower-like berry-cluster. The roots would possibly establish this point, but they are unhappily hidden by a later strip of silver.

There is a quadruped with one narrow wing on his back; there is a unicorn biped with a long twisting tail of the foliate kind, and there is a standing creature of the clutching and biting order, his belly turned towards the beholder. Finally, there is a leaping goat with shaggy hair and a fine long pair of horns. This exuberant gaiety in bird and

FIG. 24.—The design on the Ormside bowl

animal life, and the extraordinary character of so many of the creatures, have their counterpart in Carolingian zoological oddities such as the ivory panel in the Louvre [1] showing a scene from Paradise, thickly populated with a varied assortment of beasts including a lion, a leopard, a gryphon, a unicorn, a ram, a dromedary,[2] an elephant,

[1] Goldschmidt, I, 158.
[2] cf. the pair of animals on the Ormside bowl below the two birds that are pecking backwards.

and a bear. Such an array is, of course, unusual in Carolingian art ; but it is a known element in it,[1] and may be a collateral result of the same influence, perhaps something eastern, that was responsible for the character of the bowl in England. Certainly the sprightliness and violence of gesture are in keeping with continental animal-designs of the ninth century, witness the gaiety and absurd forms of the creatures adorning the calendar-tables of the Gospel of St. Thierry of Rheims.[2]

The phenomenon of Northumbrian art to which I now desire to call attention is the ' Carolingian ' phase, for so it may be called, of the high crosses themselves. What we now see, at a period of the darkest political decline,[3] is nothing less than a reawakening of the classically conceived sculptural art, and the application to carved stone of the modelled impressionist figure-style of southern illumination. From the schematic severity of the linear figure-work on the St. Andrew Auckland cross in the middle of the eighth century we turn at the dawn of the ninth to a softly modelled style of a serene and friendly sincerity, and from the almost violently barbaric harshness of the St. Andrew Auckland scroll we pass to prettiness and amusing ornament and natural gaiety.

The fragments of the beautiful cross from Easby in Yorkshire, now in the Victoria and Albert Museum, illus-

---

[1] See, for instance, the ' centaur ' ivory in the Cluny Museum, Goldschmidt, I, 157 ; note the horned curiosity below the centaur, and also the gripping and biting beats in the lower corners.

[2] Boinet, *La Miniature carolingienne*, Pl. LXXV. It is also possible to call attention to certain resemblances in detail, such as the hairy ram with a scroll tendril passing between his horns to be seen on the ivory flabellum at Florence (Goldschmidt, I, 155, on the side of the sheath, i). The ivory plaque in the Victoria and Albert Museum (Goldschmidt, I, 179), possibly English work, should also be noted in connexion with the Ormside bowl.

[3] The influence of Alcuin (a. 809), who had been Archbishop of York and remained in close touch with the north of England during the period of his residence at Aix with Charles the Great, should not be forgotten.

trate best of all the new richness of this northern ' Carolingian ' sculpture (Pl. 62). The extraordinary thin and elaborate quality of the inhabited vine-scroll on this carving, with its multiplicity of delicate tendrils, its naturalistic leaves and its corkscrew stem, represents a style that is new to England and can scarcely be divorced, as Dr. Kitzinger was the first to see,[1] from the equivalent thin-spread richness of the scroll on certain Carolingian ivories. As a test of date within the Northumbrian series we note the scale of the contained animals, which are very big in relation to their encircling volutes, as though taking their standard of size from the Heversham cross (p. 202) [2], an unquestionably late and evolved variant of the earlier tradition of the vine-scroll. But that which I regard as definitely characteristic of the age, and unknown in English art before the beginning of the ninth century, are such pretty conceits as the introduction of little gripping beasts in the spandrels of the arch above the heads of the Apostles,[3] and the intrusion of foliate details into the picture-space of the Majesty panel.[4] The Easby cross, however, is thoroughly acclimatized Northumbrian work, as may be seen by the somewhat

[1] *Antiquity*, X (1936), p. 70.

[2] Collingwood, *Northumbrian Crosses*, fig. 47.

[3] In Late Antique ivories the birds flanking the arches are dignified ornamental adjuncts to the architecture ; in Carolingian ivories of the Ada group they come to life and start pecking at the top of the arch. The interesting Lyons ivory (Goldschmidt, I, 171–2), in which the Evangelists' symbols are caught in the act of descending from the architectural frame in order to play in the picture-space, may be mentioned here, and likewise the little creatures dancing on the ends of the cornice of the canon-tables of the Gandersheim Gospels (Boinet, op. cit., Pl. XCI, A).

[4] These intrusive foliate details in figural compositions are presumably connected with those Carolingian paintings in which foreground flowers are to be found (e.g. the Godesscalc Gospels, Boinet op. cit., Pl. III). The modest appearances of leaves on the Easby carving suggests comparison with such panels as the bird-painting on folio 34*b* of Tiberius C. II (see below, p. 168) where a single vine-leaf of the conventionalized kind curls into the picture.

mannered treatment of the animals, and in its handling of interlace and of the scrolls on the narrow faces. It can be described as Carolingian only in the sense that it shows vague approximations to styles that had not expressed themselves in England before the Carolingian period, and because it shares in the Carolingian form of the newly awakened classical tradition. Thus while the Majesty does not possess the monumental dignity of the Ruthwell and Bewcastle carvings, it has the new value of the minor Carolingian effigy as seen in ivories. In fact, in the composition of this panel, with its incomplete supporters and its trivial foliate details, there is something of that ' mixture of grandeur and gaucherie ' that Mr. Hinks regards as a sign of Carolingian invention.[1] The curious and cleverly varied ' Roman ' type of the heads on the Easby cross, to which Miss Longhurst has called attention,[2] strongly contrasting with the hard ' Celtic ' manner of the St. Andrew Auckland style and the monotony of the Rothbury style to which I shall next refer, is yet another novelty in this fine carving that seems to have its counterpart in at least a few Carolingian ivories.[3]

The cross that once stood at Rothbury in Northumberland was probably the most imposing cross of all in the Carolingian series, but to-day only a few scattered pieces (Pls. 63, 64) of it are left, the foot functioning as the pedestal of the font in Rothbury Church, while the head and a part of the shaft are housed in the Blackgate Museum at Newcastle.[4] In the figure-work here we have less of the sensitive softness of the Easby style, and there is occasionally

---

[1] Roger Hinks, *Carolingian Art*, London, 1935, p. 133. In Late Antique ivories the attendants are never illogically incomplete, as here and in Carolingian work, e.g. in Lothar's Psalter (Boinet, op. cit., Pl. XXX ; Hinks, Pl. XII).

[2] *Archaeologia*, LXXXI (1931), p. 46.

[3] e.g. the Vatican ivory, Goldschmidt, I, 26, which is of general importance in connexion with the Easby style.

[4] *Archaeologia Aeliana*, 4 S., I (1925), p. 159.

a ridged and angular effect that suggests a persistence of the barbaric linear carving of the St. Andrew Auckland kind. We see this in the miracle scenes on the Blackgate fragment (Pl. 64) and also on the cross-head in the small figures (Pl. 64) that hold objects presumably intended for instruments of the Passion. It is a mannered type of English provincial carving that was not uncommon in the ninth century, for we shall see it again on the Wirksworth panel in Derbyshire (Pl. 67) and also on the beautiful shaft at Codford St. Peter in Wiltshire (Pl. 75). The Rothbury style, however, is best illustrated by the Majesty carving on the Blackgate piece. The figure is in relief to a depth of $1\frac{1}{2}$ inches and is intended to represent natural modelling, but it has in spite of this a hard ornamental Hiberno-Saxon character that is quite different from the softer and more classically sensitive Easby style ; the detail of the mouth with its long and plainly ridged upper lip helps us to appreciate this point at once. Even where the ' soft ' style was more seriously attempted, as in the Ascension panel on the Rothbury font (Pl. 64), the work is noticeably harder and coarser, and the change in the treatment of the grouped Apostles' heads when we contrast them with those of the Easby series is in the highest degree significant. Instead of the stately and varied ' Roman ' countenances we have here a much greater monotony of type, a uniform ' doll's head ' set of carvings with deep-drilled staring eyes.

The subject-matter of this cross contains much that is new, for example the peculiar arrangement of the miracle scenes in what is apparently a continuous narrative form without dividing partitions or segregation into distinct groups ; for the fragment showing the healing of the Blind Man includes a head from a second subject, perhaps that of the Woman with the Bloody Flux. The Ascension panel with its excited group of Apostles below the figure of Christ is also new in English art ; it is true that the subject had found its way into Irish iconography shortly after the middle of the eighth century [1] ; but the Northumbrian carving differs decisively from the Irish version in the tense and realistically emotional quality of the scene and must owe something to the influence of a Carolingian exemplar of the type of the well-known Darmstadt ivory.[2] Another sign of what must be, ultimately, Carolingian influence is to be discovered in the lowest of the closely fitting group of eighteen heads on one face of the Blackgate Museum shaft, because in the bottom row the hair is adorned with a jewelled fillet that leaves a fringe across the forehead, a type of ornament that is certainly Carolingian, and unknown in England before the ninth century, perhaps being a simplified form of the emperor's crown in the equestrian statuette in the Carnavalet Museum.[3] Furthermore, the setting of the Majesty carving deserves notice. The figure, which is flanked by plants, is in an arched niche in a rectangular frame, the spandrels at the top being filled by stylized sprays of fruit and leaves, and the spring of the arch being emphasized by a sheath-like ornament that robs it of architectural solidity. We have here a new type of design that can only be a rather ponderous English version of the light-hearted architectural illogicality that is found with similar floral embellishments in continental work of the ninth century.

The rest of the ornament of the Rothbury cross is no less interesting than the figure-subjects. The interlace on the font, for instance, a thick close-drawn pattern in a round-arched panel, is of a type unknown before the ninth century that has its exact counterpart in Irish illumination.[4]

[1] St. Gall MS. 51, p. 267 (Zimmermann, Tf. 188).

[2] Goldschmidt, *Elfenbeinskulpturen*, I, 20.

[3] The immediate source might be south English, for we are now in the period when the influence of West Saxon art was making itself felt in the north, and a similar crown or fillet is to be seen on the Codford St. Peter figure (Pl. 75), which, as I have already said, has a Rothbury fold-style (cf. p. 180).

[4] cf. especially the panel on the initial of folio 166a of the Armagh Gospels, dated 807 (Zimmermann, Tf. 207).

The plant-scroll, on the other hand, is in style and botanical type an off-spring of the Ruthwell and Bewcastle scrolls,[1] and the bipeds within it belong to the same series of carvings. But the contained fauna includes a new-comer in the long lean striding lion with the shaggy mane extending the length of his back. He has become enmeshed in the scroll at which he bites, and he is trapped by that uncomfortable Anglian ' lock ' of the legs ; but he is for all that a new Frankish beast.[2] A more remarkable innovation is the amazing panel on the font that presents us with a design in the form of an interlacement of long-tailed lizard-like creatures clawing and biting each other, among them being a little man who holds the feet of two of the monsters in his hands. This vicious gripping and biting composition has astonished us in the rustic construction of writhing letters in the Rome Gospels (p. 146), but it is, as one would expect, rather in the uncompromisingly barbaric world that we are likely to find the fullest expression of this horrid art, and we discover it there at once in examples of the Scandinavian ' Gripping Beast ' style.[3] This is, in our eyes, probably the ugliest and least attractive of all the barbaric forms of ornament that are known in the north, and it is explained as the result of the intrusion into Scandinavian Ribbon Style animal-pattern of a new and most unfortunate plastic taste that was derived from an increasing familiarity with the sculpturesque aspect of the lion in Carolingian

[1] cf. also the Jedburgh panel (Collingwood, fig. 57).

[2] Note especially the ' worried ' look of the brow and cf. the late eight-century manuscript, Paris lat. 12048, folio 92b (Zimmermann, Tf. 159c) and also our own Ormside bowl. In Irish art this lion with the mane stretching right down his back to his hindquarters appears in the Armagh Gospels of 807 (folio 53b). The heavily maned ox in the scroll-panel on the shaft in the Blackgate Museum is a naturalistic newcomer of the same order.

[3] Particularly in examples where the Gripping Beast style and the Ribbon Style (the Scandinavian phase of it known as Style III) fuse together. These examples may include, as at Rothbury, human masks and little clutching men.

art.[1] In England no such explanation is necessary, for the clutching and biting animal had long been known; and it is merely as a familiar barbaric drollery that this design finds its way on to a noble sculpture that also bears the Carolingian lion stalking proudly among the foliage of the English vine-scroll.

In short, the Rothbury cross is a particularly instructive example of the kind of work representing the Carolingian phase of Northumbrian art in a period that is somewhat vaguely centred upon the year 800. It teaches us that the return of the humane European tradition, in real danger of extinction as a result of the triumphantly barbaric phase of this art in the middle of the eighth century, cannot truthfully be regarded as being of a completely convincing and whole-hearted kind. The Carolingian taste had penetrated into a part of England that, owing to the unhappy vicissitudes of a long series of political disasters, was probably incapable of making more than a casual response to this second summons of classical art. Northumbria had already become barbaric in temper and was unable, even at the bidding of such men as Alcuin, effectively to renounce what was after all an ingrained aesthetic feeling for hard abstract types of surface ornament. In accepting such sculptural precepts as find expression in the modelled Romanesque figure-carvings of the Easby and Rothbury crosses, the Northumbrian artist at the same time mocks and belittles them, treating them with a humorous indifference in place of the former intense, though sometimes muddled, seriousness. He forces them into incongruous juxtaposition with the wildest conceits of the barbaric taste, and does not hesitate to intrude into the intended dignities of natural portrayal the charming and fantastic improbabilities that have their true home in Irish art.

[1] cf. *Ann-Sofi Schotte in Fornvännen*, 1935, p. 93.

IX

THE CANTERBURY SCHOOL

IN the south of England a gap of more than a century separates the Reculver cross from the earliest manuscripts of the Canterbury School.[1] No surviving antiquities of any importance can be referred to the period thus left blank, and the continuity of the Romanesque tradition during the early struggles of the Roman Church and in the period of its triumphant establishment is a matter about which we know nothing. In the Canterbury manuscripts, however, the earliest of which, the Codex Aureus at Stockholm and Vespasian A.I. in the British Museum, were written c. 750, or possibly a little later, we have a sudden revelation of the scope and content of at least one department of southern English art at the very time when, in the north, the ornamental styles were reverting to an unmistakably barbaric type ; and whatever may have preceded these manuscripts, at least we can be sure that in the Canterbury of their day the illuminators obeyed a serene and serious Romanesque discipline more than strong enough to prevent any such wholesale back-slidings there, or near at hand in the southern province.

It is, indeed, a robust classical solidity that most of all distinguishes the Canterbury work, and the antique solemnity of the figures in the Codex Aureus (Pl. 65), despite ugly unnatural drapery and the solecisms and absurdity of the architectural surroundings, is a surprise

---

[1] For the attributions to Canterbury itself of the Codex Aureus, Vespasian A.I., and Royal I.E., VI, see Zimmermann, *Vorkarolingische Miniaturen*, Text, p. 131.

to those who come to this page fresh from the mid-eighth century manuscripts and carvings of the north (cf. Pl. 55). The famous folio (Pl. 65) of the British Museum Psalter, Vespasian A.I., in which David the Harper is seen with attendant scribes, musicians, and dancing boys, most aptly epitomizes the Canterbury style. It is a gorgeous polychrome page of rich shaded colours and much gold, showing a figured scene in a broad round-arched frame, outside which are two similar detached foliate sprays, the whole having a rigidly symmetrical appearance that is curiously betrayed by the base line, which ends on one side in a solid whorl and on the other in a curling animal-head, a little flickering survival of barbarian design. The figure-drawing is an honest piece of classical painting to which perspective and modelling alike contribute ; but it is not without a somewhat harsh stereoscopic effect due to the heavy dark-edged outlines of the figures and the ponderous modelling of the drapery that is sometimes a mere tubular ribbing of the crudest northern kind, witness, for instance, the right-hand hornblower in the foreground. And this painstaking rawness is further enhanced by the over-accentuated modelling of the faces with their green shadows and white high-lights and vivid complexions. Yet if the new solidly opaque ' painterly ' style, so different from the typical patchwork tinting of the barbaric manuscripts, is by no means accomplished in manner, the artists at least knew how to handle English abstract ornament with a becoming restraint, admitting only enough of it to enliven his pages without, except in the instance I have mentioned, disturbing their equilibrium. Thus the clean competent trumpet-pattern, oddly altered by the large staring rosettes in the three biggest whorls, has here a new and restricted purpose as decoration within the arch, and it is not allowed to sprawl and spill itself over the page in the prodigal barbarian way.

The style is hybrid ; but it is hybrid in an intelligent and organized manner. The columns with their patterned gold lozenges on a background of interlace reveal a cunning southern enrichment of a northern style, and the introduction of the new animal ' portrait ' style, pictures of little Frankish beasts and birds in the roundels that purport to be the capitals and bases of these columns, is yet another sign that this Canterbury art is a disciplined hotch-potch of many fashions.[1] We see this very plainly in the initials. The normal type is a letter in heavy black line with golden or coloured terminals and modest additional ornament in the form of an open interlace and plaits and borders of red dots ; but occasionally other types intrude. In two initials we have the old barbaric animal-designs,[2] one being a serpentine creature with a body of purple and gold to which is attached an appendage of trumpet-pattern. Another Ribbon Style creature, this time drawn in black, also finds his way into these pages,[3] and there are birds with interlacing necks that were likewise derived from the north.[4] And the continued use of a long-snouted animal [5] seems to be another link with the northern school of illumination.[6]

In the panelled rows of large letters there is a certain quality of prettiness of the rustic sort, but nothing of the gripping- or biting-beast style that we have seen in northern or Mercian manuscripts. We have here letters in gold on a purple background with light-coloured animals of Merovingian type between them,[7] or letters in green, blue, and purple with heavy spotted decoration, and panels that are chequered or striped.[8] It is all rather pretentious and grand in a showy Carolingian manner of the ' Ada ' style. Considerable use is made of the new ' portrait ' type of animal, by which I mean an animal or bird drawn with

---

[1] The Merovingian origin of these creatures was first pointed out by Bröndsted, op. cit., p. 100 ff.

[2] Folios 19b and 134a ; cf. also folio 110a.   [3] Folio 47b.

[4] Folio 90a.   [5] Folios 25b and 64b (bottom terminal of S).

[6] cf. the Echternach School MS., Corpus 197, folio 2a.

[7] Folio 64b.   [8] Folios 42a and 31a.

a certain natural solidity and placed alone in a little framed enclosure without the encumbrance of interlaced appendages or the embracing meshes of a scroll. A good example is an oval panel containing a bird and a detached scroll-like plant, both in gold, against a green background, the bird standing boldly in the front and the scroll forming a distinct and insignificant space-filling detail.[1]

A later stage of the Canterbury style, perhaps to be attributed to the archbishopric of Wulfred (805–32), is represented by the Gospels, Royal I.E., VI, in the British Museum. It is a large book, and its ornament is most opulent and continentally splendid in appearance, the great purple pages in the Byzantine and Carolingian manner, and the now abundant use of gold, being largely responsible for this effect of increased richness. The folio introducing the Gospel of St. Luke (Pl. 66) is an example. Here in a sumptuous and blazing spread of colour we see the fully developed power of the mature Canterbury style. In the great arch at the top of the page and in the medallion, with their vivid rolling background of clouds in Prussian blue, purple, brown, yellow, and green, only substantial and massive figures can appear, a broad-shouldered Evangelist of solid monumental dignity and the gigantic head and forequarters of the bull, brown with a heavily shaded back and a hulking shaggy breast.

In the detailed ornament there is now a new and elaborate prettiness that has its counterpart in the contemporary manuscripts of the north. Thus there is much decorative over-painting; for instance, in the columns of the Canon Tables there are panel-borders of turquoise blue and bright vermilion with a surcharged ornament of white scrolls and

---

[1] Folio 48a. These 'portrait-studies' of animals are a direct borrowing from Frankish art, cf. Kohler, *School of Tours*, I, 34 (Paris lat. 3, folio 310b); the type is to be distinguished from panels containing a mere section, as it were, of the inhabited scroll, e.g., in Paris lat. 281, folio 137a, a manuscript ascribed by Zimmermann to the Canterbury School.

dots, following a decorative mode used in Syrian illumination as early as the sixth century. But this fussiness is admirably controlled, being shut severely within the narrow lines of the architectural frame, so that in this restricted use of excessively elaborate decoration the manuscript follows the older Echternach discipline of the north rather than the untidy lavishness of the Rome Gospels. But there is little left of the legacy of Northumbrian art. The trumpet-pattern has gone and there is no longer any animal-ornament in the Ribbon Style. The favourite animal is a naked little leonine creature of the Frankish ' portrait ' kind that has now become the victim of various barbaric mannerisms, such as the addition of interlace appendages. Often he is a biped with an absurd curly tail, and a typical new design, conceivably the result of some oriental influence, is a symmetrical pair of these creatures with eyes flashing and head and forequarters in violent postures, their tails uniting in a substantial spread of interlace (Pl. 66).[1] It is the unencumbered leonine ferocity of the heads and shoulders that distinguishes these little drawings from the older patterns of the Ribbon Style ; and though the patterns sometimes recall the Northumbrian tradition, nevertheless what we really see in this later Canterbury work is the new Frankish lion being dissolved into new types of barbaric ornament. Thus we find spiral scrolls with the heads of these creatures in the place of leaves or grape-clusters, and also animals from which plant-scrolls grow, tail-fashion.[2]

---

[1] This design is to be distinguished from the Yorkshire ' Twin Beasts ' (see p. 198).

[2] Similar variations of the animal-form can be found in Frankish manuscripts, e.g., a beast with a scroll issuing from his mouth in the Vivian Bible (Paris lat. 1, folio 9a ; cf. folio 384a). For the animal-headed scroll in Carolingian sculpture, and an apt comparison with the English version on the Cropthorne cross-head (Pl. 80), see J. Zemp, *Convent de St. Jean à Münster. Monuments de l'Art en Suisse*, V–VII (1906–10), Pl. LVI, 3.

X

EARLY MERCIAN AND ANGLIAN STYLES

THE political supremacy of Mercia lasted for more than three-quarters of the eighth century, but it cannot have been until nearly the end of Offa's reign (757–96), or just after it, that the first of the surviving pieces of Mercian sculpture were carved. In the Derbyshire hills these works prove themselves to be, as we might expect, very closely dependent upon the established precepts of eighth-century Northumbrian art, and the heavy, uncouth stone crosses of Eyam and Bakewell bear vine-scrolls that are a direct continuation of the Northumbrian series which includes the Ruthwell and Bewcastle crosses. It is true that the scroll is sadly coarsened into close pipe-like coils, more emphatically spiraliform than anything we have yet seen ; and the contained animal at the top of the Bakewell scroll (Pl. 67) is merely a graceless afterthought for which no room could be found in the main run of the plant. But the scroll is indubitably the Northumbrian scroll, a north Mercian version that may be as late as *c.* 800 or the first quarter of the ninth century.

On these crosses, particularly on the Bakewell cross, the figure-style has its own midland character, flat, silhouetted, linear, with thin fanning drapery. And midland is the rickety lightness of the architectural frames. But the inter-lace is of the Rothbury order, and so are the plant-like joints that act as capitals of the arches. When we come to the tomb-slab (Pl. 67) in Wirksworth Church we find that the ribbed figure-style is also closely related to Rothbury work. It represents a series of New Testament scenes in

164

continuous bands without dividing barriers, as in the miracle-carvings at Rothbury, and the general correspon- dence, particularly in the heads and the drapery, is so striking that exact points of resemblance, the ribbed angels and the seated Virgin of the Annunciation in the lower row with her deep massive enveloping folds (cf. the Blind Man of the Rothbury panel), need scarcely be mentioned.[1] It is a very important witness to the Northumbrian basis of the sculptural style in these highlands of Mercia, a carving of the crude jumbled order that knows nothing of the dignity ennobling such Northumbrian work as the Easby cross, nor of the hard linear tranquillity of the Mercian style then in process of formation. It is hardly likely to be later than 800, and may indeed be a carving of Offa's reign.

I have suggested (p. 147) that the Rome Gospels may also illustrate Mercian art about this time, and there is nothing remarkable in the fact that a scriptorium in the midlands should have produced a manuscript whose illumina- tion bears so openly a southern and foreign aspect ; for Offa was a continentally minded king and was in close touch with Charles the Great himself. But the first indubit- ably Mercian manuscript is the Book of Cerne. This was written at Lichfield some years after Offa was dead, for the Bishop Ethelwald mentioned in the text was probably the holder of the see of Lichfield from 818 to 830, and it is a collection of the Passion and Resurrection narratives from the four Gospels.[2] In general the style of illumination

---

[1] The iconography of this astonishing carving is obscure. In the upper row we have Christ washing the Disciples' feet, a Crucifixion with the Lamb on the cross, a scene not as yet satisfactorily explained, and (?) the Massacre of the Innocents ; below there is another unidenti- fied scene, the Ascension, (?) the Annunciation, and a scene that is perhaps the Presentation.

[2] At some time in its history the manuscript belonged to Cerne Abbey in Dorset, and it is now preserved in the University Library at Cambridge. See *The Book of Cerne*, edited by A. B. Kuypers, Cam- bridge, 1902. Also Zimmermann, *Vorkarolingische Miniaturen*, Text p. 294 ; Tfn. 293–6.

is much colder and less elaborate than that of the Rome Gospels, and it is far more barbaric in treatment than any work of the Canterbury school. Nevertheless, the aim of the principal decorative pages was to simulate the serene and spacious dignity of the Carolingian grand manner (Pl. 68), and this can perhaps be accounted for as a sign of the increasing influence in Mercia of Wessex, whose political ascendancy had been by this time (*c.* 820) established. The folios to which I have referred bear the symbols of the Evangelists under arches and their busts in medallions; but the architectural structure is light and thin, and flippantly fantastic, the capitals taking the form of such curiously unpractical conceits as a cup formed of two curling leaves, or a heart-shaped foliate sheath, or an elaborate ornament in the form of a mask from which the arch springs as an ear. The colouring is applied in the northern mosaic style rather than in the southern painterly fashion, and a warm purplish-brown assembly of cinnamon red, pink, and blue, takes the place of the rich and more varied palette of the south. Gold is used only three times in the initials, and the panel of lettering at the beginning of the extract from St. John's Gospel with its deep purple background and solid margin of vivid yellow is a solitary attempt at the opulent foreign style of colouring. There is some shading and use of high-lights, as in the hair of St. John, some plastic sensibility in the indication of the legs under the drapery of St. Matthew's angel and in the mottling of the body of St. Luke's bull; but the figure-style is for the most part conceived in a cold calligraphic manner. The figures are aloof, tranquil, with wide spaces round them. If the drapery flutters, it is frozen in the very act of swinging, and the favourite fold-style is a hard and purely linear system of expanding triangular pleats. So sincerely and so obviously are the forms envisaged as a dead pattern of lines that they can even support without incongruity the barbaric border of dots that surrounds them, a treatment (note particularly the skirt of St. Matthew's angel) that would be ludicrously inappropriate in the Canterbury figure-style. The faces are in that schematic northern tradition of drawing that we saw first upon the coffin of St. Cuthbert and was long retained by Irish illuminators. Big forward-staring eyes, pupils without irises, no modelling in the nose, the mouth a thin single line, the upper lip broad and having a central cleft ; it is all much more in the style of the Rothbury Christ than in that of the contemporary south English manner.[1]

Ornament is sparingly used. There is no real Ribbon Style animal-pattern of the earlier sort, no sumptuous inter-lace, and only one example of trumpet-pattern, which in a rather weak tumbled form is used to fill the spandrels of the arch in the St. Matthew folio. But we do observe the rustic ' Baroque ' prettiness that is characteristic of the age and had been so exuberantly expressed in the Rome Gospels ; for example, in the opening sentences of the Gospel extracts we have elaborate designs of the ' biting beast ' order. The favourite animal is the little biped with the long curly tail. Ten pages of the text, otherwise unornamented, are strangely and delightfully sprinkled with a fine company of these amusing little creatures, all vigorously moving and having wide-open mouths and ferociously glaring eyes. Their tail-forms differ. Some have acanthus leaves ; others forking plants with pointed oval leaves and a central bud, or pointed leaves with a quatrefoil base, or simple curls and twists. This free-style and haphazard sprinkling of the pages with vivacious little animals can best be matched in the most famous of all the Irish manuscripts, the Book of Kells, which is a contemporary work,[2] and it is therefore yet another sign of the barbaric

[1] The dressing of the hair of St. Matthew and of St. Luke with its first horizontally and then vertically grooved ringlets at the side of the head is the style employed on the Rothbury Christ.

[2] cf. also folio 7a of the Alcuin Bible in the British Museum (Add. MSS. 10546).

element in Mercian art responsible for the hard linear quality of the figure-drawing in the Book of Cerne.

The British Museum manuscript of Bede's Ecclesiastical History (Tiberius C. II) is another Mercian work of the early ninth century. It contains no figure-drawings, but some of the ornamental pages are of great beauty, and the best-known of them (Pl. 69) illustrates particularly well the dainty elegant drollery of midland ornament at this period. The big initial is decorated with panels that have brightly coloured borders and enclose designs, mostly interlaces and animal-headed scrolls in white on black, that were a contribution from south English art [1] ; but in general the style is little altered. The work is notable, however, for the barbaric violence of the colouring. Thus the initial on the page illustrated here is indeed an arresting ornament, the foliated cross dividing the field into four quarters coloured vermilion and bright green, each bearing a biped creature in white ; below are three panels, set at equal distances apart, in vermilion, yellow, and green, in which are spidery ' biting beast ' letters.

The development of an excessively ornate quality in Mercian illumination, with the accompanying predilection for crazy light-columned architectural designs and heraldic animal-types, was followed by a complementary change in the midland sculptural style. The ninth-century carvings in the new manner are mostly small works, such as highly decorative friezes and inset ornamental panels, that show the sculptor to have been more concerned with the minor embellishments of buildings than with the creation of imposing monumental stonework. The ponderous style of the Bakewell cross disappears, and the carvings are now gay with dainty surface-patterns, vieing with the manuscripts in their frivolous intricate brightness. In the Middle Anglian area of Mercia the Fenland school gives us the

[1] cf. the Canterbury Gospels, Royal I.E., VI. The influence of the Canterbury school in the ornamental details is much more pronounced in this manuscript than in the Book of Cerne.

'Hedda Stone' in Peterborough Cathedral, a rectangular block, 3½ feet long and 2½ feet high, with a gabled roof, that is a newly introduced form of the antique sarcophagus type of monument (Pl. 70). Its two ends are left in the rough, but on the long faces are arcades, each containing a standing figure of an Apostle that fills completely his light little architectural frame, while the roof is divided into panels in which are symmetrical designs consisting principally of pairs of animals in the now mature 'Anglian Heraldic' style. The stiffly posed and rigidly frontal figures of the Apostles have an antique sculptural solidity, as though there were some classical basis for this newly introduced arcaded series ; but, in general, the style of the carving is light and richly ornamental, with that feathery lace-like quality so typical of the period. In the roof-patterns the carving has unquestionably its own Anglian stamp. But the Hedda Stone is not too late a work to show some signs of the Northumbrian foundation of Mercian art ; thus the eyes of the figures are deep-bored, Rothbury fashion, and one of the Apostles, on the left of his row, has the heavy and narrow hanging folds of drapery looped over the arm that are to be seen on the Bewcastle cross ; furthermore, the ancient theme of the inhabited vine-scroll occurs in one of the panels on the roof and is a bleak stylized derivative of the Northumbrian series.

The Anglian decorative style used on this coping is also seen on the bone casket in the Ducal Museum at Brunswick, a little box only 5 inches in height (Pl. 70). It is edged by metal strips, and on those surrounding the base is a runic inscription from which we may infer that the casket was made at Ely, doubtless before 866, in which year the monastery was destroyed by the Danes. On the two ends are excellent examples of the new scroll, hard wiry compositions containing long-necked winged bipeds whose curling tails contribute to the interlace pattern of the scroll, and also clutching lizard-like creatures. On the panelled faces of the casket the plant-scroll vanishes and

13   169

the animals stand alone in heraldic grandeur against an interlace background formed of their own tails and lappets. One panel contains a rather clumsy interpretation of the trumpet-pattern in the form of a roundel, and the corners of the square are filled by the heads and shoulders of little lizards, seen from above, who are creeping out of the roundel, a charming conceit that is typical of the unrestrained surrealist fancy that is now so often to be found in Mercian design.

A number of metal ornaments also illustrate this delicately pretty Anglian style. Best known are the pins (Pl. 71), a linked set of three, found in the River Witham near Lincoln in 1826 and now in the British Museum.[1] They have large silver-gilt disc-heads, cast and chased, and they were probably converted by a Viking robber into the trio of pins, having been filched originally, with their connecting plates, from costly English shrines or bindings; for the three discs are not a set, that on the right, the smallest, being of different workmanship. All the roundels are divided into quadrants, and in those on the largest disc (diam. 4·7 cm.) are wyvern-like creatures in the aggressive rampant style characteristic of this Anglian art, the rigid symmetry of the pairs, the fierce cock of the little wings, the stiffly reared hind leg, and the light interlace background that issues tongue-wise from the mouths being mannerisms that are unmistakably of the period of the Brunswick casket. On the middle-sized disc there is only one animal, a creature with a fine spiral joint at the base of the wing, and in the other quadrants are wiry plant-scrolls with a triskele-like whorl of long leaves, and an interlace panel. On the smallest disc the four sections of the field contain animals, two of which are contorted quadrupeds with jewelled eyes, seen from above.[2]

[1] *Reliquary and Ill. Arch.*, X (1904), p. 52; XIII (1907), p. 134, *Archaeologia*, LXXIV, p. 241.

[2] For other examples of this Anglian metal-work see *Archaeologia*, op. cit., and *Antiquaries Journal*, XII (1932), p. 440. A new find from

There can be no doubt that in the northern and eastern tracts of Mercia, above all in Lindsey, whence came the Witham pins, and on the Fenland borders, the main tendency of early ninth-century design was directed towards further experiment with decorative themes derived from the barbaric elements in contemporary art. In these remote places the political ascendancy of Egbert of Wessex was not likely to have had any profound effect, and the influence of the fashionable designs of Frankish origin is for the most part only recognizable in the persistently Merovingian character of the head and shoulders of the favourite animal-type. As an example in sculpture of the preponderantly barbaric tastes of east Mercian art, and of its fondness for the older Northumbrian styles, we have the group of carved stone panels in the church at South Kyme, near Sleaford in Lincolnshire.[1] These bear interlace, a fret, and most remarkable of all, a fine piece of trumpet-pattern. It is likely that they are little earlier in date than such carvings as the Hedda Stone ; but not very much earlier, for the series includes part of a pretty piece of plant-scroll, a Carolingian acanthus-like thing, that it would be imprudent to date much before 800.

But in less remote places things were otherwise, and this barbaric pattern-work is not really characteristic of the sculptor's work in the midlands. We turn once more, therefore, to those more typical Mercian carvings that are distinguished for the crowded and fanciful richness of their delicate ornament and for their use of southern pictorial elements. Nothing could illustrate this type of work better than the sumptuous ' Baroque ' decoration of the friezes built into the walls of the church of Breedon-on-the-Hill

the Danish town of Hedeby has recently been published, *IPEK*, IX (1934), Pl. 44, 5. This has a central cruciform design with a boss in the middle, very like the Gravesend pendant that was found in a dated hoard of *c.* 875 ; the arms bear a two-strand interlace and there are symmetrical scrolls of the wiry Anglian type in the spandrels.

[1] *Antiquaries Journal*, III (1923), p. 118.

in north Leicestershire. Students of English pre-Conquest art owe, as we are all aware, a great deal to Mr. A. W. Clapham ; but it is probable that in no field of the inquiry has he done us a more important service than in his memorable paper establishing the date and significance of these charming sculptures.[1] It is not too much to say that in publishing them he introduced Mercian art for the first time as a rich and substantial element in our Anglo-Saxon heritage. For here we are by no means dealing with weak barbaric derivatives of northern or southern styles, nor with the determined barbarism of the eastern Mercian school. On the contrary, the friezes are crisp gaily conceived novelties, remarkable for the new types of subjects that are used and for the strange deep-shadowed fretwork-like relief that is used for them.

The friezes are all very narrow, mostly 9 or 7 inches in depth, and the longest remaining stretch, an 18-foot run on the east wall of the interior behind the altar, is a plant-scroll, old in type, but new in kind owing to the heavy cupping and under-cutting of the leaves. It contains both the running spiral and the two-stem figure of eight in an unbroken design, the patterns being cut in a high relief on an average $1\frac{1}{2}$ inches deep, which is astonishing in so narrow a strip. The single-stem pattern (Pl. 73) is a heavy scroll, but easy-flowing in loose soft coils that differ markedly from the tightly wound spirals of the Eyam and Bakewell type. The branches contain grape-clusters, trefoil leaves, and the triskele-whorl of leaves that is so often found in work of the early ninth century.

The most delightful of the friezes are those containing human figures, animals, and birds. They are of two kinds, one having a thick plant-scroll of a substance equal to that of the figures within its volutes, while the other has only a thin unobtrusive background of wiry foliage. This last is the new southern style of the animal-portrait (cf. p. 163) establishing itself in Mercia in the form of a picture-

[1] *Archaeologia*, LXXVII (1928), p. 219.

roll of living creatures. There is, for instance, a row of birds, apparently falcons and cocks, in various lively attitudes, pecking in a half-turned position with wings displayed, or strutting. The pecking attitude we have seen before, and one of the birds shows the familiar Anglo-Saxon 'lock' of the legs over the branch, the near leg passing behind it, while the off leg is pushed forward over it; but in spite of this, and in spite of the fact that there is a thin scroll in the background, the frieze is surprisingly new in concept, because of its unfamiliar pictorial quality. It is not a scroll-pattern containing birds; it is a *picture* of birds seen against foliage. In an adjacent frieze we have pairs of animals, no doubt directly based on some foreign exemplar, that are nothing less than copies of the renowned and hitherto foreign animal-combat group, a series of active little sketches that still depend for their interest on the narrative value of the creatures themselves.

The friezes showing the plant-scroll proper contain not only animals, but also human figures. On the interior of the south wall, high up so that it can best be seen from the organ-loft, is a scroll in which we find a bird, with its feet in the Anglo-Saxon 'lock', and a kneeling man holding a spear, a small carving remarkable for its thrust and vigour. Another length, probably of the same frieze, on the north wall also shows a kneeling figure, and with it is a bird having the jauntily cocked narrow wing that we see so often in the Anglian Heraldic style. Then there is a variety of the scroll in a new panel-form made up of a series of trunks that are connected at the top and bottom by a single curving branch; and this contains those long-necked creatures with little heads that are probably intended for lions. A variant of this scroll-type is peopled with human figures, most of them on horseback and carrying spears; and on the best preserved fragment there are two seated figures that are apparently the victims of the mounted warriors.

In addition to these droll storied carvings, there are panels containing interlaces, diagonal frets, deeply cupped pelta-designs, and also the trumpet-pattern. This last occurs once only and it is the poorest bit of carving in the church, a heavy tangle of stumpy peltae that are clumsily linked by roundels. It lacks not only the neatness and precision that this pattern demands, but it has lost also the background element that is necessary for its proper presentation, as the South Kyme carver well understood. It is just the bones of the ancient design, ill-distributed and poorly conceived, and in its disorganization and its use of leaf-like half peltae that are left floating at the edges, it foreshadows that incomprehensible and cheerfully muddled foliate pelta-pattern which we shall see in the Mercian Baroque work at Fletton (Pl. 74).

The Breedon carvings would be remarkable enough if there were the friezes only ; but the series also includes figure-sculpture of a more imposing kind than the minor personages of these ornamental strips. The larger carvings, it is true, occur on panels of modest size and make no pretensions to grandeur in scale ; yet they are designed as serious essays in a Romanesque style, and they help us to appreciate the extraordinary versatility and catholic range of Mercian art. They reveal, in fact, three dissimilar styles, and the most typically Mercian of these, the silhouetted and emphatically sharp-lined manner, is represented by the bust with a draped head under a round arch (Pl. 72). The panel is 24 inches in height, and is a broad-shouldered composition in a spacious frame, resolutely flat in tone, with an almost monumental dignity that is due to the impressive silhouette and to the quiet drapery with its dominant vertical lines. It is austere and restful, with great barbaric strength in the small head and the huge long-fingered hand. It recalls the figure-style of the Bakewell cross and of the Book of Cerne, and, indeed, the little triangle of frozen symmetrical drapery below the book on the Breedon carving has its almost exact counterpart in the manuscript (Pl. 68). In this same vein are the friezes that show rows of small limbed figures, each in his own niche. The arcades are peculiar, for the columns, some bearing a lozenge-pattern in light relief, have scalloped rebates and heart-shaped capitals out of which the arches spring, obviously in the contemporary manner of the Book of Cerne.[1] But the figures, again with ample space around them, are our present concern. They are little silhouetted Apostles with dancing feet that are shown against a wide skirt-opening, small sketches in stone with the whole of the emphasis upon their linear quality. In spite of the activity and motion of the feet, the figures are frozen barbaric dolls, invested with just that severity of outline, that accent on the hard edges of the drapery, which is characteristic of the popular tradition in Anglo-Saxon carving.

Another and a softer figure-style is represented by a rect-angular panel, 19 inches high. It bears two standing person-ages, each holding a stem that ends in a hollow-cut leaf. They are both remarkable for the recession of the drapery between the legs, a general cavernous relief that is in keeping with heavy-shadowed style of the principal friezes. Both figures have a light dancing stance, one foot, indeed, being shown tiptoe, pointing straight downwards and only slightly turned. The drapery is heavy ; but the figure on the right has, immediately below his left hand, a vigorously marked scalloped edge to his tunic, and there is a certain heavily modelled richness about these lightly stooping figures in their crowded panels that distinguishes them abruptly from the flatter types of carving in their roomy frames and from the other developments of the standing figure type as on the Hedda stone (Pl. 70) and at Fletton (Pl. 74) and at Castor (Pl. 69). The third Breedon style is to be seen in one carving only, and were it not that we are already prepared for an astonishing variation in the character of the carvings of the ninth century in Mercia,

[1] Cerne, folio 32b. For the lozenge and disc on the columns, Tiberius C. II, folio 94a.

we should be tempted at once to exclude from the series this panel in the interior wall of the tower. It measures 36 inches in height, and it contains a full-length figure of an angel standing in front of an arched niche, the greatest depth of relief (under the right elbow) being $2\frac{1}{2}$ inches (Pl. 72). Very nearly all that there is to be said in favour of assigning this carving to the first half or the middle and immediately pre-Danish period of the ninth century is that the architectural background is weak in comparison with the weight and solidity of the figure, and has cupped capitals, out of which the arch grows, a structural absurdity characteristic of the late eighth and the ninth century, and not, I think, known in England at any other time. For the rest the figure is work of a new order. The angel, whose hand, sceptre, wing, and cloak, overlap the architectural frame, is shown stepping forth, as it were, from the arch behind him ; but the carving is extraordinarily heavy in conception, and the width of the body, the great fleshy arm, the massive hands, and the ponderous short-necked head with its thick lumpy curls, contribute to an apparent classicism of a kind seen in Carolingian ivories, and one that is more pronounced here than in any other English sculpture. But it is an accidental classicism, a provincial experiment of the age of Rothbury ; for the flowers at the feet of the angel, the forerunners of those on the Edenham cross in Lincolnshire,[1] are stylized in the hard Rothbury way, and have thistle-like heads below which are pairs of leaves, those on the left springing diagonally upwards from thick bosses on a rectangular stem, and those on the right curling downwards towards the stem, which in this case is faceted.

The soft style of carving of the Breedon panel with the two figures is also to be seen at the church of Fletton, very close to Peterborough, where there is another set of Anglian carvings of the first half of the ninth century (Pl. 74). Here, inside the church, are two single figures in round-arched

[1] Clapham, op. cit., Pl. 21.

niches, 2 feet and 2½ feet in length, in some respects like the Breedon carvings, but flatter, less sculptural in feeling, with drapery in formal folds, softly ribbed. They still have a kindly natural stoop, have thin cloaks that are arranged in long narrow folds over the arms, and thus belong to the series of figures that begins in Mercia on the adjacent Hedda Stone. We also see this soft modelled type in the heads of the angels in the narrow friezes at Fletton ; but these smaller carvings, which are on the outside of the church, are chiefly remarkable for the bewildering deep-shadowed ornament that accompanies them, apparently a mixture of the Breedon hollow-cut pelta-pattern and a foliate scroll containing birds. This prickled senseless pattern is accompanied by other baffling panels that reveal an exuberant and almost uncontrollable phantasy in design, as though the Breedon frieze-style, which is already drolly absurd, were here purposely transformed into a humorous parade of small-scale crowded nonsense. But a square with a thin plant-scroll with a central stem, an economical and wiry symmetrical composition, is a survival from the harder, more lucid type of design that we have observed in the plant-scrolls of the Brunswick casket.

As these remarkable panels indicate, Mercian art was by this time, perhaps in the second quarter of the ninth century, moving further towards a barbaric handling of its subjects. At the beginning of the century we saw in the Breedon figure-sculpture precisely that conflict between the ' soft ' and the ' hard ' styles of figure-carving that is also, as we have learnt from the examples of the Easby and the Rothbury crosses, to be recognized in Northumbria at the same time. At Fletton the figured panels show that the final victory of a hard and barbaric mannerism was not long to be delayed, and it is therefore no matter for surprise that at Castor, near to Peterborough on the west side, there should be figure-carvings, which are probably not earlier than the middle of the century or the years immediately preceding the Danish invasion, that represent a whole-hearted return to the linear barbaric style. Inside the church there is a carving (Pl. 69) [1] that belongs to the same arcaded series of figures that we have seen on the Hedda stone [2] at Breedon, and at Fletton. It has the same stoop, flexed knees, and dancing feet, and drapery with the narrow arm-folds, and also the light crazy architecture with bulbous capitals that we have noted before ; but it is more mannered, more brittle and unsculptural, much harder and flatter in appearance, and it has a spacious silhouetted emphasis. On the outside of the church, over the south door, there is tympanum with a Christ Majesty bust that may be held to continue the tranquil and economical type of the Breedon bust with the coif, and this carving has a bordering strip of foliate decoration arranged in a series of sprays that on the West Saxon evidence [3] is unlikely to belong to a very early period of Mercian art.

[1] *Antiquaries Journal*, IV (1924), p. 421.

[2] Miss Senior, who has made a close study of this figure series, points out to me the particularly close relation between the Castor example and the figure that is second from the left end of the illustrated face of the Hedda Stone (Pl. 70).

[3] cf. ornament on the lip of the Deerhurst font.

XI

WESSEX UNDER EGBERT AND ETHELWULF

By the year 829 the political supremacy of the king of the West Saxons, Egbert, had been formally recognized not only in south-eastern England, but in Mercia and Northumbria too. We know next to nothing about the art of Wessex in the period of Egbert's rise to power ; but the manuscripts of the Canterbury school give us some notion of the general character of south English art at this time, and as Egbert, before he came to the throne in 802, had spent several years of exile at the court of Charles the Great, it is probable enough that West Saxon art in the early days of the supremacy shared to some extent the obviously Francophile tastes of Kent. Yet from the very beginning we have to reckon with a peculiarly and vitally insular quality that distinguishes West Saxon work, an inexplicable genius of this particular country-side whose influence is discernible throughout the whole of the Late Saxon period. It is something that has to be felt and not defined, for it is a spiritual mystery ; something eerily intangible, as though in secret shrines honour was still paid to older arts, and dim traditions of prehistoric and later British aesthetic sensibility lived on to guide the artist's hand. I think that the Codford St. Peter carving (Pl. 75) helps us to appreciate this ; because it is not the signs of foreign influence, though they are easily recognized, that strikes us first of all when we see this carving ; it is its extraordinary insular beauty. The work does not look foreign. It is English in its hard and robust vivacity and in its tense abstraction ; it is a stylistic precursor of the later Winchester art,[1] and a pregnant testimony to the existence of some inexplicable but long-lasting aesthetic instinct in Wessex. I cannot help regarding it as one of the tragedies of archaeology that this piece alone survives to represent the early flowering of one of the most spirited and lovely phases of pre-Conquest art in England.

Codford St. Peter is in the Wylye valley, between Salisbury and Warminster. The tapering shaft, just over 4 feet in height, has a rectangular section with a baluster moulding along the edges; but only one face and narrow strips of two sides remain, the broken portions showing the edges of thick and luscious foliate scrolls. On the face is the figure of a man with light dancing feet, who holds aloft a thick leafy branch, and, above this, in a little panel topping the baluster-columns, is an S-shaped scroll with the fat lobed leaves also to be found on the sides of the shaft, and of the kind that we see not far away at Britford (Pl. 76). The carving of the man, a fine essay in the abstract expression of human gesture, is conscientiously clean-cut work, such details as the shoes, the musical instrument [2] in the left hand, and the large T-shaped pin that secures the cloak, being of unusually scrupulous precision. The drapery is flat and closely ribbed, a rich linear pattern that interprets the folds of the garment with a harsh clarity. In this respect the carving is a southern counterpart to the Rothbury style of Northumbria, and a comparison between the arm of the Codford St. Peter dancer and that of the Christ healing the Blind Man on the Rothbury cross (Pl. 63) shows an extraordinarily close correspondence in manner; on the Rothbury cross, too, we see the same horizontal placing of the head and the same fillet or crown binding the hair, and also the same type of cumbersome

---

[1] cf., for instance, the picture of King Edgar in the New Minster Charter; it is also perhaps the foundation of the robust West Saxon sculpture later expressed at Winterbourne Steepleton (p. 219) and, afterwards, at Headbourne Worthy and Breamore.

[2] I adopt a suggestion made to me by Mrs. Kingsley Porter.

fruit on the heavy scroll. Yet in style the Codford St. Peter sculpture is plainly southern work, and to appreciate its real position in the history of English art we should do well to compare the Wiltshire dancer with the figure of the archer on the Sheffield cross-shaft in the British Museum, for the southern carving is seen to have a certain artificiality and elegance that the archer lacks. It bears, in fact, the impress of Frankish fashion, and such details as the arm bearing aloft the leafy branch and the bordering baluster-shafts were probably directly derived from continental art.[1]

Unhappily there is very little West Saxon sculpture of this period, the first quarter of the ninth century. In the church at Britford, near Salisbury, however, there are carved panels bearing the vine-scroll in the form of a close-textured running spiral, and these carvings I take to be a work of the early years of Egbert's reign (Pl. 76). The scroll is peculiar for its enclosed grape-clusters, which can only be due to Italian influence,[2] and it is further distinguished from north English scrolls by the thick acanthus-like leaves that cling to the inside curves of the volutes, as in the early Kentish form of the scroll to the seen on the Reculver cross (Pl. 46) and in the Canterbury Psalter (Pl. 65). It is not a carving of the same school as the Codford St. Peter sculpture, for it is thin and dry in a stylized Italian way, lacking rotundity and substance in the plant-stems ; but it still possesses the delicately ornate quality of the more fashionable southern art of the age, and in its rich surface-prettiness has something in common with the panelled decoration of the Canterbury Gospels.

Outside the heart of Wessex itself there were also sculptures that represent a definitely more barbaric, or perhaps I should say a more Mercian, aspect of southern art. West

---

[1] For the arm holding the scroll, cf. the Alcuin Bible in British Museum, Add. MSS. 10546, opening initial of Liber Sapientiae.

[2] cf. Sant' Apollinare in Classe, Ravenna, tympanum of the ciborium of St. Eleucadius (dated 806–10), or the Sta Sabina choir screen in Rome (dated 824–7).

of the Severn at Newent in north-east Gloucestershire there is a carving of the sort that I have in mind, a cross-shaft 4 feet 9 inches in height (Pl. 77). It has one panelled edge bearing a symmetrical wiry scroll above which is a lean long-necked animal that has the emaciated sinuosity often seen in the early ninth century. It belongs to a type that in England we recognize as the ' Carolingian lion with the worried brow ', like those we have seen in the north on the Rothbury cross and on the Ormside bowl (p. 150) ; but here the creature has an exaggerated spindle-legged thinness that belongs to a rather later stage of his history, continuing the Mercian series begun at Breedon and corresponding to the developed Northumbrian form that we shall see presently on the Closeburn cross in Dumfriesshire. The other edge and the two faces of the Newent cross bear figure-sculpture, the subject that I illustrate (Pl. 77) being the Adam and Eve group. This is a singularly impressive composition of a rich and flowery prettiness ; but it lacks the substance and the tensity and the emotional strength of the Codford St. Peter shaft ; for the two figures are neither patterns nor real people, but poor semi-naturalistic weaklings, with doll-like heads, sharp pointed faces, and enormous pit-like eyes.

This falling-off in the quality of the figure-sculpture is observable in other districts and probably reflects a general weakening in style as we approach the middle of the ninth century. The grave-stone, $22\frac{1}{2}$ inches high, at Whitchurch in Hampshire, is a case in point (Pl. 77). On the back of this is an incised symmetrical plant-scroll of the wiry kind that originated in Mercia early in the century,[1] and on the sides and top is an inscription in Roman capitals declaring that the stone marked the tomb of Frithburga. On the front is a bust of Christ in a niche recessed to a depth of 4 inches, a weak unintelligent carving that, in

[1] cf. especially in stonework the Fletton panel (Pl. 74), in ivory the Brunswick casket (Pl. 70), and in metal-work the Witham pins (Pl. 71). Cf. also the Rome Gospels, folio 18a.

spite of the projecting ears and sloping shoulders and feeble arm, was intended to suggest the classical solidity of Canterbury figure-painting.[1] The sculpture, however, has gained little in barbaric vigour by departing from natural softness and dignity ; there is no hint of the powerful and arresting qualities of the Codford St. Peter style. Yet the scroll on the back of the stone is drawn with delightful precision and strength, and the contrast in quality between the ornament and the figure prepares us for the next phase of West Saxon art ; for soon after the middle of the century the plastically conceived figure disappeared and the artist became almost completely absorbed in the perfection of a lavish system of minor ornament, chiefly intended for the embellishment of small objects. Thus we come to the West Saxon Baroque style, a phase of rich-patterned petty splendour that is happily represented by numerous surviving antiquities.

Undoubtedly southern England was rich. When Ethelwulf (d. 858), the successor of Egbert and the father of Alfred the Great, made a pilgrimage to Rome in 855, he gave to the Pope a heavy gold crown, two golden bowls, a gold-mounted sword, two small images of gold, four silver-gilt lamps (gabatae), and various sumptuous textiles adorned with golden clasps.[2] His finger-ring (Fig. 25), gold inlaid with niello and inscribed with his name, was found at Laverstock in Wiltshire and is now in the British Museum. The sumptuous design that it bears includes two confronted birds arranged in the Frankish ' heraldic ' fashion,[3] and on the nielloed gold finger-ring of Ethelswith (d. 888), who was Ethelwulf's daughter, there is an ornate quatrefoil

---

[1] cf. Codex Aureus, folio 6a, upper medallion of left column, and folio 9b.

[2] *Anastasius Bibliothecarius, Vit. Rom. Pont.*, CVI, Benedict III. Ed. Migne, sect. 575.

[3] cf. the Carolingian carved frieze on the St. Bourg-en-Andeol altar in the Ardèche. Mr. Slover has pointed out to me that the distinctive ring-terminals of the tail-feathers of the birds on Ethelwulf's ring also occur in the Book of Kells.

medallion containing an Agnus Dei of the Frankish order, flanked by two little crouching quadrupeds.[1] Both rings are in the characteristic richly decorated style, brightly patterned with copious and intricate detail.

The handsome trefoil ornament of silver (Pl. 78), found at Kirkoswald, Cumberland, in a hoard of Viking plunder hidden about 850, is a piece that aptly illustrates in its tumultuous beaded wirework, close-textured pattern, and elaborate bosses, the ' Frankish ' richness of the southern decorative style during the reign of Ethelwulf. And it is doubtless the tendency towards an overloaded small-scale prettiness here exhibited that was responsible for the cheerful ornamental system of little panels, each crowded with a fan-

Fig. 25.—Design on King Ethelwulf's ring

tastic leaf- or animal-pattern, that we see on so much West Saxon metal-work. The sword-handle from Wallingford, now in the Ashmolean Museum, with its ' Baroque ' pommel and heavy decoration of nielloed silver, is an example (Pl. 79). Its details include a prodigal display of acanthus and an extravagant animal-ornament derived from the Franco-Saxon menagerie.[2] But the distinctive feature is the close array of small crowded panels, which is rightly connected by Bröndsted with the style of the Canterbury Gospels (Royal I.E., VI) ; there is a difference, however, between the

[1] For these cf. Royal I.E., VI, folio 4a, animals in roundel at head of central column.

[2] The mannerism known as ' penetration ' is also represented on this sword : see p. 145.

Kentish work in the early decades of the century and the West Saxon Baroque of about 850 in that the quality of stateliness, of restraint, and of discipline that characterizes the Canterbury decoration is now absent ; thus, the ornamental contents of the panels, instead of being controlled by a prim and heavy frame, are now glorified as principal patterns, and appear as large jostling designs that sprawl in an unsteady assembly of chequer-like panels, swaying and bending to the outlines and contours of the shape they cover. On the Wallingford sword they bend over the lobes of the shouldered pommel and spread themselves prominently along the curving lines of the pommel-bar and the guard. In the nielloed silver mounts from the treasure deposited about 875 that was found at Trewhiddle in Cornwall (Pl. 78), the panels, here containing among other devices the animal-headed plant-scroll of the Canterbury manuscripts, sag down into the scallops of the lower edge. It is a hectic untranquil method of ornament, best adapted for little things, and it was freely used in ninth-century Wessex and Mercia, even for such tiny objects as the strap-ends, like those that were found in this Trewhiddle hoard and at many places elsewhere.

One of the most attractive small pieces in this West Saxon Baroque style is the openwork disc-brooch (Pl. 78) of nielloed silver that was found in a treasure at Beeston Tor, Staffordshire, buried between the years 871 and 874. Here the creatures in the arms of the cross have space to flounce themselves out prettily and possess the charming gaiety that is characteristic of the lighter varieties of Franco-Saxon animal-ornament,[1] while the fleur-de-lis sprays represent that smooth, fleshy type of Frankish scroll, such as is also to be seen at this same period on the seal of Ethelwald, who was Bishop of Dunwich about 850.[2] The brooch is studded and has milled edges, a typically rich minor per-

---

[1] For equivalent continental metal-work see Bröndsted, op. cit., p. 147 ff.

[2] cf. Royal I.E., VI, folio 5a, in triangle at top of central column.

sonal ornament of the age of the first Danish wars, which doubtless were the cause of the hiding of this and many other treasures in the third quarter of the ninth century.

In sculpture the West Saxon ornamental style of the period 825–50 is represented in western Mercia by the head of a cross in Cropthorne Church, Worcestershire (Pl. 80), a fragment of a cross-shaft built into the wall of Wroxeter Church in Shropshire, and part of another shaft to be seen in the Church at Acton Beauchamp in north Herefordshire, close to the Worcestershire border. The cross-head is an ornate carving with fussily ribbed and contoured details ; it bears on one face an example of the animal-headed scroll of the Canterbury kind (p. 163), and on the opposite face a leaf-tailed bird in a Mercian manner, and a lion and two scrolls bearing birds, the whole being a fusion of old and new designs welded into a characteristically sumptuous ensemble that is enlivened by copious ribbing and linear detail. The new type of animal-ornament in this rich and decorative sculpture is illustrated particularly well by the Wroxeter slab (Pl. 80) on which there is a creature that provides a sizeable length of interlace out of his own tail ; but the Acton Beauchamp carving (Pl. 80) shows us a Mercian version of the old theme of the inhabited vine-scroll, a sprawling design with huge birds and animals, that is a typical midland interpretation of the antique Northumbrian traditional pattern. In general, however, we can see easily enough that the art of this western division of Mercia was influenced principally by the art of the south, much more so than were the northern and eastern districts of the province.

That is why I place the Lechmere stone (Pl. 81) at Hanley Castle, Worcestershire, in the West Saxon context of this chapter, though it would be difficult to find anything more typically Mercian than the figure-style of this carving ; for it is in the flat silhouetted manner of the midlands and has the distinctive drapery folds in the form of spreading triangular pleats, like those in the Book of Cerne (Pl. 68) and in the Breedon sculptures (Pl. 73), while the head with the pointed face and great hollowed eyes remind us of the Newent manner (Pl. 77). But the monument is one of the small round-topped grave-stones of the Whitchurch kind (Pl. 77), and it is adorned on the back and sides with a rich and full-bodied southern ornament, an ornate cross on a thick baluster-shaft flanked by fat and fleshy plant-scrolls.

The typical elaboration of the period is illustrated by the design of this cross on the Lechmere stone, for it has little curling knobs at the extremities of the arms that we have not seen before and are perhaps in a new Italian fashion. In Wessex and Mercia, indeed, this form became a fashionable shape of cross-head for the sculptor, and we find it employed at Amesbury in Wiltshire, Rolleston in Staffordshire and at Rowsley in Derbyshire. The same shape occurs on a well-known antiquity of the mid-ninth century, the cruciform bronze brooch from Canterbury now in the collection of Dr. Wacher, a little ornament with a pretty leaf-scroll on the borders, and inset triangular plates of silver decorated with nielloed triquetrae on the arms.

Wessex itself is not rich in Saxon sculpture of the Ethelwulf Period, and the surviving pieces are not very well known. Moreover, they are puzzlingly inconsistent in style ; but I think that the reason why there are so many carvings of different kinds at a date close to the middle of the century is that these sculptures represent not a single southern art, but a variety of south English fashions, among which we should distinguish a West Saxon manner of the Mercian borders, a West Saxon manner of the Celtic fringe and of the Celtic houses in Wessex, and, lastly, an official court manner that was, no doubt, to be found in its purest form at Winchester. As an example of a West Saxon stone cross in the Mercian borderland that must belong to the mature ' Baroque ' period of the middle of the century, I cite the cross-shaft (Pl. 82) from St. Oswald's priory, Gloucester, for it exhibits to the full that lavish tumultuous style which characterizes the contemporary metal-work. The fragment is only 24 inches in height, but it is copiously ornamented with creatures of the Frankish lion type and its derivative, the biped with fiercely rearing head and shoulders and huge violently twisted tail. It represents a sculptural phase in which two dissimilar methods of carving an animal were used simultaneously, one being the smooth ' natural skin ' treatment, and the other a heavily ornate abstract manner with contours, hatching, and a spiral joint, the animal-type of Cropthorne and Wroxeter. It is a contrast belonging to the period of Ethelwulf and Ethelswith, as their finger-rings testify (p. 183). The Gloucester cross, however, owes a good deal to the Mercian basis of the art in this western area, and there can be no doubt about the midland stamp of its ' heraldic ' animal-style,[1] and the origin of the sprawling quadruped seen from above.[2] Moreover, the cross has a definitely barbaric feel, and we observe that on the back the scroll has been transformed very nearly completely into a hard interlace-pattern in which only vestiges of the original plant-form survive. Such uncouth stylization was not uncommon at this period. There is another example (Pl. 84) at Kelston in Somerset, where we see a fine leafy plant in the process of being reduced to a chilly lifeless pattern of interlacing lines.

This tendency to transmute into inanimate barbaric decoration the vivacious forms of the growing plant is further illustrated by the fragments of a cross in Minety Church, Wiltshire, and, in central Mercia, on a small piece of a ninth-century shaft at St. Peter's, Northampton.[3] The process is part of a general phenomenon of the middle

---

[1] cf. the confronted bipeds here with the Canterbury style as in Royal I.E., VI, folio 4a, bottom of left column, and then with east Mercian work, as on the Breedon cross-shaft.

[2] cf. the third disc of the Witham pins (Pl. 71), the Rome Gospels, folio 125a, ligature of VE in VERBUM, and the Wallingford sword (pommel-bar).

[3] This carving shows the ' penetration ' detail.

ninth century in the south that was to so obvious an extent a revival of barbaric forms of design that it does not astonish us to find it includes also the re-appearance of the Ribbon Style animal. It is here that we come to what I should describe as the 'Celtic' aspect of West Saxon art. The curious and peculiarly West Saxon mixture of southern continentally inspired elements and flagrantly barbaric animal-patterns in the Hiberno-Saxon tradition is aptly illustrated by the silver sword-handle (Pl. 79) from Fetter Lane in the City of London, now in the British Museum. It is typically 'Baroque' in shape, the pommel being lobed and ornamented with knobs and beaded wire, and the waisted grip having a thickened band in the centre. It bears a rich crowded ornament in nielloed silver on a silver-gilt field, and the main themes are two spreading designs, one of which is a ribbon-like biped with a long curly tail, and the other a whorl of snake-like creatures, both displayed against a background of ivy-scroll, like that on the Kelston cross. These animal-patterns represent a persistent under-current in West Saxon design of the period that must have some connexion with the ornamental repertory of the earlier barbaric manuscripts ;[1] but this West Saxon Ribbon Style is very far from being a mere revival of antique designs, for we have a series of stone-carvings in the south that show similar decoration and teach us that in reality the apparently ancient Ribbon Style animal now appearing in West Saxon art is the result of a ribbon-like and fluid treatment of the ninth-century Mercian 'lizard' and the biped derivative of the Frankish lion.

These West Saxon sculptures in the definitely barbaric or 'Celtic' manner are of considerable importance in the history of art in north-west Europe,[2] for they represent an expression of southern English taste in the second half

[1] cf. the terminal whorl of the P in the monogram of folio 18a of the Rome Gospels (Pl. 56) with the whorl on this sword-handle.

[2] Mr. F. Cottrill has published a valuable study of the Ribbon Style series in Wessex, *Antiquaries Journal*, XV (1935), p. 144.

of the ninth century that cannot have been negligible as a factor controlling the general styles of the period. This new fondness for the Ribbon Style formula in animal-design was probably a result of continued contact with the Celtic west, and it is a notable fact that its appearance in England coincides with what I may describe as the beginnings of the 'Jellinge' tendency in Hiberno-Scandinavian design, and also with the development of a continental art having a strong northern or Celtic bias, as exemplified by the older of the covers of the Lindau Gospels in the Pierpont Morgan Collection at New York. One of the finest and earliest English crosses in this series stood at Colerne in northern Wiltshire. It is now represented by three fragments in the church, a part of the head and two pieces of the panelling on the faces, 15 inches and 19 inches in length (Pl. 83). These bear flat animal-patterns, cut to a relief of about half an inch, in the form of creatures with glaring leonine heads, and bodies that are rich with heavy hatching, chevron ornament, beading, and a tightly wound spiral joint. This overloaded decorative style of 850–75 continues the manner of the Cropthorne cross (Pl. 80) that belongs to the first half of the century, and the animal is a form of the heraldic type of biped to be seen on the Gloucester carving (Pl. 82); but it is now plainly in the process of dissolving into broad ribbon-designs of sweeping unruly convolutions. The rod-like fore-legs of the beasts with crossed necks, and the absurd legs of the bending body on the second fragment, have become mere meaningless appendages of the pattern, and thus illustrate the nature of the change that is here altering these once fiery alert creatures into smooth-flowing ribbon-scrawls.[1]

---

[1] The resemblance to older manuscript-types of animal-pattern is probably accidental, e.g. the late eighth-century Cuthbert Gospels, folio 71b, bottom panels. In a Mercian example of the same sculptural style at Tenbury Wells in Worcestershire we have, however, one of those back-to-back compositions that does seem to be based on an established manuscript convention ; cf. Rome Gospels, folio 11b, right-hand border.

In spite, however, of this marked barbaric trend in Saxon design during Ethelwulf's reign and just after it, there were other sculptures of mid-ninth-century Wessex that made no use of this Ribbon Style animal-ornament, but instead sought to reproduce a fashionable and continental type of scroll-pattern, as though reflecting the more sophisticated Francophile taste of the court circle. There is, for example, the cross, now represented by two fragments each 3 feet in height, at Littleton Drew in Wiltshire (Pl. 84). On its faces we have a fleshy foreign-looking scroll with repeated thickenings of the stem and curly ends to the leaves ; and on the edges are other scrolls with complicated interlacing branches, a type of design that is not infrequent in Carolingian art. Another instance of a West Saxon carving of this kind comes from royal Winchester itself and is to be seen in the garden of Prior's Barton at the end of the College Fields.[1] It is a fragment of a pillar with a round shaft, and its ornament is arranged in an arcade of round-arched panels (Pl. 85). It bears the closely assembled tumultuous type of ornament with which we are already familiar in this period, but it has nothing of the flat ribbon-quality of the Colerne carving. The work is, on the contrary, thick, rounded, and robust, and one of the foliate scrolls is a rich symmetrical pattern that has great spreading acanthus-leaves at its base, an unmistakable indication of Frankish influence. But the carving is English and barbaric in the varied nature of its ornament, for other panels contain interlace and a fine animal-study, a splendid smooth-bodied stag caught up in the meshes of an interlace. This is one of the best surviving examples in Saxon sculpture of the partly barbarized portrait-manner in animal-design ; but it does not belong to the same series as the leonine and bird portraits of the late eighth and early ninth century. What we have now is the curious and often unidentifiable forest-fauna of stags and the like

[1] I have to thank Major J. R. Pinsent for permission to examine and photograph this important carving.

that appear in northern sculptures about the same time, as on the round-shaft cross at Masham in Yorkshire and on the Ilkley crosses. The Winchester carving shows us the southern beginnings of this short-lived style, and we may be sure that these new animal-types, like the acanthus, comes to us from Frankish art and were a part of the fashionable repertory of continental designs that first found an English home in the royal capital of Wessex.

There is, however, only one carving in England that really gives us an adequate impression of the southern continental-style ' Baroque ' art of the middle of the ninth century, and that is the enigmatic Mercian pillar in the graveyard of Wolverhampton Church (Pl. 86). This fine sculpture is 14 feet in height, and is almost completely covered by decoration arranged in zones, with pendent triangles of ornament beneath the lowest belt. There are no figures, and nothing that is conceived in a mood of the more serene and monumental classical grandeur. It is a rich jostling array of minor patterns. Two of the zones, the second from the top and the bottom one, contain animals and birds in a strap-work frame of lozenge-shaped partitions, a decorative arrangement that is characteristic of the ninth century ; [1] but the carvings that contribute most of all to the continental character of the pillar are the rich and foreign-looking acanthus-ornaments to be seen in a narrow band of formal sprays and in handsome spiraliform scrolls that fill the top zone and the third from the top. [2] The Wolverhampton shaft is unquestionably the noblest monument that has come down to us from the pre-Alfredian sculptures of the West Saxon supremacy, and it illustrates

[1] The immediate source is probably Frankish ; cf. the northern French Sacramentarium Gelasianum, folio 131b (Zimmermann, Tf. 137a), an eighth-century manuscript. In England cf. the Beeston Tor brooch (Pl. 78), and in Scandinavia the bronze tortoise-brooches of the Vikings (see H. Shetelig, Osebergefundet, III, p. 271).

[2] For the ragged rolling magnificence of this scroll-type cf. Corbie School illumination, e.g. Paris lat. 1141, folio 6b. Ivory carvings like the cup at Deventer (Goldschmidt, I, 152) should also be noted.

better than all else the gaily ornate style of the period of Ethelwulf and his sons, a style that sought so often to express itself in the terms of the then fashionable continental art. There is nothing else quite like it in England, though it is possible that the heavily decorated round-shaft crosses in the north, such as that at Masham (p. 195), may to some extent reflect an analogous contemporary taste in another province. In the south, at the end of the ninth century, we have the Deerhurst font, one part of which looks like a piece of a round-shaft cross, as an apparent survival of the Wolverhampton style ; but the spontaneity and gaiety of the earlier work are gone. It is duller, more subdued, and more even-textured ; for we shall presently learn that in Alfred's reign West Saxon art had lost the vivacity and charm of the Ethelwulfian ' Baroque '.

XII

LATER NORTHUMBRIAN SCULPTURE

THE influence of the gaily ornate southern art of the middle
of the ninth century could scarcely fail, at a time of the
political ascendancy of Wessex, to make itself felt in Northumbria. But it did not easily penetrate into the more
remote provinces of the district, where the northern tradition
developed with much less interruption and change than
we might expect, and I do not think it is of any considerable
importance except in the country round York and Ripon.
In general, the alteration in style took the form of an
increasing lightness in treatment and a greater extravagance
in the use of elaborate detailed ornament, which is now
close-packed in a sumptuous lace-like spread ; but we
notice also an appreciable loss of sculptural quality in the
work and of Romanesque grandeur in the figure-style, the
noble Majesties of the Easby and Rothbury kind being
supplanted by personages on a smaller scale, by unpretentious busts, and by miniature scenes in tiny panels.
The well-known ' Angel ' cross at Otley, a carving of the
early ninth century, provides a very good illustration
of this increasing insignificance of the Northumbrian
effigy in the York area, and we have a further example
in the round-shaft cross at Dewsbury. The chief influence
with which we have to reckon in this matter is undoubtedly that of the Mercian series of arcaded figures,
as on the ' Hedda Stone ', at Breedon, and at Fletton.
This must have been a considerable factor in the development of the York school, and at Hovingham there is a
very beautiful slab (Pl. 87) on which, above a border-

ing strip containing a highly decorative Northumbrian scroll, there is an arcaded series of figures in a light architectural frame that is directly connected with the Mercian style (p. 178). The same sort of work occurs at Masham, where there is a round-shaft pillar (Pl. 87) on which are figures and animals that are arranged in zones and contained in a similar arcade of thin-lined niches with wiry foliate sprays in the spandrels of the arches. The figure-style is typically slight and unimportant, and consists of small-scale narrative groups and a row of single figures, probably Christ and the Apostles.

The animals on this Masham pillar also deserve notice ; for they likewise testify to the new southern character in Yorkshire sculpture. They are very badly weathered, but we can discern the fantastic forms of the Carolingian ' forest fauna ' to which I have already alluded (p. 191), and can see their thin spidery legs and their delicate floral background. These are not ' Anglian Beasts ', which is the name given by Dr. Bröndsted to the emancipated fauna of the Northumbrian vine-scroll (pp. 198–9), but a night-mare array of foreign creatures, comparable with that which adorns the pages of Frankish manuscripts, and here, no doubt, to be connected with one of the styles of the Breedon friezes [1] (Pl. 73). The appearance of the stag, however, shows that we have to do with a series of creatures that is not quite the same as any that we have seen before in Mercia or the north, and suggests that the date of the Masham cross must lie near the middle of the ninth century ; for we may remember that in the south this new-comer occurs for the first time on the round-shaft fragment at Winchester (Pl. 85), a sculpture that is not likely to be earlier than 850.

No doubt some Northumbrian crosses still preserved a

[1] Compare the combat scene on the Breedon frieze (Pl. 72) with the animal carving on the cross-shaft from Crofton, West Riding (Collingwood, fig. 64). For the Frankish source of the ' forest fauna ' see the Fountain of Life folio (6b) in Paris Bib. nat. lat. 8850.

predominantly Celtic style and seem to have been the work of Hiberno-Saxon sculptors with little experience of southern art. A fragment of a shaft at Brompton, North-allerton, is an example (Pl. 90). Here the square panelling with the unusual and interesting bird-studies, cut flat and silhouette-fashion, is clearly barbaric in feeling,[1] and though the 'portrait' type of bird came ultimately from Merovingian ornament, I cannot help thinking that it came to Yorkshire through the medium of Celtic art. Indeed, birds of very much the same kind appear in an obviously Celtic composition on a Welsh grave-slab at Caerleon.[2] The stylized scroll on this Brompton piece is pure Northumbrian work ; but the human figures upon it are hard and mannered in a definitely Celtic way, and the general impression is one of a cross that was scarcely affected by the southern fashions then becoming popular.

Nevertheless the advent of the southern style into this Yorkshire area did bring about a very important change. The best example that I know of the influence of West Saxon ornament is a cross (Pl. 88) of which a part is at Cundall and a part at Aldborough, places near to one another on either side of the boundary between the North and West Ridings. The face that shows the changed manner best, the close-panelled decorative system favoured in Ethel-wulf's day, is divided into small compartments by stepped partitions and in them are wiry symmetrical scrolls or large smooth-skinned animals with a ' portrait ' emphasis. The stylistic bond between this ornamental arrangement and that to be seen on some of the West Saxon metal-work like the Trewhiddle mounts (Pl. 78) is surprisingly close, and, though in detail the cross is only vaguely influenced rather than directly inspired by the art of Wessex, the southern stimulus responsible for its unusual decoration must have been of con-

---

[1] cf., for instance, the style of carvings like the Banagher cross in the National Museum, Dublin.

[2] I have to thank Mr. Nash-Williams for sending me a picture of this carving, which I should not otherwise have known.

siderable strength. It is true that the panels on the back and sides include short lengths of vine-scroll in which are pecking birds and a large uncomfortably leaping beast, plainly contributions from Northumbrian art ; but the stiff wiry scrolls, symmetrically arranged around a central stem, that alternate with the animals on the step-panelled face, though they have a family alliance with the Croft type of scroll, are here seen in a special form not found elsewhere in Yorkshire, but to be seen in Mercia at Fletton (Pl. 74) and in Wessex at Whitchurch (Pl. 77).

A particularly interesting variant of this mid-ninth-century Yorkshire style is to be seen in the fragment of a recumbent tomb-slab (Pl. 88) at Melsonby in the North Riding, which is perhaps one of the best-preserved and most beautiful carvings in the county. Its single ' portrait ' animal and its pair of beasts are obviously of the Cundall type, but they are arranged in an uninterrupted composition ; not I think because the sculptor had forgotten the southern panelling, but because in this instance the slender tomb-length was itself a sufficiently constricted area. The slab is bordered by interlace and a running plant-scroll, both crisp and clean-cut like the animal-pattern, and on its vertical edge it has pairs of human heads set within little oval ' windows '. The significance of this I do not know ; but it reveals that lack of respect for heavy and solemnly sensible figure-work that is typical of Saxon art at this period, and it has its match both farther north, as at Heysham, and also in Mercia, as at Sandbach. I may add that even on the Cundall cross the figure-sculpture is relatively insignificant and consists of a bust of an angel and two small carvings of the Masham order. One of them is a representation of Samson and the gates of Gaza, and the other a scene in which a figure emerges from a canopied arch and turns towards a group of personages outside.

By comparison with an animal in a vine-scroll on one of the Ilkley crosses (Pl. 89, 2), Dr. Bröndsted was able to show that the violently contorted beast in the uppermost of the stepped panels at Cundall is a vine-pattern animal released from encumbering stems and foliage. It is an example, therefore, of the emancipated ' Anglian Beast ', the importance of which he was the first to realize. But this same cross also shows us short lengths of the ancient scroll-pattern in which we see the preliminary stages of this release of the contained fauna. We observe single birds and beasts grossly overemphasized at the expense of the scroll that supports them, and also symmetrically placed pairs of animals, likewise treated as more important elements in the picture than the straggling lines of the plant behind them. We are here at the starting-point of two types of ninth-century pattern, one the solitary ' Anglian Beast ' proper, and the other the enmeshed pairs of animals or ' Twin Beasts ', in which a scroll-effect is still preserved by the elaborate interlacements of the beasts themselves.

The origin of this last-named pattern is to be sought in such carvings as that on the cross-shaft (Pl. 90) at Nunny-kirk in Northumberland where we have a figure-of-eight scroll containing a pair of birds and a pair of beasts, prob-ably of much the same age as the Heversham cross (Pl. 92), on which we see the initial magnification of the single animal. But these Twin Beasts of Nunnykirk do not free themselves in the manner of the Anglian Beast. Even on the stepped face of the Cundall cross where there are examples of the unencumbered Anglian Beast, the Twin Beasts of the bottom panel preserve a part of their scroll-background, and their normal tendency is to re-dissolve into a mesh of ribbons. There is an excellent illustration of this more bar-baric version of them on the Thornhill cross at Nith Bridge.

The probability is that whereas the Twin Beasts are from start to finish a Northumbrian concept,[1] the Anglian

---

[1] The possibility of a connexion with the heraldic pairs of animals as seen in Mercian and Canterbury art (p. 163) should not be neglected ; but we have here in the north so clear a persistence of the scroll-back-ground, that it seems to me the Yorkshire ' Twin Beasts ' are not directly derived from the southern types of opposed creatures.

Beast emerges from the scroll largely as a result of the influence in the north of southern design in the early ninth century. The forward-facing ' lion ' on the Cundall cross is not an Anglian Beast but a Frankish type animal-portrait, and in recording the emancipation of the vine-pattern animal from his encircling scroll we should do well to make allowances for the influence of the Frankish manner of animal-drawing, such as we have discovered intruding in the Cuthbert Gospels [1] and in Mercian manu-scripts.[2] The Anglian Beast is, in short, a somewhat grudging northern concession to the continental taste and is perhaps the result of the influence at York of Francophile ecclesiastics like Alcuin.

It is certainly in the area of which York and Ripon are the centres that the development of the Anglian Beast is best studied. We have, for instance, the three crosses in the churchyard at Ilkley (Pl. 89), all dating from the first half of the ninth century. On the easternmost, which bears on the edges a tightly coiled vine-scroll, the faces show a panelled arrangement with Twin Beast designs and sections of vine-scroll, one of which contains the violently straining quadruped that appears in unrestricted freedom on the Cundall cross. On the central and tallest,[3] where the vine-scroll on the edges, now more tightly spirali-form than before, breaks its pattern in a gauche response to southern fashion,[4] we see two Anglian Beasts, one an ugly rearing brute with his tail functioning as a thin wisp of scroll, and the other a winged biped, looking very like a derivative of the Anglian Heraldic style. It is scarcely to be doubted that southern fashion led to this prominence of the single creature in a panel ; and on the same face of this cross, above these two single animals, there are the

---

[1] e.g. folio 20a.

[2] Book of Cerne, folio 3a ; Cotton, Tiberius C. II, folio 94a.

[3] The head does not belong to the shaft.

[4] cf. the Sandbach scroll, and the break in the pattern of the Breedon frieze ; for the origin see the Canterbury and Carolingian manuscripts.

Twin Beasts plainly designed according to the formula already evolved in the south, whereby two fiercely erect bipeds are united by the interlacement of their tails. On the third Ilkley cross we have several examples of the Anglian Beast, but it is at once noticeable that they have acquired something of a southern atmosphere following their liberation, and now have a suggestion of the fantastic oddity of the Masham creatures. It is wellnigh certain, therefore, that some potent extraneous influence was responsible for this northern development of the single-animal unit, and though Dr. Bröndsted is undoubtedly right in maintaining that the subject of the experiment was primarily the fauna of the vine-scroll, the fact of the emergence of the solitary beast is best explained as a result of the example of southern English art.

There is further evidence in the fragment of a cross-shaft (Pl. 93) found at Dacre in Cumberland, a middle ninth-century carving with a conjoined vine-scroll and key-pattern on the edge. The faces bear elaborate floriated scrolls, very prettily cut with something of the Easby foliate richness, and among the contained beasts is one of a kind new to northern sculpture, a little winged lion with a long neck and a 'regardant' head, assuredly a version of the Frankish lion. He stands with the Saxon 'lock' and has suffered a certain native stylization ; but for all that he is an intruder in the scroll-pattern, and he appears at just the time when the Anglian Beast emerges as a single ornamental theme. Then, again, the well-known 'Dragon' cross (Pl. 91) at Otley in Yorkshire shows that this theme in the north did not by any means depend on the quadruped out of the vine-scroll. The 'dragon' is an heraldic portrait-version of the winged biped, done with an impressive rigid dignity that is utterly foreign to the capering and contorted animal lately released from his struggles among the stem and tendrils of a climbing plant. Yet this sculpture is clearly of the same date as the tallest Ilkley cross, which has also its dragon and, as on the side of the

Otley shaft, a pair of miserable beasts united by the convolutions of their tails.

The Yorkshire style at the time of the Danish Conquest was, however, very uncertain in intention and manner. The elaborate work of Masham and of Cundall had seen its day, the little figured scenes had disappeared, and we are left with ragged ill-organized versions of the old vine-theme and of panelled beasts. There is a good example of the type at Collingham (Pl. 91), which is situated between Otley and York. On the edges are lengths of the vine-scroll and of a heavy interlace, and on the faces are panels containing animals in pairs and singly. One Anglian Beast is a huge-headed ugly monster with the normal smooth skin of his kind ; but others of the creatures, following that southern hesitation which we have already observed at Gloucester (Pl. 82), are stiffly schematic and are enriched with contour-lines and joint spirals. Moreover, the Twin Beasts have the grimly ferocious leonine heads that we see so often in southern and Mercian work. Once again we find evidence of a response to the ornate fashions of the midlands and of Wessex ; but the Collingham cross preserves in spite of this its own northern harshness, a gaunt uncouth savagery that turns the spitting and hissing comicalities of the south into terrifying and menacing giants.

The southern influences that operated with such noticeable effect in the country around York did not, as I say, everywhere interrupt the development of the older Northumbrian art, nor did they lead to the widespread use throughout all the northern counties of what we may call the ' York Styles '. In some districts, for instance the north-west coast, a frankly barbaric system of ornamenting crosses still found favour in the first half of the ninth century and perpetuated an ' Irish ' style that had already found expression in Northumbria at an earlier date (p. 137). Thus at Irton, close to the Cumberland coast, there is a tall and splendid cross (Pl. 92) that illustrates particularly well the survival of the ancient barbaric decoration. It has, it is true, long runs of the vine-scroll on the edges, work of the harshly mannered type that is to be seen on the tallest of the crosses at Ilkley ; but on the face and back there is nothing but geometric ornament in a carpet-like arrangement of panels within a marginal border of interlace. On the front we have a sunk-field step-pattern, a diagonal fret, and two ornamental roundels of the inward-pointing pelta variety. These last are perhaps of southern origin,[1] but the step-pattern, though it has its match in later West Saxon work at Bradford-on-Avon (Pl. 104), is an established Celtic ornament ; and, as there is no serious modification of the barbaric manner, I have little doubt that the main inspiration of the Irton ornamental style is Irish.[2] We are here on the Celtic fringe of England, and in the presence of an established type of decoration that had a long life in the Celtic lands, not only in Ireland but also in Wales, where it is abundantly represented by sculpture of the late ninth and the tenth centuries.

The continued survival of the original 'Ruthwell–Bewcastle' type of Anglo-Saxon ornament in the more remote schools of Northumbrian sculpture is not a very surprising instance of conservatism ; but it is interesting to watch the fate of the ancient theme of the inhabited vine-scroll in the first half of the ninth century. One of the early stages in degradation of this pattern is to be seen on the fragment of a cross-shaft (Pl. 92) at Heversham in Westmorland. The animals are very large, very insecurely perched in their thin containing volutes, and obviously preparing for their future freedom in the form of Anglian Beasts. This isolation of the animal is carried a stage forward on a carving at Lowther Castle in the same county (Pl. 90), for the animals on it are shown portrait-

---

[1] cf. the well-known Carolingian device of the four inward-pointing hearts, as seen in the Kettlach group enamels (e.g. Riegl, *Spätrömische Kunstindustrie*, II, Pl. XIX, 8).

[2] cf. the step-pattern and fret in the Mac Regol Gospels of the early ninth century, e.g. folio 84*b* (Zimmermann, Tf. 199).

fashion in a figure-of-eight scroll that is a further adaptation of the familiar vine-pattern, though it has now become
little more than a framework of medallions in which the
animals are posed.[1] But here this particular tendency to
enlarge and isolate the fauna of the scroll came to a stop,
and north of the Border we find that an exactly opposite
process was in operation, a barbaric reaction against this
encroachment of the southern ' portrait ' treatment. This
led not to the magnification and eventual liberation of the
animal, but to its closer imprisonment; and the first signs
of this desire to reduce the Northumbrian vine-scroll fauna
to something that is little more than an inorganic element
in the pattern can be seen on the Morham cross (Pl. 93)
from East Lothian, a carving that may perhaps be as early
as the late eighth century. It shows us a thin, hard scroll
in which there is a series of vigorously violent and eccentric
creatures whose convolutions and excited gestures contribute to the apparently foliate prettiness of the whole
design. They function very much as binding sprays and
leaves and flowers had previously functioned, and so con-
trive to give an effect of animated richness to this face of
the cross. In the same way the carving at Thornhill in
Dumfriesshire, generally known as the Closeburn cross and
now in the Grierson Museum, bears on one edge a scroll
of the full-length inhabited type containing birds so intricately involved in the pattern of the scroll that they are
not very much more than binders connecting one volute
of the vine-stem to the next ; thus the neck that protrudes
from the containing scroll, and the wings and the legs,
have a value and accent equivalent to that of the scroll
details and are no longer clearly differentiated parts of an
emphatically stated creature.

This cross (Pl. 93) is certainly ninth-century work.
Though the scroll is in a purely northern barbaric manner,

[1] *R.C.H.M. Westmorland*, Pl. 6. A further development of this same
design occurs at Ramsbury in Wiltshire (Pl. 99) on a cross of the
Alfredian period (p. 212).

it also bears a panel in which is a forward-facing ' Carolingian ' lion that is not unlike the Newent type of beast (Pl. 77), and it is probable that much of its ornament was influenced by the sculpture of the York district. In another panel, for instance, we have a straddled creature seen from above, not long released from the vine-scroll in which he was formerly climbing and now displayed in a torturingly geometrical exercise, a design of the type that was to be seen on the Cundall shaft (Pl. 88) and on the eastern cross at Ilkley. The adjacent Nith Bridge cross at Thornhill shows the influence of the southern Yorkshire area to an even greater extent ; and the vine-scroll on the Closeburn cross is, therefore, all the more interesting as a North British example of a barbaric tendency to imprison the creature of the scroll, and to reduce him to a tangled pattern ; for it was a tendency against which, in this area, such strange new-comers as the Anglian Beast and the Twin Beasts were destined to struggle in vain.

XIII

MERCIA BEFORE THE DANES

EVEN in Mercia the supremacy of Wessex and the influence of southern art did not completely interrupt the Northumbrian tradition of sculpture. The north Derbyshire school of the Eyam and Bakewell crosses (p. 164) is not likely to have been a negligible factor, and a little farther to the west of this group, on the other side of the Peak country in the Cheshire plain, there are two justly renowned crosses that testify to the continued survival of certain elements of the Northumbrian style. These are the twin crosses [1] (Pls. 94, 95) at Sandbach, a few miles north-east of Crewe. On the smaller of them we have again that lozenge-shaped strap-work which came to our notice first of all on the Wolverhampton column (Pl. 86), though here it is a stylized stringy version of it; and on both crosses we observe a rich style of closely assembled multitudinous ornament that can only be a reflection of the West Saxon taste of the middle of the century; but, in general, there is an unmistakable Northumbrian flavour about these sculptures, and the principal reason for this is the important part that is played by the old theme of the inhabited vine-scroll.

It is certainly a late and derived version, a coarse ragged pattern of the running spiral type, with a population of large uncouth creatures that leap crazily at the fruit in the

[1] The two crosses are stylistically similar and contemporary, and form a single monument, for they stand side by side on one great plinth. There are several other instances of pairs of crosses in north-west Mercia and in north England, but they are of a later date (tenth–eleventh century).

ninth-century manner without waiting to secure a foothold in the branches. The use of floating bosses as space-filling details heightens the sprawling formless character of the design, and its general lanky, straggling unsteadiness is typical of a small group of carvings of the period.[1] But the scroll has also a few distinctively southern features. The volutes, for instance, occasionally end in animal-heads, an obvious sign of influence from the south,[2] and across one volute is the figure of a man, lightly held in position by the drapery folds at his shoulder, who has two long legs that trail off into tendrils, again suggesting a connexion with what was originally the Canterbury style.

On the other hand, a sign of northern influence is the narrow interlace border on the west face of the smaller cross, which reminds us of the Irton cross (Pl. 92).[3] And a detail such as the combination of plant-scroll and interlace in the same run, which is also to be seen at Ilkley (Pl. 89) and Dacre (Pl. 93), is further evidence of a fashion from outside the province intruding upon the Mercian style.[4] Yet the Sandbach crosses have an unmistakable midland character, and the creature in the Anglian Heraldic Style on the bottom of the west face of the taller cross (Pl. 95) is purely Mercian.[5] So is the figure-style. It is true that the abundance of the figure-carvings and

[1] cf. a fragment of a shaft from St. Peter's, York, now in the Yorkshire Museum ; also the scroll on the Hilton of Cadboll stone at Edinburgh.

[2] In Mercia cf. the Cropthorne cross-head (Pl. 80).

[3] cf. also the Closeburn cross (Pl. 93). The interlace border is an antique element first seen in English sculpture on the Reculver cross (Pl. 46), and it also occurs in the south at Shaftesbury and at Bradford-on-Avon. I think, however, that the Irton-Sandbach type is a distinct northern version that has its own Irish background.

[4] In origin this is a south English mannerism, but it is possible that in this instance it is derived from the York area. The best match to the Sandbach version is, however, to be seen on the Penally cross in Pembrokeshire, where the vine-scroll is of the same ragged type.

[5] cf. a similar animal on a cross-shaft at Breedon, *Archaeologia*, LXXVII, Pl. XXXV, *b*.

the prominence given to them may perhaps owe something to Northumbrian tradition ; but there is no doubt
that the manner in which the principal figures are presented is Mercian in kind, and in the great medallion on
the larger cross we come very near to the simple linear
dignity of the Lechmere sculpture (Pl. 95). Nevertheless,
the Sandbach style has its own rugged and barbaric strength
in the treatment of the human form, and the harshly outlined personages with big heads and weak doll-like bodies
are a new invention because they are here arranged in a
most unusual surface-covering pattern of people. Thus on
the sides of the smaller cross and on one face of the big
cross there are series of these little figures in double rows,
either in unevenly opposed panels or in niches on the
same level. It is an essentially calligraphic and decorative style, almost Irish-looking in kind, and it may well
be a sign that we are here in a borderland region which
lay within the shadows of the western and north-western
Celtic and Hiberno-Saxon world.

The direction in which central Mercian art had been
moving since the period of the Breedon and Fletton friezes
is illustrated by a fine cross of the middle ninth century at
Rothley, near Leicester (Pl. 96). It has a tall and slender
shaft that bears ornament arranged in panels, one of which
has a gabled head. Following the tradition of most of the
Mercian sculpture of this area in the first half of the ninth
century, the ornament is slight, pretty, and crowded, with
no ambitious figure-carving ; and now that the sparkling
relief and heavy under-cutting of the earlier work are gone,
the load of detailed ornament that the column bears is a
lifeless and rather uninspiring spread of pattern. The
favourite motives are interlaces and plant-scrolls, the latter
being of a rich and elaborate type that includes the characteristic whorl of long leaves, as on the Croft cross (Pl. 61)
and the Witham pins (Pl. 71). One panel contains a
winged dragon with an interlacing tail, a good example
of the Anglian Heraldic beast ; and another, that above the

gable, bears a handsome symmetrical foliate ornament, which, though the design seems to be connected with the plant-scroll canopies on the ' Angel ' cross at Otley, has a peculiarly curly ' acanthus ' look that is probably the result of West Saxon influence (cf. the Littleton Drew shaft, Pl. 84).

Nearer to the time when Mercia east of Watling Street passed under the dominion of the Danes, we find a sculptural style of greater austerity and simplicity that is distinguished for its returning interest in flat, barbaric animal-pattern. In the Derby Museum there is a piece of a shaft (Pl. 97), which comes from St. Alkmund's in the town, that illustrates the extraordinarily spirited drawing of the Mercian lion-form that is the principal mannerism of this new style, and also the new Ribbon Style treatment of the animal that, following the fashion of ' Celtic ' Wessex, simultaneously makes its appearance in Mercian sculpture. The lions are carvings in the barbaric flat style and have lifeless contoured bodies ; but they are magnificently posed, and possess all the savage vigour that we associate with the English version of the Frankish animal. They are not Anglian Beasts ; for they are not derived from the traditional fauna of the Northumbrian vine-scroll, but are descendants of the southern quadruped (Pl. 66) and of the same family as the beasts of the Gloucester cross (Pl. 82).[1] As examples of abstract and symbolic design their importance is considerable ; but, historically, their principal interest lies in the fact that they represent the type of animal-drawing which was the source, as Dr. Bröndsted long ago perceived, of the Great Beast of Scandinavian art, such as we see later on the renowned memorial (c. 980) of Harald Gormsson at Jellinge in Denmark. Inasmuch as Derby was one of the Five Boroughs, the midland centre of Danish power in England, we may well have here one of the sculptures that was directly responsible for the adoption of this animal-type by the invaders.

[1] Note the foot that hangs over the edge of the panel, and compare this with similar details on the Gloucester cross.

The 'combat' scene of the Breedon frieze (Pl. 73) and of the Crofton cross-shaft (p. 195) is carved on the edge of the St. Alkmund's fragment. It is strung out and much stylized,[1] ribbon-fashion, but it is undoubtedly a version of this splendid theme of the battle of the beasts, and here again is an element that was destined to make a profound appeal to the aesthetic tastes of the vikings. It is possible, however, that the Scandinavian and Danish carvings of the death-struggle between the lion and the serpent has another source, and in this book we have no need to examine the problems of the emergence of the Viking styles. Above all, I want to insist that the time has not yet come to talk about the influence on Saxon sculpture of Scandinavian art. In fact, if there is any influence here at all, it is, ultimately, Irish ; and my point is simply that the St. Alkmund's cross-shaft is English in the sense that it had been carved before the Danes took possession of Derby. This is important because it means that the Ribbon Style panel of this shaft need not be connected with the contemporary taste for such patterns in Scandinavia and the subsequent emergence of the ' Jellinge ' style. Mr. Cottrill, in a paper that I have already quoted (p. 189), has made an extremely valuable contribution to our knowledge of ninth-century art by insisting on the priority of the English version of the new Ribbon Style such as we see on this Derby cross. It is, in fact, entirely typical of the increasingly barbaric manner in English sculpture which is characteristic of the period immediately before the great invasion of 865, and the Mercian example can only be the direct counterpart of the West Saxon carvings that led Mr. Cottrill to conclude, quite rightly so I think, that in relation to the art of the Vikings the style is English-born.[2]

The Mercian sculpture of the period of the Great Invasion

[1] Note the ' penetration ' detail where the foot of the victim pierces the neck of his aggressor.

[2] In this connexion I may call attention to the Ribbon Style animal-pattern on the north face of the north cross at Sandbach.

is work of an outstanding merit, and even among the finest of the purely barbaric genre of carvings in England, the St. Alkmund's cross at Derby is pre-eminent. It belongs to a new style ; for, making an end of the last traces of the Carolingian mood of the first half of the ninth century, and rejecting the prodigal and too diffuse richness of ornament that was still fashionable when the Rothley cross was carved, we now find the midland sculptors returning whole-heartedly and with a most successful clarity of statement to the severest abstractions of an uncontaminated barbaric art. Here in the country east of Watling Street the carvings of the St. Alkmund's type can only represent a short-lived phase, since they first appear on the very eve of the disasters of the Danish Conquest ; but their style, and the mood that they reflect, is, as we shall see, of general importance in England. In Mercia we can measure the force and brilliance of this barbaric revival by the truly admirable lion-mask (Pl. 98) that has been lately discovered by Mr. T. C. Lethbridge on a stone at Glatton in Huntingdonshire, a truly remarkable carving that also bears an example of the ribbon-necked beast. The mask-type stands half-way between the earlier Mercian designs of the Book of Cerne (Pl. 68) and the later English versions such as are to be seen in the tenth-century Athelstan Psalter ; and it is seen here in a noble and most austerely formidable guise. Indeed, I rank this carving as nothing less than a masterpiece ; for it is conceived and executed according to the grandest traditions of the barbaric style.

XIV

WESSEX IN THE TIME OF ALFRED

THE West Saxon version of the Ribbon Style animal had been established as one of the sculptor's favourite patterns in the days of Ethelwulf (839–56) and of his successors Ethelbald and Ethelred, and it was probably still in use when Alfred came to the throne in 871. The later examples of what we may call the Colerne type of design (Pl. 83) can be seen on fragments of crosses at West Camel and Rowberrow in Somerset, at Steventon in Hampshire (Pl. 98), and at Ramsbury in Wiltshire ; best of all, perhaps, at this last place where a remarkable group of carvings is preserved at the west end of the north aisle of the church. This collection gives us a very valuable indication of what West Saxon art was like in the second half of the ninth century,[1] and as it forms a link between the age of Ethelwulf and the age of Alfred, it is the natural starting-point for this chapter. Three large fragments of a big cross-shaft (Pls. 99, 100) are to be found in this series of sculptures, and on the lower fragment, which is 35 inches in height, there are ornamental panels that are directly connected with the Colerne style, though the former ' Baroque ' enrichments are no longer to be seen

[1] The usual dating is early tenth century, i.e. temp. Edward the Elder. This seems to depend on the argument that as Ramsbury was made the see-town of a new bishopric of Berkshire and Wiltshire in 909, there can have been no church nor carvings there previously, surely a most unreasonable assumption. Bröndsted puts these carvings much earlier (late eighth century). My own view is that they should be assigned to the period 860–80, certainly not later than the beginning of Alfred's reign.

and only a thin chevron-hatching survives on the bodies of the beasts. On one panel there is a looped, limbless and very clumsy serpentine body with the head seen from above, entangled in an untidy mesh of interlace, and on another face (Pl. 100) we have an S-shaped animal with a head, drawn in profile, that bites its own body, an archaic Durrow-like pattern (cf. Pl. 37) which can be matched on one of the faces of the contemporary cross-shaft at Tenbury Wells in Worcestershire. The work is lifeless and ugly, without the elasticity and tautness of early Ribbon Style design, and the creature that I have just mentioned has pitifully feeble limbs, one a miserable jointed bar and the other a stump that trails off into interlace.

Here we are at the end of a series of West Saxon designs. But the interesting thing about the Ramsbury carvings is that the sculptor now makes elaborate use of new interlace patterns of foreign origin, which he copied with great skill. On three panels of the main shaft there are admirable designs, one of which is the distributed Stafford knot, probably a design derived from ninth-century Italian art and not an English invention,[1] while another is one of the Italian or Carolingian ' wheel ' series of interlace patterns.[2] But all this is surpassed by the superb, and so far as England is concerned, entirely new version of the old theme of the inhabited vine-scroll. It is a sculpture of surprising vigour and originality. I am not quite certain that it is a development of the ancient pattern, though a comparison with the Lowther Castle scroll (Pl. 90) suggests that the design comes from the north ; but it is possible that we ought to take into account the influence of a pattern that comes from the East or the Mediterranean, in which animals are enclosed in an interlace figure-of-eight. But whatever its source, this West Saxon version of the design is incon-

[1] This type of interlace is well established in Italian art. A good example will be found on the cross-head from S. Giulianna di Budrio in Bologna, dated 827.

[2] cf. the design on the Santa Sabina choir-screen in Rome (824–7).

testably one of the noblest works of the age, and I know little
that is finer in all Anglo-Saxon art than the grotesque leonine
beasts in these medallions, for they are masterpieces in
that strongly silhouetted hard, cold abstract style that
barbaric sculpture achieved only in the periods of its
greatest purity and power. We may even say of them that
they represent a most remarkable new adventure in the
symbolizing deformation of the organic shape ; for they
are phantasies that are half-animal and half-scroll, the
body looking like a great dead leaf from which the neck
and fore-legs protrude stem-wise.

The simplicity of the pattern-statement in this very
beautiful panel and the crisp decorativeness of the adjacent
interlace are witnesses to the dignity and greater austerity
that now becomes, so I think, the predominant feature of
West Saxon art in this phase. It would not, of course, be
true to say that the earlier types of ornament and the
Ethelwulfian system of overloaded decoration had disappeared. On this cross there are the panels containing
degenerate Ribbon Style designs, and there is a grave
cover in the Ramsbury series, a slab 25 inches long bearing
a raised cross, that is copiously and heavily ornamented
according to the manner of the middle of the century.
Yet we cannot be mistaken about the change in taste that
is suggested by the panel with the lions in medallions, and
the same feeling for a bold and tranquil declaration of the
pattern without the embarrassment of fussy detail can be
seen again on another Ramsbury tombstone (Pl. 99), a
mostly nobly designed domed slab, 45 inches in length,
that bears a spacious scroll-pattern, symmetrically arranged,
with interlocking volutes and large triangular leaves. We
have already observed in Mercia, as we may see by looking
back, first, at the Rothley cross (Pl. 96) and then at the
St. Alkmund's shaft (Pl. 97), a similar reaction against
the over-elaborate ornamental style of the first half of the
century.

Like the animals on the St. Alkmund's shaft, the creatures in the medallions on the Ramsbury cross are not Anglian Beasts but Frankish lions. On the grave-cover that bears the raised cross there is one of the animals in this Carolingian series playing the rôle of the Agnus Dei and occupying, as on the Wirksworth slab (Pl. 67), the position of the crucified Saviour. It has the typical fiercely posed neck, and is no doubt to be connected directly with the type of Agnus Dei on Queen Ethelswith's finger-ring. As on the St. Alkmund's shaft, the animal-ornament at Ramsbury shows the ninth-century detail that we call 'penetration' (p. 145), for on the slab with the Agnus Dei the tongue of the animal passes right through its body, and on the large cross-shaft the head of one of the Ribbon Style beasts emerges from under the contour-line of the body that it bites. The Ramsbury carvings, therefore, most plainly belong to the ninth-century series of barbaric Saxon sculptures that have their Mercian counterpart at Derby, and inasmuch as the midland series was cut short by the Danish invasion of 865 or very soon afterwards, it is in Wessex alone that we may expect to find the further history of this south English barbaric style uninterrupted by such a disturbing factor as the settlement in the province of invaders of another race. I doubt very much, however, if after what we may describe as the Ramsbury period in Wessex, there was much more sculpture done in the manner of this and the equivalent Mercian group of carvings. On the contrary, I think that in the south the change in style which we see actually in the process of taking place at Ramsbury, led to the gradual abandoning of themes such as the Ribbon Style animal. There is certainly no evidence suggesting that this particular type of barbaric ornament continued to be used in southern sculpture in the period following the death of Alfred (899), and though at Ramsbury itself the confusion of styles and types there represented warns us against positing any clean-cut break with the older traditions, it is by no means improbable that at the end of the century, perhaps as a result of the influence of

Alfred himself, a humane and dignified new art was already bringing the barbaric phase to a close.

It is very difficult to form a just estimate of Alfredian art, and there are, indeed, two pieces of evidence that seem to run counter to the view that I have just expressed. The manuscripts, for instance. Admittedly, we know very little about the art of illumination in southern England in the late ninth century ; but if we may judge by the disparaging remarks that King Alfred himself makes about the ignorance prevailing among his clergy, it may at least be inferred that men thought little of books and of the decoration of them during the period of the wars between Wessex and the Danes. And in the Bodleian Library we have the copy of Alfred's own translation of St. Gregory's Pastoral Care that was sent by the king to the Bishop of Worcester. It must have been written under the king's supervision in Winchester during the last decade of the century, and though it contains very little ornament and was probably never intended to be richly decorated in the manner reserved for Gospels and Psalters, it must represent as good a style of illumination as the king could command in his own capital. Yet its ornament (Pl. 101) is far from being impressive, and it is clear that the scribe, who was obviously Celtic in his sympathies, merely used as a basis for his humorous little inventions the trivialities of early ninth century South English and Mercian illumination. It would be unfair to pretend that the scratchy, crudely coloured initials in the Pastoral Care do not possess both gaiety and charm ; but there is something about the work that suggests a general poverty-stricken bleakness in this branch of the arts. One initial in black ink recalls the delicacy of Carolingian work ; and a little polychrome jewelled panel survives from the Mercian manuscripts ; [1] a quatrefoil

---

[1] So, too, in the Durham *Rituale* (Durham MS. A. IV, 19), a manuscript of the late ninth or early tenth century, where the panel is to be found among a series of scratchily drawn little initials that seem to be in a midland or southern style.

initial contains a clumsy version of the little Frankish lion ; in others there are human faces, one with the Codford St. Peter fillet (p. 180), that are very roughly done with crude complexion-spots on the cheeks. But there is no sign of a new style emerging, and I do not think that it is possible to pretend we have more here than the thin and unsatisfactory remnants of a manuscript-art that was already a century old.

In the second place there is the evidence of the renowned Alfred Jewel (Pl. 101) in the Ashmolean Museum, which is supposed to have been an ' aestel ' or page-weight for the heavy vellum leaves of a manuscript. Though its cloisonné might be held to be foreign work, the main body of the jewel is unquestionably English, as is proved by the form of the animal-head terminal ; and the point about it that interests us here is the excessively elaborate style of the golden frame and terminal, which are enriched with every possible embellishment in the form of filigree, granulation, and toothed edges. But the barbaric character of this rare example of the goldsmith's art is scarcely, I think, to be regarded as important evidence revealing the general trend of West Saxon art in King Alfred's time. The piece is unnaturally rich simply because it is a tiny jewel and seeks to express within a minimum space the maximum of magnificence. Furthermore, this piece is not in its entirety English. The introduction of cloisonné enamel must certainly have been a result of continental example, and the half-figure of Christ that is depicted in this new medium is, though possibly English in type,[1] undoubtedly influenced by Frankish and Italian cloisonné. Similarly, the sleek and fleshy floral scroll on the back of the jewel is proof of the persistence of the Frankish trend in West Saxon ornament.

I must admit that it is hazardous to set aside the evidence

[1] The Christ-figure holding two flowers had already appeared on the Sandbach cross.

216

of the Cura Pastoralis and the Alfred Jewel, and the truth may be that southern English art at the end of the ninth century was more complex and more varied in character than what I am now going to say suggests. But I am inclined to think that the real significance of the period and of the influence of King Alfred himself lies in the fact that the older kinds of trivial ornament were for the most part rejected in favour of a new and quieter statement of more impressive subjects than those popular in the middle of the century. To claim this is to claim more than the surviving monuments can be expected to show convincingly ; but if we are right in attributing, as every indication suggests, the angel-panel in the wall of the apse at Deerhurst (Pl. 103) to the closing days of Alfred's reign, we should be ill advised to ignore the lesson of this noble work of art, one that is distinguished alike for its incisive clarity and its tranquil imposing solemnity. The flat linear quality of the earlier Mercian sculptural style is abandoned, and this grave mask-like countenance with the wig of heavily ribbed locks, a gaunt and Celtic-looking masterpiece of the west, is invested with a truly monumental solidity, and must be ranked as the grandest carving on this side of the Danelaw boundary. It marks the beginning of an entirely new tradition in south English sculpture.

The word ' Romanesque ' is the core of the matter. Alfred sought to give his country a nobler art than that which he had found, an art that had a greater purpose than the parade of multitudinous ornament and aspired to the full majesty of a figural art grandly conceived. Deliberately he tried, as it were, to light and to hold aloft the torch of Romanesque classicism in defiance of the barbarous northern arts of the Danes. And he did not fail. Within ten or fifteen years of his death (899), Queen Aelflaed of Wessex (d. 916), the wife of Edward the Elder, had a stole and maniple embroidered for Frithestan, Bishop of Winchester, who was enthroned in 909. These two vestments, which bear inscribed tablets stating by whose order and for whom they were made, were subsequently (934) given by King Athelstan to the shrine of St. Cuthbert and were enclosed in the coffin with the Saint's body, then at Chester-le-Street. In 1827 they were found therein, and they are now in the Cathedral Library at Durham (Pl. 102). As there are no manuscripts of this early date in the tenth century, these noble embroideries, with their careful figure-drawings, are of extraordinary importance ; for they represent beyond all doubt the fashionable court art of Winchester about 910. No surviving sculpture and no piece of minor metal-work can reveal to us more plainly than do these vestments the trend and inclinations of the palace style. We have no authority whatsoever for positing any remarkable stylistic revolution in the early days of Edward the Elder, and therefore it is only by unworthy cavilling that we can resist the natural conclusion that this style is in harmony with, and indeed a direct continuation of, the art of this same court a decade or so earlier when Alfred the Great was still alive.

Both the stole and the maniple are $2\frac{1}{4}$ inches in width and are bordered by braids in red silk and gold thread that are decorated with tiny free-style acanthus sprays and pairs of animals in repeating sequences of seven. Between the braids they are ornamented with full-length figures of saints and prophets, though in the centre of each vestment is a quatrefoil containing one of the Christian symbols, and at the ends are square panels containing busts. All this decoration is in coloured silks, enriched with gold, and outlined, and laid upon a resplendent golden ground. Even now, though the colours are faded, the effect is one of the utmost glittering magnificence. The figures stand on little scalloped rocks, which divide the length into panels in the coulisse manner ; but in spite of this partitioning there is an extraordinary sense of freedom about the composition, since there is abundant space at the side of the figures for lettering, and above the haloes for a bushy spray of acanthus foliage.

The figures are fully and impressively Romanesque in quality. They have a certain gracious listlessness, as though belonging to a school of drawing already represented in England on the Alfred Jewel ; but they stand with solid dignity and in solemn calm. Only rarely, as in the drawing of the prophet Nahum, does that emphasized pointed oval tightening of the drapery over the thigh, also to be observed at Bradford-on-Avon (p. 220), hint at the quickened and acutely modelled draughtsmanship that was the delight of the later Winchester artists. Yet there is an English freedom of treatment in the work, and in the use of the trembling, untidy acanthus that occupies with inconsequential prettiness the space above the heads of the figures, we may recognize a particularly English feeling for a type of design in which the effigy is released from an imprisoning architectural frame and stands unconfined in a golden flower-decked space.

The West Saxon sculpture that follows the Deerhurst angel (Pl. 103) does not have the same simple and majestic grandeur as the Winchester work embroidered on the stole and maniple. There is not, it is true, very much of this sculpture left, and I know of two places only where there are carvings that belong to the period of Alfred's death or to the early years of his successor's reign ; but at one of these, Winterbourne Steepleton in Dorset, there is a piece of sculpture that has merits of no ordinary kind. I refer to the little flying angel (Pl. 103), now built into the outside wall of the church. Here movement, a really full-bodied strength of gesture, gives a new interest to the developing Saxon style ; for the head and the legs are bent sturdily upwards almost at right angles to the trunk, and the eager face is turned to look backwards over the shoulders. The carving has substance ; it is taut and powerful like the Codford St. Peter dancer ; and in this respect it is better work than the figure-sculptures at the second place I have in mind, the beautiful little Saxon church at Bradford-on-Avon in Wiltshire. Here, set high above the chancel-arch, are two very well-known flying angels (Pl. 103) that formed part of what must have been a rood or other figural composition on a grandiose scale ; for these two supporters measure each about 5 feet in length. They are probably later in date than the Winterbourne Steepleton angel, maybe nearer 950 than 900, and they lack the vitality and thrust of this carving ; but though they are by comparison listless and insipid, though the earlier sculptural robustness is gone, they are exercises in a new linear style of such an airy lightness and grace that we know them to be connected with the figure-drawings on the Cuthbert stole and in the later manuscripts of the developed Winchester style. They represent, however, a deliberate return to the linear silhouetted manner of carving, a more barbaric handling of the theme, and it is not simply because they are sculptures, but because of the noble and truly grandiose nature of the subject portrayed that these two angels play their part in the Romanesque revival of the tenth century.

The decoration of the Bradford-on-Avon church included geometric ornament that provides evidence of the seemingly incradicable taste for Celtic and Hiberno-Saxon pattern. It is a slab (Pl. 104) that bears within a bordering strip of interlace two panels, one containing a sharp-cut step-pattern, and the other a spiraliform design based on the old trumpet-pattern, very like an ornament used on the Deerhurst font. The appearance of this elaborate work, very plainly suggesting that the Bradford school of sculptors was influenced from outside the West Saxon centre at Winchester,[1] together with the mannered linear style here used for the figure-subjects, cannot fail to remind us of the barbaric background against which the new Romanesque art of Wessex has to be seen. We do not need to be told that the house of Alfred the Great could not at a single word destroy an aesthetic consciousness that was already centuries old ; nor is it even likely that the court at Win-

[1] For the step-pattern panel cf. the Irton cross (Pl. 92).

chester ever sought to discredit openly the Celtic and Hiberno-Saxon elements in southern ecclesiastical art. In the initial stages of the restoration of the Romanesque concept that it has been my purpose to describe, we cannot expect to find more than a royal example and the gradual acquiescence of the people ; and of both these we have here, I think, pertinent illustrations, firstly in the Cuthbert stole, which was embroidered at the capital itself, and, secondly, in the carvings of this little western church that was situated so close to the boundaries of the Celtic world.

My last picture in this book leads us back, therefore, to that barbaric ornament which has provided the main subject of our survey. I think it is right that this should be so, for in the long struggle between the naturalistic and the geometric forms of aesthetic expression that has provided our central theme the instinctive urging of the barbaric northerner to make use of vividly patterned spreads of inorganic decoration has continually triumphed over the rare and timid experiments in organic art. Deep in the hearts of the people the inextinguishable spirit that had inspired Early British art endured as a perpetual source of the cunning invention and gross travesty that came into operation whenever opportunity occurred for classical forms to be changed into the native idiom. In the Roman Period, when classical art had its firmest hold upon our land, the undercurrent of the barbarian aesthetic temper was easily apparent beneath an uncongenial burden of official classicism. As Roman power wanes, so British barbaric art rises to its noblest maturity, using as its material the very patterns and pictures that the Empire had endorsed. And, later, when the Romanizing influence of the Golden Age of the Church fades, once more barbaric art in its brilliant Hiberno-Saxon guise dominates the mason's yard and the illuminator's cell. Even the Carolingian renaissance can command no more than a transient respect, and it was not, I think, until the shattering disaster of a great invasion by other barbarian peoples turned the course of English history, that the issue was raised to a different plane, classicism then standing for the stability of inherited culture, and barbaric art for the evil forces that then threatened English society with disruption. In that hour of sore trial the champion of English liberty was Alfred the Great, the ' darling prince ' of an afflicted people. And it is Alfred, and the house of Alfred, that brought about the profound change that I hope it will be my task to describe in another volume. For consciously, so I think, the Alfredian kings made English art Romanesque, and made it so in a way that no one before had achieved, as a standard, as a challenge. At their command the wilder ornaments of the barbaric world fall into gradual disuse, and, instead, the saving and impressive dignity of the central civilization of the Holy Roman Empire itself was reflected in the art of the Alfredian English who confronted the hostile barbaric world now advancing menacingly against the frontiers of Wessex. The Bradford panel represents no serious back-sliding from this high purpose. It is an ornamental adjunct, a subsidiary detail in a church that contained a huge and impressive figure-sculpture, nobly planned. The very contrast between it and the figure-carvings is an indication of the colossal revolution then in progress. If we are to look forward, it is from these angels to the splendours of the matured Winchester style and to our later Romanesque sculpture. But if we look backwards, it is from the panel to the mighty traditions of the barbaric manuscripts and to the full magnificence of Celtic art. It is a parting of the ways, and the whole imponderable strength of the barbarian aesthetic consciousness was pitted against the West Saxon Court. I take it to be one of the most significant facts of our story that the saving of Wessex and the establishment of the English kingdom under Alfred and his sons made possible the accomplishment of that Romanesque beauty which awaits us in the Winchester art of the second half of the tenth century and is the veritable foundation of the English medieval style.

INDEX

Printed in Great Britain by
Butler & Tanner Ltd.,
Frome and London

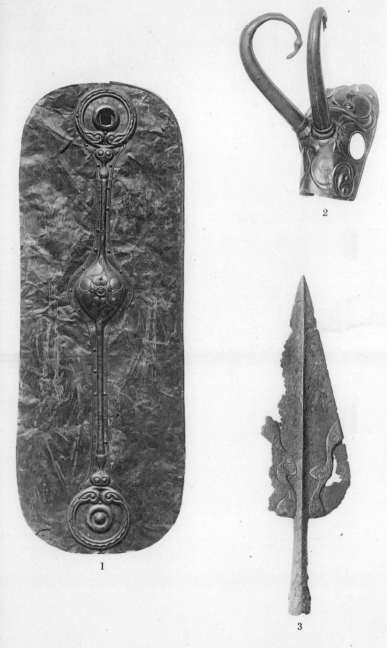

1. SHIELD, R. WITHAM. (Ht. 45 in.) 2. CHAMPFREIN, TORRS. (Ht. 10½ in.)
3. SPEARHEAD, R. THAMES. (Ht. 12 in.)

1. BRONZE BOAR, HOUNSLOW. (Ht. 1½ in.) 2. BRONZE BOAR, LEXDEN. (Ht. 3 in.) 3. & 4. AYLESFORD BUCKET, details (x⅔)

1. MIRROR, DESBOROUGH, NORTHANTS. (L. 14 in.) 2. SHIELD, THAMES
AT BATTERSEA. (L. 30 in.) 3. & 4. ENAMELS, POLDEN HILL (x¼)

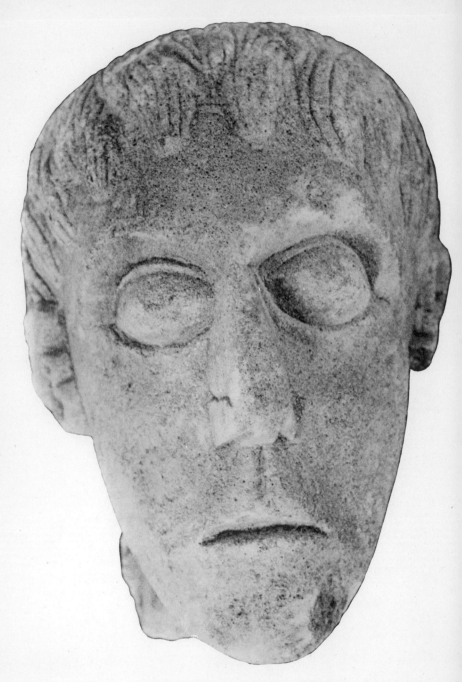

HEAD IN CHALK, GLOUCESTER. (Ht. 8 in.)

1. BROOCH, SILCHESTER. (L. 3½ in.) 2. SEAL-BOX LID, CHESTER. (D. 1.1 in.) 3. AESICA BROOCH (L. 4 in.) 4. SEAL-BOX LID, LINCOLN (L. 1½ in.) 5. DRAGONESQUE BROOCHES, N. ENGLAND (x⅘)

1

2

DETAILS OF TYMPANUM, BATH
1. Ht. 5 ft. 2. Ht. 3 ft. 2 in.

1. STONE ANTEFIX,
TOWCESTER,
NORTHANTS.
(Ht. 22 in.)

2. STONE CARVING,
WALLSEND,
NORTHD.
(L. 16 in.)

1

2

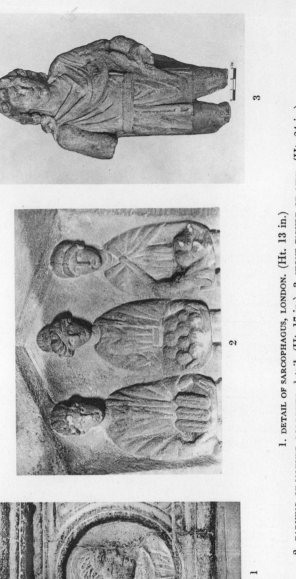

1. DETAIL OF SARCOPHAGUS, LONDON. (Ht. 13 in.)

2. CARVING OF MOTHER-GODDESSES, detail. (Ht. 17 in.)   3. STONE FIGURE OF ATYS. (Ht. 24 in.)

1. STONE HEAD, BENWELL. (Ht. 12 in.) 2. STONE HEAD, CORBRIDGE. (Ht. 6 in.) 3. STONE HEAD, CORBRIDGE. (Ht. 7 in.) 4. STONE HEAD, CARLISLE. (Ht. 8 in.)

X

TOMBSTONE OF LONGINUS, COLCHESTER. (Ht. 6 ft.)

2. TOMBSTONE, CHESTER, detail
(L. of male figure 43 in.)

1. TOMBSTONE OF PERVICA, detail
(L. of figure 2 ft. 9 in.)

XII

2. MOTHER GODDESS, NETHERBY. (Ht. 38 in.)

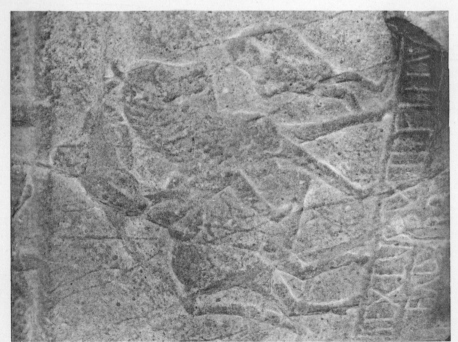

1. DETAIL FROM TOMBSTONE, CHESTER. (Ht. of mounted figure 19¼ in.)

1. SOL INVICTUS, CORBRIDGE. (Ht. 20 in.) 2. DETAIL, RISINGHAM. (Ht. 18 in.) 3. TOMBSTONE, CAERLEON. (W. 30 in.) 4. MOTHER GODDESSES, WELLOW. (Ht. 12 in.)

1

2

1. CHESTER, detail of FRIEZE. (Ht. 28 in.)
2. BATH, detail of CARVING. (Ht. 9 in.)

XV

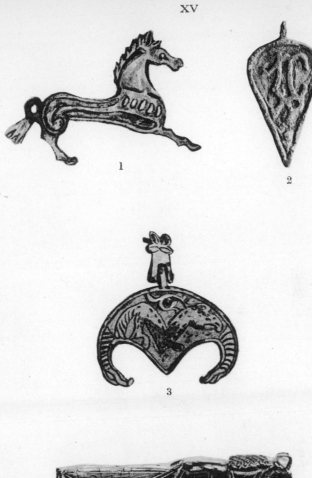

1

2

3

4

5

1. BROOCH, PAINSWICK.   2. PENDANT, SILCHESTER.   3. PENDANT,
MARGIDUNUM.   4. KNIFE-HANDLE, CORBRIDGE ($\frac{1}{4}$).   5. SPOON-HANDLE,
BARHAM, KENT (enlarged).

1. BRONZE HANDLE, COLCHESTER. (Ht. 6 in.) 2. PART OF CHAIR-LEG,
DORSET. (Ht. 11 in.) 3. STONE CARVING, CORBRIDGE. (Ht. 38 in.)
4. STONE CARVING, HEXHAM. (Ht. 12 in.)

1

2

MOSAIC PAVEMENTS. 1. SILCHESTER. 2. COOMBE ST. NICHOLAS

MOSAIC PAVEMENT, LEADENHALL STREET, CITY OF LONDON

1

2

MOSAIC PAVEMENTS. 1. LEICESTER. 2. MEDBOURNE

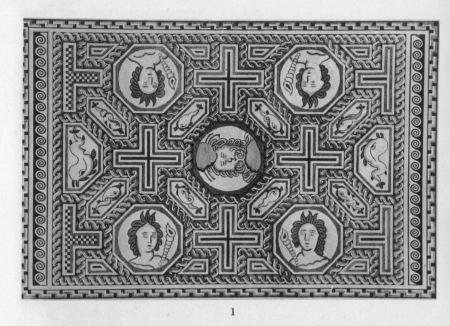

1

2

MOSAIC PAVEMENTS. 1. FRAMPTON. 2. BRISLINGTON

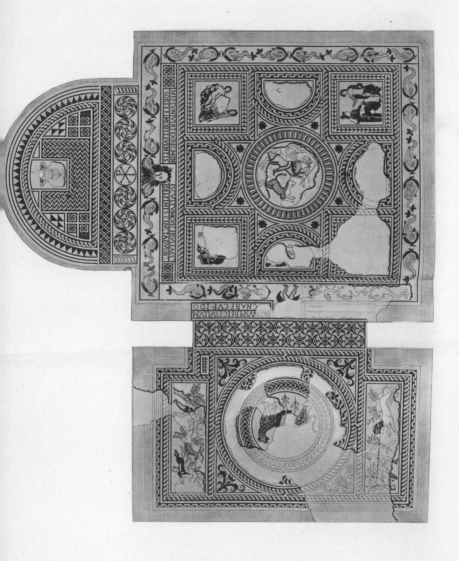

MOSAIC PAVEMENT, FRAMPTON, DORSET

1. SILCHESTER. (L. 4¾ in.) 2. SILCHESTER. (D. 1.6 in.) 3. ASHDOWN. (L. 2.2 in.) 4. ICKLINGHAM. (D. 2.4 in.) 5. BATH. (L. 2.7 in.)

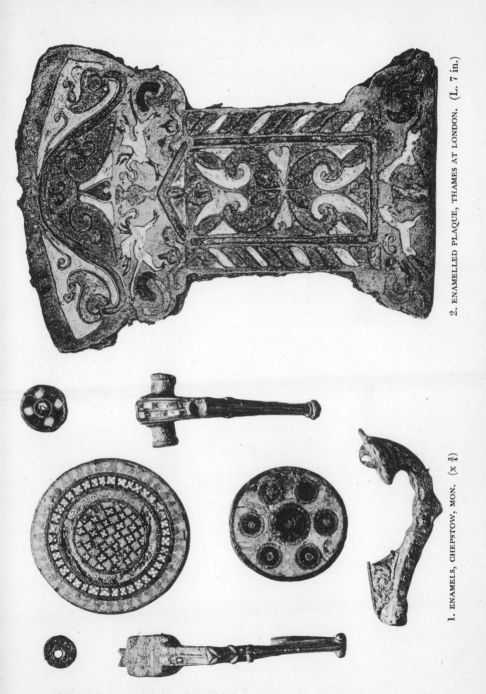

2. ENAMELLED PLAQUE, THAMES AT LONDON. (L. 7 in.)

1. ENAMELS, CHEPSTOW, MON. (× ¾)

1

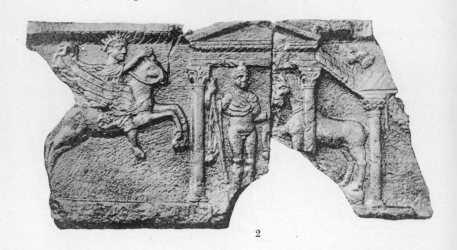

2

1. CAPITAL, CIRENCESTER. (Ht. 41 in.)   2. CARVED SLAB, CORBRIDGE. (L. 42 in.)

MOSAIC PAVEMENT, RUDSTON, YORKS.

BOWL-ESCUTCHEONS. 1. BAGINTON (enlarged). 2 & 3. DOVER (D. 2 in.) 4. EASTRY. (W. 1.7 in.) 5. BARLASTON. (D. of ring 2.6 in.)

BOWL-ESCUTCHEONS. 1. & 2. FAVERSHAM (enlarged). 3. NR. OXFORD. (D. 2 in.)
4. DISCOVERY NOT RECORDED. (D. 2 in.) 5. HITCHIN. (D. 2 in.)

1

2

HANGING-BOWLS
1. LULLINGSTONE. (D. 10 in.)   2. WINCHESTER, with "prints". (D. 11¼ in.)

1

2   3

4

1. EQUAL-ARMED BROOCH, DÖSEMOOR. (L. 3.7 in.) 2. STRAP-END,
SARRE. (L. 2.1 in.) 3. WRIST-CLASP, S. ENGLAND. (L. 2.3 in.) 4.
SHIELD-BOSS, BIDFORD-ON-AVON. (D. 6½ in.)

1. CHESSEL DOWN. (L. 5.5 in.). 2. LAKENHEATH. (L. 4.2 in.) 3. SOHAM. (L. 6.4 in.) 4. CHESSEL DOWN. (L. 1.5 in.) THE REST, GRAVE-GROUP, CHESSEL DOWN. (c. $\frac{1}{2}$)

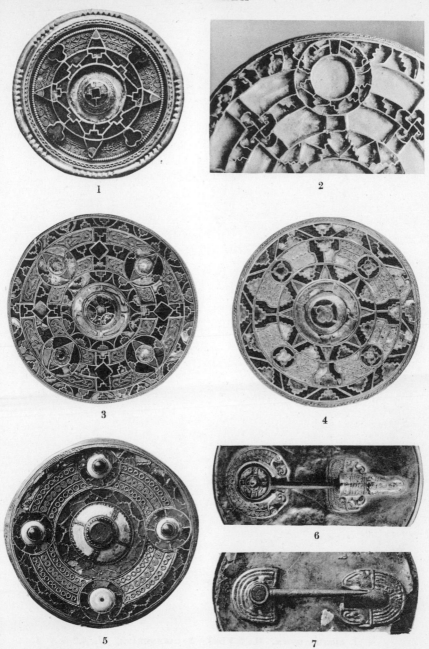

KENTISH BROOCHES. 1. FAVERSHAM. (D. 1.6 in.) 2. FAVERSHAM,
detail (enlarged). 3. KINGSTON. (D. 3.4 in.) 4. SARRE. (D. 2.4 in.)
5. SARRE. (D. 2.5 in.) 6. KINGSTON, back. 7. SARRE (No. 5), back.

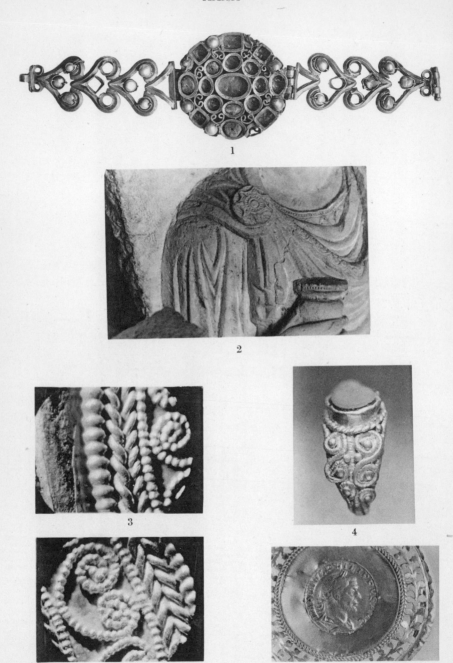

1. BRACELET, TUNIS. (L. 6½ in.) 2. DETAIL OF BUST, PALMYRA. 3 & 5.
DETAILS OF BROOCH, OTTERHAM, KENT. 4. FINGER-RING, NEW GRANGE.
6. DETAIL OF BROOCH WITH COIN OF PHILIP

1. BROOCH, LONDON. (L. 1¼ in.) 2. ESCUTCHEON, FAVERSHAM. (L. 2½
in.) 3. BROOCH, HOWLETTS. (D. 2.4 in.) 4. SWORD-POMMEL, CUNDALE.
(L. 2½ in.) 5. POTTERY BOTTLE, FAVERSHAM. (Ht. 11 in.)

1. BUCKLE, FAVERSHAM. (L. 2.7 in.) 2. JEWEL, MILTON. (L. 1.9 in.)
3. ST. CUTHBERT'S CROSS. (W. 2.3 in.) 4. PENDANT CROSS, IXWORTH.
(W. 1.5 in.) 5. BUCKLE, TAPLOW. (L. 4 in.)

1. & 2. MOUNTS, TAPLOW. (¼) 3. MEDAL OF CONSTANTIUS. 4. DETAILS OF DRINKING-HORN, TAPLOW. (Width of mount on rim 3 in.)

1. MOUNTS, FAVERSHAM. (L. 5 in.) 2. MOUNT, HARDINGSTONE. (D. 3¼ in.) 3. MOUNT, ALLINGTON HILL. (D. 3 in.)

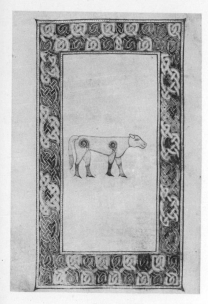

folio 116b.

folio 174b.

folio IIIa.

folio Ib.

BOOK OF DURROW

1   2

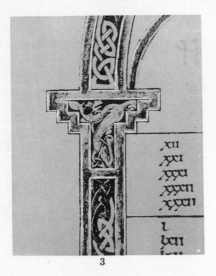

3   4

1. BOOK OF DURROW, folio 245b.   2. LINDISFARNE GOSPELS, folio 93b.
3. LINDISFARNE GOSPELS, folio 11b, detail.   4. LINDISFARNE, GOSPELS,
folio 139, detail.

LINDISFARNE GOSPELS, folio 29

LINDISFARNE GOSPELS, folio 94b.

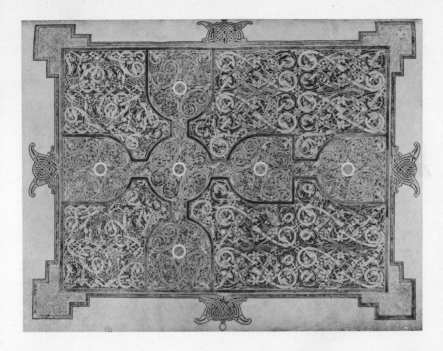

LINDISFARNE GOSPELS, folio 26b and detail

CODEX AMIATINUS, folio 796b

1

2

1. BINDING OF STONYHURST GOSPELS. (Ht. 5½ in.)
2. FRAGMENT OF ST. CUTHBERT'S COFFIN. (Ht. 8½ in.)

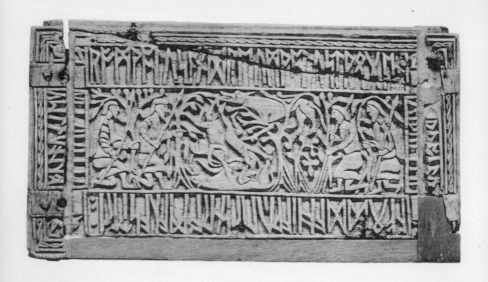

DETAILS FROM THE FRANKS CASKET. Left side: right side. (L. 7¼ in.)

DETAILS FROM THE FRANKS CASKET. Front: top: back. (L. 9 in.)

FRAGMENTS OF THE RECULVER CROSS. (Ht. of each 12 to 14 in.)

XLVII

1. & 2. DETAILS OF CROSS; RUTHWELL. 3. & 4. BEWCASTLE CROSS

1

2

1. DETAIL OF RUTHWELL CROSS.   2. DETAIL OF BEWCASTLE CROSS

THE ACCA CROSS, HEXHAM: Fragment of shaft

ABERCORN CROSS, CO. LINLITHGOW

ABERLADY (CARLOWRIE) CROSS, EAST LOTHIAN

ST. ANDREW AUCKLAND CROSS, CO. DURHAM

ST. CHAD GOSPELS (LICHFIELD CATHEDRAL), folio 218

folio 81b

folio 172b (detail)

CASSIODORUS IN PSALMOS (Durham B. II 30)

folio 75b

folio 18b

ECHTERNACH GOSPELS (Paris. Bib. Nat., lat 9389)

folio 18a

folio 11v

ROME GOSPELS (Vatican, Barb. lat. 570)

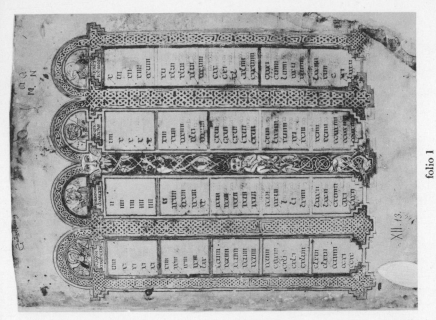

folio 1

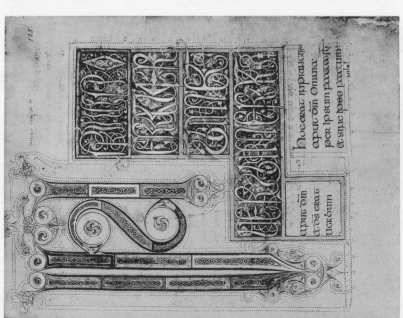

folio 125

ROME GOSPELS (Vatican, Barb. lat. 570)

CUTHBERT GOSPELS (Vienna. lat. 1224), folio 71b

3. LENINGRAD GOSPELS, folio 18

2. ECHTERNACH GOSPELS, folio 20a

1. LINDISFARNE GOSPELS, folio 27

THE ORMSIDE BOWL. (D. 5½ in.)

CROSS-SHAFT, CROFT, N.R. YORKS.

FRAGMENTS OF CROSS-SHAFT FROM EASBY, N.R. YORKS.

PART OF CROSS-HEAD AND FRAGMENT OF SHAFT (FOUR FACES),
ROTHBURY, NORTHUMBERLAND

SHAFT OF CROSS, ROTHBURY, NORTHUMBERLAND. (Ht. 28 in.)

2. CANTERBURY PSALTER (British Museum, Vespasian A.1), folio 30b

1. STOCKHOLM. CODEX AUREUS, folio 9b

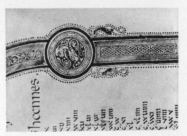

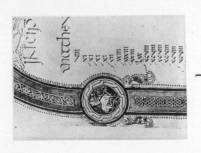

CANTERBURY GOSPELS (British Museum, Royal I.E.VI): 1–4. folio 4a (details), 5. folio 43a

2. CARVED SLAB, WIRKSWORTH, DERBYSHIRE

1. CROSS-SHAFT, BAKEWELL, DERBYSHIRE

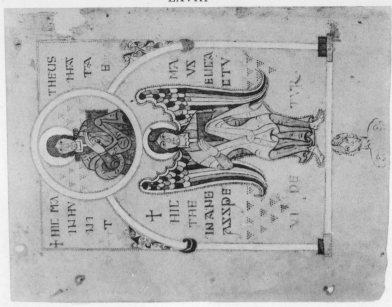

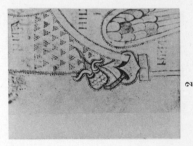

1

3

2

4

BEDE'S ECCLESIASTICAL HISTORY

(British Museum, Tiberius c. II, folio 5b).

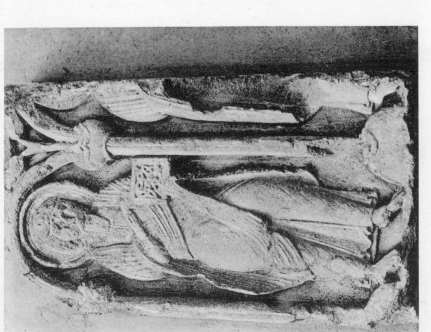

STONE CARVING, CASTOR, NORTHANTS.

1

2

1. "HEDDA" STONE, PETERBOROUGH CATHEDRAL

2. IVORY CASKET, BRUNSWICK MUSEUM. (Ht. 5 in.)

SILVER-GILT MOUNTS (used as heads of pins), RIVER WITHAM, LINCS.

(slightly enlarged)

STONE CARVINGS, BREEDON-ON-THE-HILL, LEICS.

STONE CARVINGS, BREEDON-ON-THE-HILL, LEICS.

STONE CARVINGS, FLETTON, HUNTS.

CARVED SHAFT, CODFORD ST. PETER, WILTS.

CARVINGS IN BRITFORD CHURCH, WILTS.

1

2

1. CROSS-SHAFT, NEWENT, GLOUCS.

2. TOMB-STONE, WHITCHURCH, HANTS.

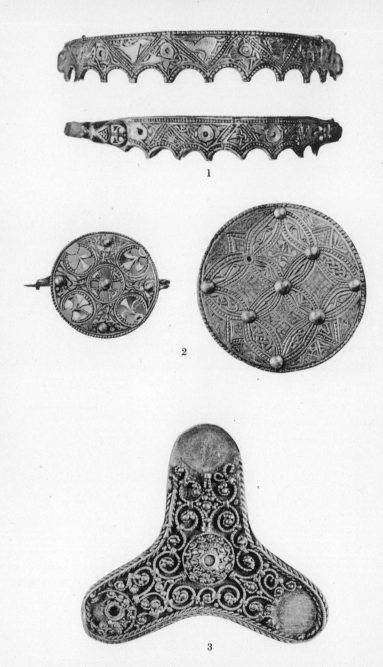

1. MOUNTS OF DRINKING-HORN, TREWHIDDLE, CORNWALL (slightly reduced)

2. SILVER BROOCHES, BEESTON TOR, STAFFS. (x$\frac{2}{3}$.)

3. SILVER ORNAMENT, KIRKOSWALD, CUMBERLAND (L. 3.5 in.)

1

2

1. PART OF SWORD-HANDLE, FETTER LANE, CITY OF LONDON. (x½.)

2. SWORD-HANDLE, WALLINGFORD, BERKS. (L. 8 in.)

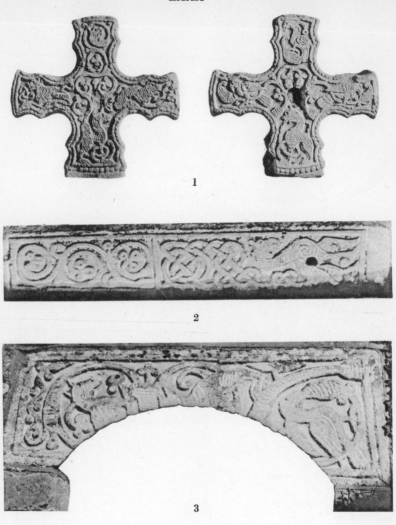

1. CROSS-HEAD, CROPTHORNE, WORCS.   2. CARVING, WROXETER, SALOP

3. CARVING, ACTON BEAUCHAMP, HEREFORD

THE "LECHMERE STONE", HANLEY CASTLE, WORCS.

FRAGMENTS OF CROSS-SHAFT, COLERNE, WILTS.

1. STONE-CARVING, KELSTON, SOMERSET. 2. & 3. FRAGMENT OF SHAFT, LITTLETON DREW, WILTS.

FRAGMENT OF CROSS-SHAFT, WINCHESTER

CARVED PILLAR, WOLVERHAMPTON

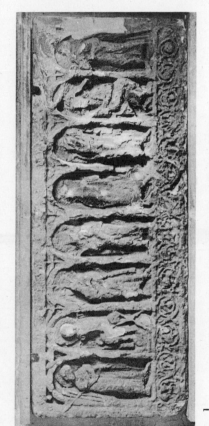

1. CARVED SLAB, HOVINGHAM, YORKS.   2. & 3. SHAFT, AND DETAIL, MASHAM, YORKS.

1. & 2. FRAGMENTS OF CROSS, ALDBOROUGH (1) AND CUNDALL (2), YORKS. 3. & 4. GRAVE-STONE, MELSONBY, YORKS.

DETAILS OF CROSSES, ILKLEY, YORKS.

1. BROMPTON, NORTHALLERTON, YORKS. 2. NUNNYKIRK, NORTHUMBERLAND

3. LOWTHER CASTLE, WESTMORLAND

1. COLLINGHAM, YORKS.   2. OTLEY, YORKS.

1. HEVERSHAM, WESTMORLAND   2. IRTON, CUMBERLAND

1. & 2. DACRE, CUMBERLAND   3. MORHAM, EAST LOTHIAN

4. THORNHILL, DUMFRIES

CROSSES, SANDBACH, CHESHIRE

DETAILS OF CROSSES, SANDBACH, CHESHIRE

CROSS-SHAFT, ROTHLEY, LEICS.

FRAGMENT OF CROSS-SHAFT, ST. ALKMUND'S, DERBY

2. GLATTON, HUNTS.

1. STEVENTON, HANTS.

CROSS-SHAFT AND TOMB-STONE, RAMSBURY, WILTS.

DETAILS OF CROSS-SHAFT, RAMSBURY, WILTS.

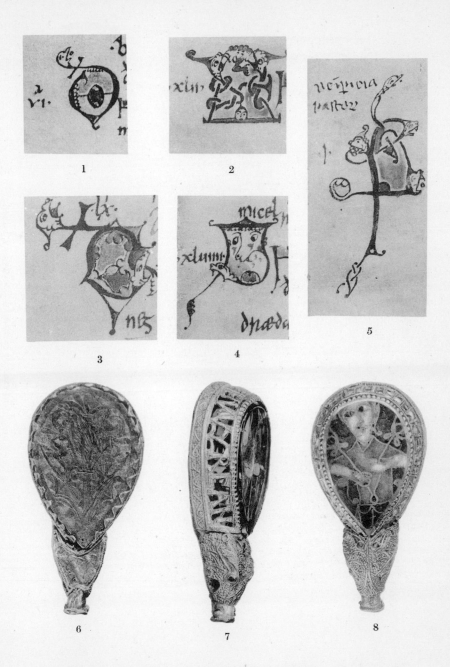

1–5. INITIALS FROM ALFRED'S "CURA PASTORALIS" (Bodleian, Hatton MS. 60)

6–8. THE ALFRED JEWEL. (L. 2.4 in.)

ST. CUTHBERT'S STOLE, details

1

2   3

1. BRADFORD-ON-AVON, WILTS.   2. DEERHURST, GLOUCS.

3. WINTERBORNE STEEPLETON, DORSET

BRADFORD-ON-AVON, WILTS.